D0990840

The
Cuban-American
Experience

The Cuban-American Experience

Culture, Images, and Perspectives

THOMAS D. BOSWELL
JAMES R. CURTIS

Rowman & Allanheld
PUBLISHERS

ROWMAN & ALLANHELD

Published in the United States of America in 1984
By Rowman & Allanheld Publishers
(A division of Littlefield, Adams & Company)
81 Adams Drive, Totowa, New Jersey 07512

Library of Congress Cataloging in Publication Data
Boswell, Thomas D.
The Cuban-American experience.

Bibliography
Includes index.
1. Cuban Americans. I. Curtis, James R., 1947–
II. Title.
E184.C97B67 1983 305.8′687291′073 83–16042
ISBN 0–86598–116–7

86/ 10 9 8 7 6 5 4 3 2

Printed in the United States of America

For our children,
Brandon Joaquin Boswell
and
Courtney Elizabeth Curtis

Contents

Tables and Figures ix
Preface xi

1. **Cubans in Contemporary American Society** 1
   Cuban-Americans as an Ethnic Minority, 1; A National View of Cuban-Americans, 3; Notes, 10

2. **Cuba: Revolution and Change** 11
   An Historical Perspective, 11; The Period of Spanish Domination, 12; The Period of United States Influence, 16; The Castro Revolution, 19; Major Social Changes Since Castro, 24; Conclusions, 34; Notes, 36

3. **History of Cuban Migration to the United States** 38
   The Early Trickle, 39; Period of the "Golden Exiles," 41; Missile Crisis Hiatus, 47; Period of Freedom Flights, 48; The Interlude from 1973 to 1980, 50; The Flood from Mariel, 51; Summary of Historical Trends, 57; Notes, 58

4. **Cuban Settlement in the United States: Patterns and Processes** 61
   Concentration in a Few States and Large Cities, 61; The Return Flow to Miami, 66; Ethnic Segregation, 67; Summary and Conclusions, 69; Notes, 69

5. **Miami: Cuban Capital of America** 71
   Growth and Expansion of the Cuban Population, 72; An Economic Enclave, 85; The Cultural Landscape of Little Havana, 89; Notes, 98

6. **A Demographic Profile of the Cuban-American Population** 100
   Cuban-Americans, Spanish-Americans, and Non-Spanish Americans, 100; Florida, New Jersey, New York, and Other Origins, 108; Summary and Conclusions, 111; Notes, 113

7. **Language and Religion** 115
   Language, 115; Religion, 124; Notes, 133

8. **Cuban-American Artistic Expression** **136**
Music, 136; The Visual Arts, 141; Creative Literature, 151; Theater and Dance, 154; Notes, 155

9. **Cuisine and Foodways** **158**
Historical Roots of Cuban Cuisine, 159; The Cuban-American Diet, 160; Grocery Stores and Restaurants, 164; Notes, 166

10. **Politics and Ideology** **168**
Exile Politics, 169; United States Politics, 173; Cuban Municipalities in Exile, 175; Notes, 178

11. **The Cuban-American Family and Youth: Acculturation and Assimilation** **180**
The Cuban-American Family, 180; Cuban-American Youth, 184; The Question of Assimilation, 187; Notes, 192

Index **195**

Tables and Figures

Tables

3.1 Estimates of the Cuban-American Population, 1870–1982 40

3.2 Cuban Migration to the United States, 1959-1981 42

3.3 Comparison of the Occupational Structure of Cuba in 1953 with the Occupations of Cuban Refugees at the Time They Migrated to Miami Between 1959 and 1963 46

4.1 Cuban-Americans Living in the United States, by Selected States, 1970 and 1980 62

4.2 Metropolitan and Nonmetropolitan Residences for Families in the United States, March 1980 65

4.3 Cuban-Americans by City of Residence, March 1981 66

5.1 Dade County Population, 1950–1980 73

5.2 1980 Cuban and Haitian Immigration to Dade County After the Federal Census 81

5.3 Dade County Cities, 1980: Selected Population Characteristics 82

6.1 Age Structure of Cuban-Americans Compared to the Total Spanish Origin and Non-Spanish Origin Populations in the United States, 1980 102

6.2 Occupation, Employment, and Income Characteristics of Cuban-Americans Compared to the Total Spanish Origin and Non-Spanish Origin Populations in the United States 105

6.3 Population 25 Years Old and Over by Years of Completed Schooling, March 1979 107

6.4 Selected Social Characteristics of Cuban-Americans by State of Residence, 1970, 1980 110

6.5 Occupation and Income of Cuban-Americans, 1970 111

7.1 Anglicisms in Spanish Spoken by Cubans in the United States 123

Figures

1.1 Mariel refugees aboard *Jennifer y Naty*. 5

1.2 President Kennedy at the Orange Bowl in 1961. 8

2.1 Map of Cuba. 13

3.1 The Freedom Tower, Miami, Florida. 44

3.2 Refugees housed in the Orange Bowl, Miami, 1980. 54

3.3 "Tent City," Miami, 1980. 55

4.1 Distribution of Cuban-Americans in the United States, 1980 63

5.1 Distribution of Cuban population in Dade County, 1970. 76

5.2 Distribution of Cuban-American population in Dade County, 1980. 80

5.3 The Jordan and Rowntree model of a ghetto or ethnic neighborhood. 84

5.4 Exterior of a cigar factory in Miami. 87

5.5 Inside a cigar factory in Miami's Little Havana. 88

5.6 Street scene during *Calle Ocho* open house. 90

5.7 Bay of Pigs memorial in Miami's Little Havana. 93

5.8 Wall mural in Miami's Little Havana. 95

5.9 Yard shrines. 97

7.1 Interior of a *botanica* in Miami. 132

8.1 Drawing by Rafael Soriano. 144

8.2 Artwork by Enrique Riverón. 146

8.3 Painting by Emilio Falero. 148

8.4 Pencil drawing by Juan Gonzalez. 149

10.1 Headquarters of the *Municipio de Santiago de Cuba en el Exilio* in Little Havana. 177

Preface

Since the Castro Revolution the number of Cubans living in the U.S. has ballooned from about 40,000 to approximately 1,000,000. This extraordinary increase is the result of one of the largest, most dramatic, and at times controversial immigrations to this country since the last decade of the nineteenth century. It is not surprising, therefore, that a considerable body of literature on Cuban-Americans has accumulated over the last twenty-four years. Yet, many important aspects of the Cuban-American experience have been neglected, and there is a noticeable absence in the literature of a comprehensive, balanced survey. This situation exists largely because a majority of Cuban-Americans are relatively recent arrivals. It further is related to the fact that professional and scholarly works, in addition to suffering from limited accessibility, have tended to focus on highly selected research topics. Consequently, our purpose in writing *The Cuban-American Experience* was to offer a broad, systematic overview that incorporates some of the themes that previously have been neglected.

In the eleven chapters that follow we discuss the major social, economic, political, and geographical topics relating to Cuban settlement and culture in the U.S. We begin by examining Cuban-Americans as an ethnic minority, as well as some of the events and people that have helped shape the popular images that Americans may have of this group. As a background for understanding the Cuban emigration, the focus then shifts to Cuba itself for an historical overview of the country's changing political, economic, and social systems. A chronological account of Cuban immigration to this country follows. In the next three chapters we analyze the distribution and residential patterns of Cuban-Americans nationwide, the growth and impact of Cuban settlement in Miami, and the demographic characteristics of Cuban-Americans. Attention then turns to Cuban-American language and religious patterns, artistic expression, and cuisine and foodways. In the final two chapters we examine Cuban-American politics and ideology, the family, and youth, and close with a discussion of the processes of acculturation and assimilation.

Our major problem in striving to present the larger picture of Cuban settlement in the U.S. was deciding what *not* to include. The subject matter is rich and varied, and the range of potential topics worthy of inclusion in this study is virtually limitless. Though space limitations precluded in depth discussions of many subjects, we have attempted to offset this inherent disadvantage of the survey approach by citing additional references that would facilitate further investigation.

From its inception *The Cuban-American Experience* has been a joint venture for us. We worked together to organize the project, and to find a publisher, and have shared ideas and research materials. The scope of the book, however, coupled with our own professional interests and specializations, led us to divide the primary research and writing responsibilities. Specifically, Boswell wrote Chapters 2, 3, 4, 6, 10, and 11, as well as the section on the Cuban economic enclave in Miami in Chapter 5. Curtis wrote Chapters 1, 5, 7, 8, and 9, as well as contributing the sections on Cuban municipalities in exile in Miami in Chapter 10, and on Cuban-American youth in Chapter 11.

We are grateful to a number of people who assisted us in various ways during this project and would like to acknowledge their contributions. Certainly we are indebted to the staff of the Richter Library at the University of Miami for their help during the research phase. In particular, Ana Rosa Nuñez, Lyn MacCorkle, and John Damore of the reference department, and Sara Sanchez of the periodicals department were extremely helpful in providing critical source materials. Ms. Sanchez also graciously agreed to read and offer suggestions on the original draft of Chapters 5, 7, 8, and 9. Jaime Suchlicki, Robert L. Levine, and Barbara Cruz of the University of Miami read and commented on Chapters 2, 3, and 9, respectively. Guarioné M. Diaz of the Cuban National Planning Council in Miami critiqued earlier drafts of several chapters, and also provided access to the C.N.P.C. library. Ileana Fuentes-Pérez of Rutgers University and Richard F. Rose of Miami-Dade Community College offered suggestions on Chapter 9, and provided important reference materials. At Florida International University, Antonio Jorge provided information of the economic contributions of Cubans living in Miami, and Nancy Erwin made available the results of her study of several Cuban neighborhoods in Dade County. Alejandro Pórtes of Johns Hopkins University provided information on the social characteristics of Cuban immigrants during the 1970s. Monsignor Bryan O. Walsh offered information on Cuban Catholics in Miami. Juan Espinosa of the Bacardi Art Gallery, Dora Valdes-Fauli of the Forma Art Gallery, and Jeff Murphree contributed gratuitously several outstanding photographs. Don Watler and Peggy Post were responsible for the cartography. The manuscript was typed by Patty Wilson and Kathy Kelleher of the Word Processing Center, College of Arts and Sciences, University of Miami. We also would like to thank the staff at Rowman and

Allanheld, especially Paul Lee, Senior Editor, and Jim LeMaire and Nancy Amy for their work on *The Cuban-American Experience*. Last, but most important, we are grateful to our wives, Marilyn and Patti, for their constant encouragement and understanding during the writing of this book.

Thomas D. Boswell
James R. Curtis

or parentage are surpassed in number only by Mexican-Americans and Puerto Ricans. Excluding illegal aliens, Cubans represent approximately 5.5 percent of the total Hispanic population.[2] While at a national level this figure is not impressive, it is regionally significant in light of the concentrated pattern of Cuban settlement in south Florida. Largely as a consequence of Cuban immigration to the greater Miami area, south Florida has emerged as an important and distinctive island of Hispanic culture.

Although Cuban-Americans represent less than one-half of one percent of the current population of the United States, they nonetheless are a significant and interesting ethnic minority. There are several important reasons why this is so. First, and perhaps most importantly, the number of Cuban-Americans is now equal to about 10 percent of Cuba's present population, a sizeable proportion for Cuba, if not for the United States itself.[3] Second, the emigrants have not, until recently, been representative of Cuba's population composition (see Chapter 3). The earliest waves of emigrants who fled the island in the immediate aftermath of the Castro revolution were predominantly upper- and middle-class professionals and entrepreneurs. The departure of this well-educated and skilled population created a serious "brain drain" in the country which intensified the impact of emigration on Cuba's population, even beyond what might be normally expected by a figure of 10 percent. Third, the characteristics of the migrants have changed considerably through time, so that recent arrivals are significantly different from those who migrated during the 1960s. The Cuban-American population is now more representative of the total population of Cuba. Fourth, the concentration of Cuban emigrants in a few American destinations has enhanced their visibility and influence. More than 6 out of every 10 live in just two metropolitan areas: Miami and Union City–West New York in New Jersey. In Dade County, Florida, for example, the Cuban population has ballooned from about 20,000 in 1959 to nearly 600,000 in 1983, which represents an increase from less than 5 percent of the total county population to approximately 39 percent (see Chapter 5). In both metropolitan areas, Cuban-American settlement has had a tremendous social, economic, and political influence on the respective host communities. Fifth, Cubans represent the first large group of refugees who have moved to the United States as their country of first asylum.[4] In the past, most other refugees have come to America indirectly, after spending time in an intervening third country, with the exception of the refugees from Viet Nam who arrived during the middle 1970s. Although some Cubans have also entered in this fashion, the vast majority has moved directly from Cuba to the United States. They have, as a consequence, been accepted automatically (until recently) as refugees who have been motivated by political persecution in a communist country. This status has entitled them to federal government benefits that were not available to most other immigrant groups, who have migrated primarily for economic reasons. In fact, the federal Cuban assistance effort was the largest in the history of the country. (There is a considerable body of scholarly literature which suggests that migrants who emigrate as political refugees are often significantly different from those who move in response to economic opportunities.)[5] Sixth, Cuban-Americans have made remarkable progress in adjusting to living conditions in the United States. Though argumentative, it is probably correct to suggest that there has never been a large non-English speaking immigrant group in this country that has exhibited more rapid upward socioeconomic mobility. In comparison with most other Spanish-speaking minorities, for example, Cuban-Americans clearly have a higher per capita income and have achieved higher levels of educational attainment. Seventh, many of the traditional Cuban institutions and elements of culture, both material and nonmaterial, are better preserved in the Cuban-American community than in Cuba itself. This is related primarily to the sweeping societal changes implemented by the Castro regime. An eighth reason why persons of Cuban descent warrant attention is because their large-scale movement to the United States is still recent, it is a current problem that is being grappled with by United States Immigration authorities, urban planners, and surveyors of social services today.

A National View of Cuban-Americans

It is axiomatic that the popular conception of most, if not all, American ethnic groups is fraught with stereotypes. These images are at best simplistic; at worst, they are without basis in fact. In a majority of cases, they tend to be shaped more by secondhand knowledge and hearsay than by personal experience or objective analysis. Increasingly, these views are formed, or at least enhanced, by the coverage that ethnic groups receive in the mass media, coverage that is often fragmentary, and at times purely misleading. Clearly any attempt to construct a "national view" of an ethnic group is admittedly a subjective undertaking, a task that is virtually impossible to adequately document. Yet, to the extent these views may reflect prevailing American attitudes toward ethnics, which may in turn influence an ethnic group's perception of its own sense of identity in American society, they are worth exploring. This section is not meant to critically evaluate how the American public feels about Cuban-Americans. Rather, the intention is to briefly highlight selected aspects of the Cuban-American experience which have gained national attention, and which might, therefore, have been instrumental in shaping the views that some Americans have of the Cuban minority living in the United States.

Cuban-Americans, like other ethnic groups, have been stereotyped. Yet, it is probably fair to suggest that their composite image at the national level remains vague. If this is true, it is related primarily to the fact that most Cuban-Americans are recent emigrants, having settled in the United States only in the last 20 years. Their concentration on the fringe of the U.S. (south Florida) has perhaps further clouded the picture of Cubans as an ethnic group.

If one aspect of the Cuban-American experience can be singled out as having received the greatest share of national attention, it would have to be the emigration process itself. (A detailed account of this emigration will be provided in Chapter 3.) From the first hurried flights out of Havana in the waning days of the Batista regime in late 1958 and early 1959 to the chaotic mass emigration in 1980 via the Mariel boatlift, Americans have watched with fascination the dramatic unfolding of the Cuban exodus to the United States. In general, it is probably correct to assume that Cuban emigration to this country has been seen in a favorable light by most Americans, as least prior to the Mariel boatlift. This positive attitude is reflected by the fact that Cubans have been as well-received in the United States as any immigrant group has in recent history. Their flight from communism and the iron-clad rule of Castro struck a responsive chord in Americans. It pulled at the very heart of American patriotism and sense of justice and compassion. Cubans were welcomed with open arms and generous federal assistance.

Unfortunately, this receptive posture was tainted by the events surrounding the Mariel boatlift and its aftermath. From April 21 to September 26, 1980, the "Freedom Flotilla," as it was labeled at the time, brought nearly 125,000 Cubans to the docks of Key West, Florida. Yet, even before the refugees were processed, the boatlift raised serious questions concerning the effectiveness of our immigration laws and policy. In the view of many Americans, including high-ranking government officials, our Cuban emigration policy seemed to be controlled less by the federal government than by Castro himself. This concern was compounded by the fact that in a time of recession and high unemployment, Americans were sensitive about protecting the nation's borders from the influx of illegal aliens and refugees, especially those migrating essentially for economic reasons. Following the disclosure that a sizable proportion of the Mariel refugees had criminal records (approximately 26,000, though most for petty crimes),[6] that others were patients from mental institutions, and that others were homosexuals, prostitutes, or elderly and disabled individuals, public opinion toward Cuban refugees deteriorated. Subsequently, the well-publicized disturbances at various camps where the refugees were being housed while awaiting resettlement–most notable at Fort Chaffee,

Figure 1.1 *During the massive Mariel exodus, Cuban refugees, such as these aboard the* Jennifer y Naty, *crowded into hundreds of small craft bound for Key West and a new life in the United States. (Photo courtesy of the U.S. Coast Guard.)*

Arkansas, and Indiantown Gap, Pennsylvania—worsened the situation. Then, a spree of violent crimes especially in Miami and New York, which was attributed to a small core of hardened criminals among the refugees, clearly had a negative impact. Public perception of the refugees, and perhaps by extension the greater Cuban-American community, reached its nadir. In a Roper Poll conducted in late March 1982, for example, only 9 percent of the respondents felt that Cuban immigration to the United States had been "a good thing for the country," and 59 percent felt that it had been "a bad thing for the country."[7] On both of the questions, Cubans were ranked last out of a total of 15 immigrant groups included in the survey. This regrettable shift in attitude was fueled to a certain extent by vivid, if not sensationalized, accounts of the criminal activities associated with the Mariel refugees. One representative example is an article that appeared in the December 1982 issue of *Reader's Digest* entitled, "From Cuba with Hate: The Crime Wave Castro Sent to America."[8] The article begins with a graphic description of the murder of a Cuban girl in Miami involving three Mariel refugees. The author then states, "They had come in the thousands . . . gaunt men with stone-hard eyes and crude tattoos on their bodies." While the veracity of the article is not in question, its tone and mere appearance in a magazine with the circulation of *Reader's Digest* most likely contributed to the negative image of Cuban-Americans as a result of the Mariel exodus.

Although the 1980 Refugee Act—which greatly lowered the number of Cubans allowed to legally enter the county—was in effect when the boatlift occurred, the Mariel refugees were granted a special status ("entrants") which allowed them to enter the country. But since October 1980, Cubans seeking to emigrate to the United States have had to apply for entrance on an individual basis, like all other nonrefugees. And while the flow of Cuban emigration to this country since that date has been greatly reduced, the situation could change almost instantly (or at least the law would be severly tested) if Castro were to open the gates of another Mariel.

Beyond the issue of emigration, other aspects of Cuban-American settlement and culture have received comparatively minor attention in the national mass media. This unbalanced treatment may further explain why the national view of Cuban-Americans remains unclear and easily swayed by events like the Mariel exodus. It might also explain why the perception that some Americans have of Cubans living in the United States continues to be colored by the flamboyant and enigmatic figure of Fidel Castro (bearded, dressed in fatigues, and invariably smoking a cigar) as well as the exotic images of the nightlife in pre-revolutionary Havana, such as those depicted in the movie *Godfather II*. Yet, in spite of the fact that coverage of Cuban-Americans in the popular media has been rather sparse and uneven, it nonetheless has been essentially positive, with the exception of the attention given to the wave from Mariel. This observation is based on coverage accorded Cuban-Americans in fields as diverse as politics, business, and entertainment and sports.

On various occasions, Cuban-Americans have captured national attention in the area of politics and political ideology. (Chapter 10 will provide a more detailed discussion of this topic.) Although comparatively few Cuban-Americans have been elected to public office, especially outside of Miami or at the national level, they still have assumed a relatively active role in a range of political activities, some of which have generated considerably controversy, if not intrigue. Unlike a majority of other Hispanics or black-Americans, for example, Cuban-Americans, as a group, are politically conservative. Since the earliest wave arrived after the Castro takeover, they have been staunch supporters of Republican party candidates and causes. This stems ideologically, at least in part, from the wide-held perception among most Cuban-Americans that Republicans are more closely aligned and sympathetic to their own fervent anti-communist, and more precisely anti-Castro, sentiments.

The ill-fated Bay of Pigs invasion in April 1961 surely contributed to this feeling. Although the invasion was a great disappointment and embarrassment to the United States, and clearly was one of the low points of the Kennedy Administration, the valor and courage of the Cuban-Americans who participated in the poorly conceived invasion was never questioned. They were fighting communism only 90 miles from the shores of the United States, while receiving financial assistance and supervision from the United States government. The failure of the invasion damaged the image of the United States government, but not necessarily that of Cuban-Americans who, in fact, gained widespread sympathy and respect from many Americans for their valiant efforts. It was this feeling that prompted President Kennedy to come to Miami to personally welcome home the Bay of Pigs veterans, over 1000, who had been held prisoners by Castro and then suddenly released on Christmas Eve in exchange for money, supplies, and equipment.

At other times, however, the anti-communist posture and politically motivated zeal of some Cuban-Americans have exceeded the accepted bounds of political dissent and behavior in the United States. This extremist position surfaced, for example, when Cubans from Miami were implicated in the scandalous break-in of the Democratic headquarters in the Watergate complex during President Nixon's term in office. The bombings and other terrorist activities aimed at alleged sympathizers of the Castro regime by militant anti-Castro organizations, such as Omega 7, illustrate the

Figure 1.2 President and Mrs. Kennedy came to the Orange Bowl in Miami in late 1961 to welcome the Bay of Pigs veterans. (Photo courtesy of the Historical Association of Southern Florida.)

extremes that political ideology and activism reach in certain quarters of the Cuban-American community.

In the business world, the entrepreneurial accomplishments of Cuban-Americans only recently have begun to capture attention beyond the principal areas of Cuban settlement, most notably in Miami and Union City–West New York. This is not to ignore, however, that the premium cigar manufacturing industry has long been associated with Cubans, especially the Tampa-based companies, or that individual Cuban businessmen have attained prominent positions in some of the nation's largest corporations, men such as Roberto Goizueta, current chairman of the board of the Coca-Cola Company. In the past decade, Cuban-American businessmen have played a crucial role in transforming Miami's economic structure from a position of regional importance to one of national and international recognition. The heralded rise of Miami as a center of banking and trade for much of the Caribbean Basin and South America, for example, is attributable in no small measure to the Cuban-American influence.[9] This has led to a host of interrelated economic developments, widely discussed within the business community, including the growing choice of Miami and Coral Gables as the Latin American (and even global) headquarters of a number of multinational corporations. (Chapter 5 will elaborate on the economic impact of Cuban-Americans on metropolitan Miami.) The generally positive news coverage that these and other business successes have received both nationally and abroad have served to increase the visibility of Cuban-Americans, while enhancing their image as an industrious and success-oriented minority.

The national image of Cuban-Americans, like that of other ethnic groups, has undoubtedly been molded to some extent by their exposure in the realm of entertainment, including the popular arts and professional sports. Clearly the most recognizable and influential Cuban-American personality in the entertainment field over the past thirty years has been Desi Arnaz. Son of a former mayor of Santiago de Cuba, Arnaz worked the spectrum of popular entertainment. But it was television that brought him to the forefront of public attention. During the 1950s and 1960s, Arnaz teamed with Lucille Ball in one of the earliest and most popular situation comedies in the history of television, *I Love Lucy*. The character he played, Ricky Ricardo, was much beloved by the viewing audience. Perhaps he, too, contributed to a positive impression of Cuban-Americans.

Though certainly less familiar to the American public than Desi Arnaz, other Cuban-American entertainers, particularly musicians, have occasionally managed to bridge the gap between the Latin and Anglo audiences. (This topic will be discussed more fully in Chapter 8.) In the case of musicians, many of their successful "crossover" songs often coincided with various Cuban dances, which enjoyed brief periods of popularity in the United States, including the *rumba* craze of the 1930s, the *mambo* fad of the late 1940s, and the *chachachá* rage of the mid-1950s. The names of Don Azpiazu for his *rumbas*, Machito (a.k.a. Frank Grillo) and his Afro-Cubans for their *mambos*, and Pérez Prado for his *mambos* (particularly "Cherry Pink and Apple Blossom White" and "Patricia") were prominent in this respect.

In the highly visible world of professional athletics, Cuban-American athletes have achieved their greatest success and recognition in baseball. In Cuba, baseball was and still is the favorite national sport. In the United States, Cuban-born baseball players played in the major leagues as early as 1912, although most began only after the "color line" fell in the late 1940s. Some of the more notable Cuban-American baseball stars include Pedro Ramos, Luis Tiant, Mike Cueller, Tony Pérez, and Tony Oliva, who won three American league batting titles.

In summary, prior to the massive immigration from Mariel in 1980, the national view of Cuban-Americans was generally positive. This perception was shaped primarily by the favorable and relatively extensive coverage of Cuban immigration in the mass media. Beyond the immigration process itself, the popular image of Cuban-Americans and the overall pattern of Cuban culture and settlement in the United States was vague. The events surrounding the Mariel boatlift and its aftermath had an extremely negative impact on the perceptions that Americans held regarding the value of Cuban immigration to the United States. That a single episode could have such a deleterious effect, we feel, is related to a lack of knowledge concerning the nature of Cuban settlement and culture in this country. It is hoped that the general survey of the Cuban-American experience which follows will be one step in correcting that situation.

Notes

1. The 1980 U.S. Census data do not include the approximately 125,000 Cuban refugees who arrived shortly after the census enumeration.

2. If illegal aliens of Hispanic descent, mostly Mexicans, were included, the percentage would be significantly reduced. See, for example, "It's Your Turn in the Sun," *Time*, October 16, 1978, pp. 48–61.

3. The Population Reference Bureau estimates that the mid-1981 population for Cuba was 9.8 million. *1981 World Populations Data Sheet* (Washington, D.C.: Population Reference Bureau, April 1981).

4. Rafael J. Projias and Lourdes Casel, *The Cuban Minority in the United States: Preliminary Report on Need Identification and Program Evaluation* (Boca Raton: Florida Atlantic University, 1973), p. 1.

5. William S. Bernard, "Immigrants and Refugees: Their Similarities, Differences and Needs," *International Migration* 14:267–280 (no date), 1976; and Egon F. Kunz, "Exile and Resettlement: Refugee Theory," *International Migrational Review* 15:42–52, Spring-Summer 1981.

6. Juan M. Clark, Jose I. Lasaga, and Rose S. Reque, *The 1980 Mariel Exodus: An Assessment and Prospect* (Washington, D.C.: Council for Inter-American Security, 1981), p. 7. They report that according to the Immigration and Naturalization Service a total of 1761 refugees, representing 1.4 percent of the emigrants, were classified as felons (i.e., convicted of murder, rape, or burglary), with another 23,927 (19.1 percent) classified as non-felonious criminals or political prisoners.

7. The poll was conducted between March 20–27, 1982. See "A Nation of Immigrants," *Public Opinion* 5:34, June-July 1982.

8. Peter Michelmore, "From Cuba with Hate: The Crime Wave Castro Sent to America," *Reader's Digest*, December 1982, pp. 223–248.

9. Andrew Neil, "Date Line: Miami, April 15, 1992," *The Economist*, October 16, 1982, pp. 3–26; Robert Stickler, "Latin Clout," *The Miami Herald*, Business Monday Section, pp. 1, 8–9.

2
Cuba: Revolution and Change

The island republic of Cuba achieved a level of prominence in 1959 that was much larger than its areal extent or population size alone could justify. In this year it became the first country in the Western Hemisphere to experience a socialist revolution. Today it represents a controversial communist stronghold in the Caribbean Sea and has had a major impact on the politics of an area that used to be considered as being solely within a capitalistic sphere of influence dominated by the United States. As a result, a great deal has been written about Cuba. The purpose of this chapter is not to provide an exhaustive and authoritative review of all the characteristics of Cuba's economy and society because this has already been done several times in the literature.[1] Instead, the goal is to summarize those conditions that have been most influential in affecting the attitudes of Cubans toward the United States and to describe some of the changes that have taken place in Cuban society, especially since 1959. The first part of the chapter will assume an historical perspective, while the second will focus on some of the more important social changes that have occurred since Fidel Castro's government took control.

An Historical Perspective

Most of the history of Cuba has been characterized by foreign domination. It was ruled by Spain from 1511 to 1898, making it one of the first colonies in the New World to be established by the Spanish and the last (along with Puerto Rico) to be lost. Between 1898 and 1902 it was occupied and run by a United States military government. It became politically independent as a capitalistic state in 1902 and remained so until 1959. However, during this 57-year period it was extremely dependent economically upon the United States as its primary trading partner. Since 1959 the island's foreign trade partners have been almost totally realigned toward the Soviet Union and communist countries of Eastern Europe. Today, Cuba is as economically dependent of the Soviet Union as it was on the United States during the 1950s.

The Period of Spanish Domination

Columbus was the first-known European to discover Cuba during his initial voyage to the New World in 1492. However, Spain did not begin to colonize the island until 1511. By 1515 seven cities had been founded, including Havana and Santiago, which are Cuba's two largest metropolitan centers today (Figure 2.1). At the time the Spanish first arrived, there were somewhere between 100,000 and 200,000 Indians living on the island. As was tragically the case throughout the rest of the Caribbean islands, the Indian population did not last long in Cuba. By the time Cortez was planning his expedition to Mexico in 1519, the number of Indians had declined to about 3000 due to the effects of war, forced labor, and European-introduced diseases.[2] Most historians agree that they ceased being an identifiable group by the end of the sixteenth century.

During the first two hundred years of its existence as a Spanish colony, Cuba functioned primarily as a supply and communications center between Spain and its mainland colonies in Mexico, Central America, and South America. Since wealth and fame were more easily obtained in the mainland empires, they were much more attractive than Cuba to new colonists. As a result, the island's population grew very slowly during this early period. Due to the initial decimation of the Indian population and the continual siphoning off of many of its former residents to the mainland, it was not until around 1725 that Cuba regained its pre-conquest population size.[3]

Although sugar cane was introduced early in the sixteenth century and African slaves were first introduced in 1517, neither were of major importance in Cuba until the latter half of the 1800s. Cattle raising and the growing of tobacco and various food crops dominated the agricultural sector of the economy during the earliest years of settlement. The Seven Years War (1756–1763) between Great Britain and France, in which Spain aided the French, initiated a new era in Cuba. In 1762 the British captured Havana and occupied it for ten months. Through the Treaty of Paris (1763) Cuba was returned by England to Spain in exchange for Florida. However, the impact of the defeat of the Spanish, followed by the rapid succession of revolutionary changes in the United States, France, and Latin America during the next 60 years, created a new economic structure and society in Cuba. The American Revolution opened the United States market for the importation of sugar and coffee from the island. The introduction of steam-powered mills in 1819 gave further impetus to the expansion of the growing of sugar. The production of coffee also increased rapidly until 1833, after which it began to decline in importance. The cultivation of tobacco began in the seventeenth century and during much of

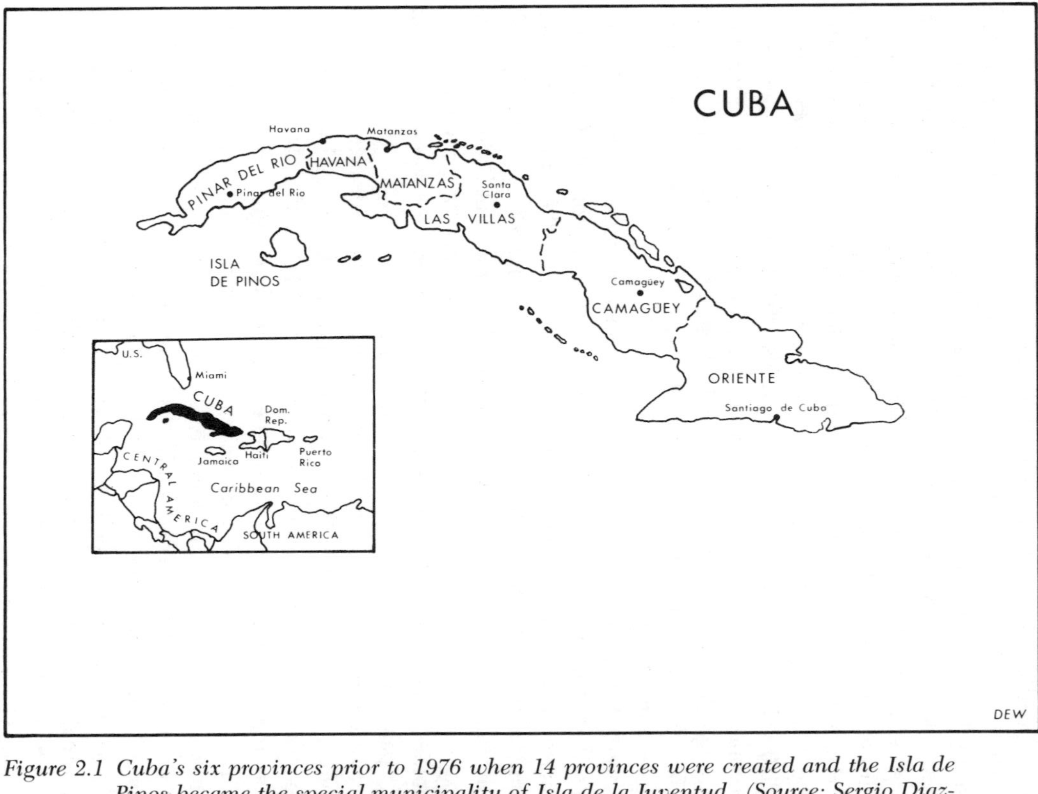

Figure 2.1 Cuba's six provinces prior to 1976 when 14 provinces were created and the Isla de Pinos became the special municipality of Isla de la Juventud. (Source: Sergio Diaz-Briquets and Lisandro Perez, Cuba: The Demography of Revolution *(Washington, D.C.: Population Reference Bureau, Vol. 36, No. 1, April, 1981), p.2.)*

the 1600s and 1700s it ranked as Cuba's leading export, followed by beef and hides. However, tobacco growing did not receive much impetus initially from the new United States connection, so it began to slowly decrease in importance after reaching its peak in 1788. Tobacco production would again experience a spurt in activity in the 1830s that would last throughout the rest of the nineteenth century.

The labor demands created by the growing sugar and coffee industries led to the large-scale importation of African slaves. An emancipation law was enacted in 1880 under which slavery was finally ended in 1886. It has been estimated that close to one million slaves were transported to Cuba during the island's 369-year history of slave trading, with the vast majority arriving during the last 100 years of this period. The 1846 census indicated that Cuba's population at that time was composed of 565,000 whites, 220,000 free blacks and mulattoes, and 660,000 slaves.[4] As the slave trade declined after the middle 1800s, the demand for inexpensive labor was met through the importation of indentured laborers from China, the arrival of a few thousand Indians from Mexico's Yucatan Peninsula, and continued Spanish immigration.

By 1825 the flames of revolution against Spanish domination had largely run their course throughout the Latin American mainland. Only Cuba, Puerto Rico, and the Philippines remained within the Spanish colonial empire. However, the Cubans had the same complaints against Spanish rule that the rest of Latin America had. The mercantilistic policies of Spain controlled trade and the development of industry in favor of the mother country at Cuba's expense. All power of control was in the hands of Spaniards who had migrated to the island and a serious rift developed between these people and the *criollos* (persons of Spanish ancestry born in Cuba). The close alliance between the Catholic church and the Spanish-dominated government was also a target of criticism. Freedom of education from state and clerical control became another major issue.

The question of Cuba's independence from Spain in the years before the American Civil War was complicated by the issue of slavery. The first insurrections were carried out by Cubans who wanted the island to become annexed to the United States, rather than become independent. The goal was not only political liberty and freedom of trade, but also to ensure the preservation of the institution of slavery. At this time the American South still practiced slavery and there was some sentiment in the U.S. to add Cuba as a slave state. The Cuban planting aristocracy was well aware that if the island were to become independent, slavery would be abolished and they would loose their main source of cheap labor. The United States did make several offers to buy Cuba between 1848 and 1898, but they all were rejected by the Spanish.[5] These purchase attempts later proved to be very unfortunate for future relations between the United States and an independent Cuba. Henceforth, the intentions of the U.S. government with respect to the island's sovereignty were questioned and its initial support of slavery was used as evidence of racial discrimination. After the American Civil War and the abolition of slavery in the United States, interest in annexing Cuba declined.

From 1865 until 1898 Cuban history is primarily a chronicle of political and economic woes interspersed with rebellions. In 1868 a creole plantation owner, Carlos Manuel de Cespedes, initiated the Ten Years War in Cuba's most remote eastern province at the town of Yara. After several years of success, the offensive lost its momentum by attrition and a truce was signed finally in 1878 (the Pact of Zanjon). Spain promised political reforms and a number of other concessions, but few were actually carried out. Although Cespedes was killed in the Ten Years War, the rebellion did serve to popularize two leaders who would subsequently become famous leaders in the future struggle for Cuban independence. One was Antonio Maceo, a black who was raised in the city of Santiago, and the other was Maximo Gomez, an exile from the Dominican Republic.

In 1879 a young poet and intellectual who had organized a revolutionary committee in Havana was deported to Spain. This was José Martí, who would become the chief spokesman and organizer for renewed efforts to liberate Cuba. From Spain he moved to New York City and remained in the United States for 15 years. His activities through the Revolutionary Junta in New York City became the nucleus for renewed revolutionary action. Contact was made with groups of Cubans throughout the United States and money, arms, and recruits were collected for another assault.

By 1895 the Cuban economy was in dire straits. Sugar prices had fallen to low levels and slavery had been abolished. The coffee and tobacco industries had not recovered from the disruptive effects of the Ten Years War, especially in the island's eastern provinces. Unemployment and dissatisfaction were at high levels. Martí recognized this as a propitious time to launch a final rebellion. The insurrection began in the eastern province of Oriente on February 24, 1895. Maceo arrived in Cuba on April 1, and Gomez and Martí joined the battle eleven days later. Slowly, the rebel forces pushed westward, concentrating their activities in rural areas because the Spanish troops were stationed mainly in the cities. Both Martí and Maceo were killed but the rebels were beginning to wear down the Spaniards through a process of attrition.

When it became apparent that the fighting between Spain and the rebels had become serious, the United States sent the battleship *Maine* to Havana in 1898, in case it might be needed for the protection of Americans living in Cuba. As the ship lay at anchor in the mouth of Havana harbor it blew up, killing 260 sailors. Recent research suggests that the cause of the explosion came from within and was most likely an accident. In any event, the Spanish forces were blamed for the disaster and shortly thereafter the United States declared war on Spain. The entire episode of the Spanish-American War lasted less than four months, with intense fighting taking place for only about two weeks. An armistice was signed in August 1898 and a final agreement was reached through the Treaty of Paris, which became effective on April 11, 1899.

The United States created a remarkable diplomatic error in its handling of the armistice. Little respect or sympathy was shown for the Cubans who had fought so long and hard for their independence. The Spanish army surrendered to the American forces, not the Cubans. Rebel Cubans were not allowed to participate in the surrender ceremonies. Because neither rebel representatives nor their flag were present when the agreement was signed, the United States gained the undying enmity of the Cuban people. Cubans rightly claim that they fought a lot longer and lost far more lives seeking their independence than did the Americans. They feel that the Americans intervened at the last minute, once it was clear that the rebels would win. They resent their rebellion being called the Spanish-American War, instead of the Spanish-Cuban War. Given a history of racial prejudice, attempts to purchase the island, and big business ventures in the sugar industry, the motives of the United States are easy to question. Needless to say, the present Castro government has given great emphasis to this episode of Cuban history.

The long period of Spanish domination played a major role in forming Cuban culture. The language, religion, economic institutions, and social structure of Spain were transferred to the island. Spanish law and policy kept the government highly centralized and, along with trade, in the hands of Spaniards. Virtually no industry developed. Sugar and, to a lesser extent, tobacco became the major cash crops. Society was highly stratified, with relatively few rich families and a large mass of poor people, many of whom lived as peasants in a predominantly rural environment. In short, it was not a life of equal opportunities for all individuals. Sixty years later a socialist revolution would occur that would seek to address some of these inequalities. Those who chose to migrate to the United States instead of suffering through the changes and dislocations created by communism would carry with them many of the social and cultural attributes that their parents and grandparents had acquired during the Spanish phase of Cuba's history.

The Period of United States Influence

While United States intervention quickly ended the war for independence, it left considerable confusion regarding American intentions for Cuba's future. President McKinley resisted pressures from business interests to annex the island, but he was not yet prepared to accept the government formed by the Cuban rebels. For the next four years Cuba was governed by the United States Army. When the Spanish had withdrawn their forces they had looted as they left. Disease and starvation were widespread and the economy was in ruin. Under tight-fisted control, roads, bridges, hospitals, post offices, and a public school system were built. In addition yellow fever was virtually eradicated.

In 1901 a controversial addition to an Army Appropriation Bill for that year was enacted, which was known as the Platt Amendment. Its provisions were reluctantly accepted by the Cuban representatives as a condition for their independence one year later. The controversy focused on an article that allowed the United States to intervene in Cuban affairs, if it was felt that such action was necessary to maintain order and protect the island's independence. It also obligated Cuba to provide land for a military base. The latter provision soon led to the establishment of the United States Naval Base at Guantanamo Bay on Cuba's southeastern coast. The United States still occupies this installation and it has become a major irritant in current United States–Cuban relations, although the Platt Amendment was abrogated in 1934. During the 33 years that it was in effect, the Amendment permitted the United States to send troops into Cuba, which it did a number of times "to protect American lives and property." It also was a constant threat to Cuban governments that considered following policies of which the United States did not approve.

Given the promises to protect and defend the island, there were great hopes that Cuba would use its natural and human resources wisely and thus experience rapid economic growth. Unfortunately, the island had no history or experience with democracy and as a result that institution failed almost from the beginning. Sadly, between 1902 and 1959 Cuban leadership was characterized by intermittent indifference and ineptitude, as well as almost continuous corruption. Obtaining a national political office almost always guaranteed wealth. In 1909, for instance, José Miguel Gómez entered the office of President as a poor man and left a millionaire. Mario Garcia Menocal was worth perhaps one million dollars when he entered the Presidency in 1913. He left office eight years later with a fortune estimated at $40 million.[6] The situation reached an intolerable level during the later stages of the dictatorship of Fulgencio Batista, who dominated the political scene between 1933 and 1959. He was chief of staff of the army from 1934 to 1940 and in fact was in a stronger position than the President. In 1940 he was elected to the Presidency and served until 1944. In 1952 he again became President, but this time he did so through a coup d'etat. He legalized his position in 1954 when he was re-elected to the office, although he was the only candidate.

Batista was opposed by numerous groups as his rule became increasingly brutal. As suppression of the opposition became ruthless, the general populace began to give their support to the several revolutionary movements emerging on the scene. On July 26, 1953, a young University of Havana-trained lawyer, Fidel Castro, led what at first appeared to be a disasterous attack on the Moncada Army Post in the city of Santiago. Many of his followers were killed in the battle or tortured to death later. The rest were captured and given prison sentences. Castro himself was sentenced to 15 years in the infamous prison located on the Isle of Pines.

In 1955, shortly after he had assumed his second elected term as President, Batista declared a general amnesty for all of his former enemies, including Fidel Castro. The next year Castro spent in the United States and Mexico organizing another invasion force. He left Mexico in late 1956 with 83 men crowded aboard an aging yacht, the *Granma*, for the southeastern coast of Cuba. The rebels, called the 26th of July Movement, were forced to withdraw to the Sierra Maestra Mountains. They waged a battle that gradually gained support as the Batista government became more desperate in its attempts to repress the rebellion. On January 1, 1959, Batista and his cabinet fled the country and Castro and his army marched triumphantly into Havana on January 8th. A new era was about to begin for Cuban society.

Despite the poor quality of Cuba's leadership between 1889 and 1959, there was tremendous growth in the Cuban economy during this period. The American influence was particularly critical in promoting this development. The United States market for Cuba's sugar caused a rapid expansion in the amount of land used for its production.[7] American capital (close to $2 billion) was used to construct new sugar mills and plantations. By the late 1950s sugar accounted for about 80 percent of Cuba's total exports. Americans also owned most of Cuba's electrical industry, the railroads, the nations' telephone company, most of the mining facilities, and even much of its tobacco industry. The United States purchased about 75 percent of the island's total exports and provided about 65 percent of its imports.

Between 1901 and 1932, close to 850,000 Europeans migrated to the island to take advantage of its booming economy. In addition several hundred thousand migrant workers from Jamaica and Haiti also arrived, but most returned when the sugar harvests and planting seasons ended.[8] However, the Great Depression of the 1930s curtailed this movement and after this period immigration has not played a major role in Cuba's population growth. The 1953 Census for Cuba indicated that approximately 73 percent of its population was white and about 27 was either black or mulatto. This turn around in racial composition from what was reported in 1848 was due to the ending of the slave trade in the 1880s and the immigration of whites between 1900 and 1930. By the late 1950s Cuba had a larger proportion of its population classified as white than almost any other of the Caribbean islands.

By the late 1950s Cuban quality of life compared favorably with most of the developing countries of the Western hemisphere. The island's life expectancy was over 60 years and both its birth and death rates were declining. By Latin American standards, Cuba had relatively high levels of average income and consumpsion, fairly advanced medical and sanitary standards, a relatively well-developed system of education, and a moderately urbanized society. In addition, a significant middle class had emerged.[9]

Unfortunately, the benefits derived from Cuba's economic growth during the period of United States influence were not equally distributed among the island's population. There was plenty of money, tourism was booming, the big spenders came to the gambling tables, large profits were derived from the sale of sugar, and the United States was nearby with investment capital and managerial expertise. But most Cubans did not function within this system. Most were poor, not as poor as Haitians, but poor nonetheless. In 1953 the poorest 40 percent of the population received only 6.2 percent of the country's income. Conversely, the wealthiest 20 percent controlled 60.0 percent of the income.[10] Over one-fourth of the population was illiterate. Unemployment usually was close to 30 percent. Employment for hundreds of thousands of low-paid sugar cane cutters was highly seasonal, with the average period of employment normally being between four and six months. The rest of the year they usually were without a salaried income. The gulf between the city and rural areas was great. High school attendance was low in rural areas and college was primarily for the wealthy. Close to half of the doctors lived and worked in Havana, and health care was, at best, unreliable outside the cities. As long as most could remember there had been a privileged class, first of Spanish rulers and later composed of the family and friends of a series of dictatorships. For all but the wealthy and upper-middle class, being Cuban meant living without any great prospect for the future.

The Castro Revolution

When Fidel Castro arrived in Havana in January 1959, he had the support of nearly everyone on the island, except for the supporters of Batista who were quick to leave for the United States. Gradually, however, the radical nature of the economic, social, and political changes that the new government began to promote became increasingly apparent. As a result, the support of those who had the most to lose, such as the upper-middle class liberals who had remained and some of the middle class, began to wane. In the ensuing years close to a million of these people would emigrate to the United States and several other countries. (This mass migration will be discussed in Chapter 3.) Many of those who did not leave, but instead chose to remain on the island and criticize the government, were jailed. One of the first acts of the new government was to conduct public tribunals for those supporters and officials of the Batista regime who had not been able to escape. Many were executed in summary fashion. Although these actions received much adverse publicity and criticism in the American press, there is little doubt that most of the Cuban people considered this to be just retribution for the past brutality of the Batista dictatorship.[11]

In May 1959, the Castro government implemented its First Agrarian Reform Law. At that time only 8 percent of the landowners controlled 70 percent of the cultivated land. About 40 percent of this was farmed by poor sharecroppers and 25 percent of the best sugar acreage was in foreign hands.[12] The 1959 law placed a limit of about 1000 acres, with some exceptions, on the amount of land that could be privately owned. It also created the National Institute of Agrarian Reform (Institution Nacional de Reforma Agraria—INRA) that was to become responsible for planning future agricultural development. Most of the land that was confiscated was consolidated into large state farms, modeled after those established in the Soviet Union. About 100,000 sharecroppers were given "vital minimum" plots of approximately 67 acres to farm, if they wanted to work on their own land instead of a state-operated farm. Although the law provided for some compensation to be paid to the former landowners, almost all of them left the country and never received any payment.

In October 1963 a Second Agrarian Law became effective. Its purpose was to deal with the rural bourgeoisie not affected by the first law. It further reduced former large private holdings to about 167 acres, but only if there was evidence that the landowning family supported the revolution (otherwise they lost all of their land). Immediately, the vast majority of the large landholding operations, such as sugar plantations and cattle ranches, were taken over by the state. However, many of the smaller enterprises, like tobacco and coffee farms, were left largely intact. In fact, by the middle 1970s almost a third of the agricultural land in Cuba was still in the hands of 162,000 private owners who raised 26 percent of the island's livestock, 18 percent of its sugarcane, 80 percent of the tobacco, 75 percent of its coffee, and about 50 percent of its fruits and vegetables.[13]

The United States, who had been buying most of Cuba's sugar crop through a quota agreement, suddenly cut the island's sugar allotment by about 95 percent in July 1960. Shortly thereafter, the Soviet Union agreed to purchase the sugar that the United States refused to buy and also announced that it would defend Cuba against any foreign attack. In August, Castro stated that most of the United States-owned businesses on the island were being nationalized. In total, about 1.8 billion dollars worth of property and equipment were seized. In October, the government also nationalized 382 Cuban-owned companies, including all the banks. In addition, an Urban Reform Law was implemented that would eventually turn over ownership of homes and apartments to those who rented them, putting an end to Cuba's landlord class.

As a result of these nationalization activities and the growing alliance between Cuba and the Soviet Union, the United States placed a partial embargo on exports to the island in November 1960. In February 1962 a complete embargo was imposed on trade between the United States and Cuba. The result of this action was the almost complete realignment of the island's foreign trade. By 1980, 75 percent of Cuba's foreign trade was with the communist countries of Eastern Europe, 65 percent alone being with the Soviet Union.[14] In addition, during the nineteen years between 1960 and 1979, the Soviet Union provided $16.7 billion in economic assistance to Cuba.[15]

Diplomatic relations between the United States and Cuba were severed in January 1961. When it became apparent that a group of Cuban exiles were preparing to invade the island, Castro announced on April 16, 1961 that his was a socialist revolution, with Marxist-Leninist ideals. The exile soldiers who were about to launch the assault had been trained in Guatemala and were given financial and material support by the United States. On April 15th, the troops rendezvoused in Nicaragua. Eight of the exile force's planes bombed Cuba and a land invasion was begun on April 16th at Playa Giron, Bay of Pigs. The invasion lasted three days; the exiles were soundly defeated, in part because they had counted on American air support that never arrived.

In October 1962 United States reconnaissance pilots photographed missle launching pads that had offensive capabilities in Cuba. The U.S. took the issue before the United Nations and later that month announced a quarantine on all offensive military equipment being shipped to the island. Soviet ships were stopped at sea, under orders of their government. The Soviets agreed to withdraw their missiles and dismantle their bases. In return the United States gave assurances that it would not invade Cuba. Castro saved face by refusing to allow a land inspection, but this was accomplished by air reconnaissance and inspection of Soviet ships at sea.

From the beginning of the Castro Revolution it was decided that Cuba's economy would become centrally planned. For this purpose the Central Planning Board (Junta Central de Planificacion-JUCEPLAN) was created. Between 1960 and 1963 a plan was followed that was designed to make

Cuba self-sufficient in the production of both food crops and manufacturing. It was decided to try to diversify the island's exports by de-emphasizing the production of sugar and expanding industry. For the most part this policy was a failure. Only a few of the factories were completed before monetary reserves ran out. Costs were not effectively calculated, and in some cases prices for raw materials exceeded the cost of importing the finished product. Results in the agricultural sector were just as disappointing. New crops were slow to be accepted and little additional food was grown. The de-emphasis on sugar eventually caused yields to plummet, with the result that Cuba's major export declined, adversely affecting the country's balance of international trade. In 1963 a new economic policy was proclaimed. It was decided to re-emphasize sugar and other traditional exports, such as tobacco and nickel. Plans called for a 10 to 15 percent expansion in the land used to produce sugar and a goal of a 10-million ton harvest in 1970 was announced. This overly ambitious target was not reached, as the harvest in 1970 fell short by 1.5 million tons.

There were a number of factors that severely limited Cuba's economic growth during the 1960s. Most of the machinery that had been built by the Americans was beginning to wear out and replacement parts were difficult to obtain as a result of the economic embargo imposed by the United States. The exodus of experienced managerial, technical, and professional personnel created a serious "brain drain" for the economy. The collectivization of production, with the aim of achieving a greater equality in wages and living standards, removed some of the incentive for efficient production by eliminating the profit motive of the former capitalistic structure. Low sugar output in various years, combined with low prices for sugar in the international market, further aggravated the island's infavorable balance of trade. The costs of new social programs in education and health, the providing of free utilities, subsidizing prices of consumer goods, agrarian reform, and programs to create jobs were an expensive drain on monetary reserves.[16]

Seeking to remedy problems resulting from labor inefficiency and absenteeism that had accompanied the abolition of the profit motive, the Cuban government began, in the early 1970s, to reduce its emphasis on equality. Wages were more sharply differentiated according to type of work, production levels, and hours worked. Higher prices were charged for consumer goods and utilities started charging fees for services that were free during the decade of the 1960s. The aim was to establish a system of material incentives to increase labor productivity.[17] In 1976 a new law was enacted legalizing limited private enterprise. Although it is still illegal to buy a product and resell it at a profit, individual operation of certain small businesses is permitted. Some examples of these newly allowed private services include gardeners, automobile mechanics, shoeshine boys, and hairdressers. All are required to pay a monthly tax to become licensed to practice their private trades.

The first half of the 1970s witnessed a partial economic recovery, spurred by higher sugar prices and increased output, as well as by Soviet economic assistance. However, starting in 1976 the Cuban economy again went into a tailspin. A drastic decline in world sugar prices occurred and plagues affected the sugar and tobacco industries. Also, two hurricanes (Frederick in 1979 and Allen in 1980) wrecked havoc with much of the agricultural production and caused other disruptions. Serious difficulties in the nickel and fishing industries and military involvement in Africa also detracted from economic progress.[18] The realities of the late 1970s substituted for the brief euphoria of the early 1970s and led to a more cautious and reserved outlook for the 1981 to 1985 period. Cuban planners have scaled down their expectations for economic growth and are beginning to realize the magnitude of the economic problems they face, such as the lack of a diversified export base, the need to import almost all of the island's oil from the Soviet Union to meet its energy needs, the need to import 30 to 35 percent of Cuba's food, and an overwhelming reliance on Soviet assistance (especially when other Third World countries are increasingly competing for this same source of assistance).

Still, despite these setbacks there is no doubt that most Cubans (especially those from the lower class) are enjoying higher economic standards of living today than they did during the 1950s prior to the Castro Revolution. The gains in health standards and education levels have been especially noteworthy. In addition, there is less inequality in income now than there was in the 1950s. In 1973, the poorest 40 percent had 20 percent of the total income, compared to 6 percent in 1953. Conversely, the wealthiest 20 percent of the people received 35 percent of the income in 1973, compared to 60 percent in 1953.[19] In addition, the Cuban government has tried assiduously to reduce the gap in the standards of living between rural and urban areas by promoting rural development. Rents have been lowered and home ownership is more common. The costs of electricity, water, and telephone service have been reduced greatly through government subsidies. Unemployment, particularly in the sugar industry, has been reduced from about 30 percent before the Revolution to less than 6 percent today. One interesting way in which Cuba has been able to lower its unemployment is to temporarily export redundant workers as assistance to friendly Third World countries. It is estimated that between 15,000 and 20,000 Cubans are working currently in two dozen such countries.[20] The emigration of hundreds of thousands of people of labor force age to the United States has also eased the strain on Cuban labor force capacities.

Major Social Changes Since Castro

MASS ORGANIZATIONS

Today everyone living in Cuba belongs to at least one of its large government-sponsored organizations.[21] In such a revolutionary society it is very difficult to be a loner, which is exactly what the government wants. This system demands active participation, to the point that if an individual does not participate, his or her loyalty to the Revolution is questioned. In fact, passivity is considered to be one way of dissenting. Childhood is usually spent in the Young Pioneers. Many teenagers subsequently are selected to join the Union of Young Communists. A few ultimately rise to membership in the Communist Party. In addition, most adults belong to their neighborhood Committee for the Defense of the Revolution and most women are members of the Federation of Cuban Women.

The Young Pioneers was founded in 1961 and is patterned after similar organizations in other communist countries. It admits children between 5 and 13 years of age. Typically, a child enters the first grade of elementary school and the Pioneers during the same year. Meetings are held either in or after school. The goal is to teach the children to be good students and to be loyal to the Revolution. Political indoctrination plays a major role in their activities and the revolutionary leader Che Guevara is their idol. It is during this youthful age that Cubans are introduced to the "New Man" concept. The New Man is supposed to behave altruistically. He or she is a moral individual who is truly concerned for the welfare of others and is not motivated by self-interest or the desire to obtain profits.

The Union of Young Communists was founded in 1962 and is regarded as being a training ground for the desired goal of communist party membership. Not all members of the Young Pioneers join the Young Communists because membership is decided on a compatitive basis. Young people between the ages of 14 and 27 years compose the Union. They are further indoctrinated with the ideals of the Revolution and participate in a number of service projects. They help run the island's school system as teacher's aides and voluntary teachers, they participate in the harvesting of crops, they take part in reforestation projects, and they helped build the Havana-to-Santiago railroad.

The first communist party was formed in Cuba in the 1920s but it played only a very minor role in the island's politics until the 1959 victory of Castro's rebels. In fact, this old communist party did not at first support Castro's revolutionary activities. In the years between 1959 and 1961, when the tone of Castro's movement became increasingly socialistic, a number of old communists played significant roles in guiding the policies of the new government. However, since 1962 most of the old communists have been pushed aside in favor of many of the participants in Castro's 26th of July Movement. In 1965 a new communist party was formed, known as the Communist Party of Cuba. The new party was designed to join together several political factions that had supported the Revolution. This is now the only officially recognized political party in Cuba.

The Cuban Communist Party is an elite organization that is made up of less then three percent of the island's population. Cuba's percentage of party membership is one of the lowest of any of the world's communist countries. A rigorous screening procedure is followed that takes about six months before an individual can become a member. Supporters of this elitism argue that the emphasis is on the quality of its membership, rather than quantity. It is this organization that controls the governing of the country.

Since only a very small proportion of the Cuban population belongs to the Communist Party, another organization was needed to allow majority adult participation in government activities. The Committees for the Defense of the Revolution (CDRs) were organized in 1960 to fulfill this purpose, even before the new communist party was formed. Each block in Cuba has a CDR and there are close to 80,000 of them. They are tightly knit, all pervasive, neighborhood organizations. Approximately 5,000,000 persons are members, which is close to 80 percent of Cuba's entire population over 14 years of age. Anyone can join, unlike the restrictive membership policy of the communist party.

The CDRs are the mass activists of the Revolution. They perform a number of community service tasks, such as administering oral polio vaccine to children, mobilizing women to receive pap smears and breast cancer checks, organizing blood donor rallies, keeping school records for every child on the block, and organizing parents for volunteer school projects. More controversially, they are also the eyes and ears of the Castro government. They watch for any suspicious activities and maintain a system of surveillance that violates privacy, causes suspicion , and often generates difficulties among the block's residents. They are incessantly busy promoting the Party line with propaganda messages and touting the virtues of the idealistic New Man. In short, they are everywhere, watching to make certain that there is conformity in keeping with the goals of the Revolution. The president of each CDR maintains a "Book of the Block," which represents an inventory of all that takes place there. When someone leaves the block, either for prolonged travel or permanently, this fact is recorded. Each person's responsibility for tasks on the block is written down and checked off when completed. Births, deaths, and marriages are also recorded, as are such facts as number of children and their attendance in school.

The CDRs hold frequent meetings to seek public opinion and are supposed to provide a platform in which grievances can be aired. However, the CDRs and the labor unions also vote to put citizens on the buying list for rationed goods, such as appliances. As a result, there is a reluctance to voice serious complaints for fear of being left off these lists. As a consequence of the vigilance of the CDRs, most observers agree that there is no organized resistance to the Castro government inside Cuba. Although many resent the lack of privacy, and will say so in private, there is very little open complaining. Dissent is manifested more often by subtly withdrawing from activity, working slowly, and doing only the required minimum.

EDUCATION

By 1958 Cuba had acquired a relatively high standing among Third World countries in terms of its average level of education. A United Nations report ranked the island second in Latin America in its teacher-pupil ratio and third in its percentage of literates.[22] Still, there were serious problems with the country's educational system at that time. The last census taken before the revolution in 1953 showed that about 24 percent of all persons ten years of age or older were illiterate. Furthermore, there were notable regional differences. Havana, the most modern province, had an illiteracy rate of only 9 percent, while the most backward province of Oriente had a rate of 35 percent. The gap between the urban and rural populations was even greater. The percentages of people that were not able to read or write in urban areas was 11 percent, but in the countryside it was almost 42 percent. Corruption was widespread in the ministry of education. The rich and middle class sent their children to private schools either in Cuba or abroad. The public schools were left largely to the children of the working classes.

In 1961 the Castro government entered into a literacy campaign. Close to 280,000 teachers and students were sent around the country to instruct approximately 700,000 persons how to read and write. At the end of the year-long effort, it was claimed that illiteracy had declined to 3.9 percent, the smallest percentage for any country in the world. However, Cuban educators who left their country assert that in reality this was an overly optimistic estimate because the tests given to determine whether or not a person could read and write were not valid according to United Nations standards. Nevertheless, it is clear that a great deal of progress had been made through the campaign's efforts. Also in 1961 the government nationalized all private schools as a means of further eliminating some of the inequalities within the educational system.

The most controversial educational innovation of the Castro government was initiated in 1968, with the creation of secondary schools in the countryside. These are large boarding schools for about 500 seventh- to tenth-grade boys and girls. The idea is to combine work and study and bring together students from both urban and rural areas. The facilities are all laid out in a standard format with rectangular buildings that are three to four stories high and have classrooms, dormitories, a cafeteria, and surrounding recreational facilities, including a swimming pool. Each of these schools is located near the center of a plot of agricultural land of about 1250 acres. The average day is split between studying for about four hours and working in the fields for another three hours. The time a student spends in school is highly regimented from the time the day begins at 6 A.M. until bedtime at 10 P.M. The work that students do in the field each day is designed to provide them with an appreciation for agriculture, to instill a work ethic, and to produce crops that can be sold to help defray some of the costs of running the school. Typically, a child stays at school from Sunday evening until noon on Saturday. They are home with their parents only for parts of Saturday and Sunday. This bothers some parents who feel that their freedom of authority to raise their children as they see fit is being seriously compromised.

Currently, school attendance is mandatory for children through the sixth grade, however there is a strong revolutionary moral code that pressures most youth to remain in school until they are 15 or 16 years old. The goal is to eventually raise the average educational level until the completion of high school is the standard of achievement. In 1978 approximately a third of Cuba's entire population was enrolled in some type of organized education program. In addition to the schools provided for children, adults have been able to benefit from night school programs and opportunities to combine schooling with employment. To pay for such enormous involvement, approximately ten percent of the island's gross national product is spent on educational activities.[23]

Questions can be raised regarding the quality of Cuba's revolutionary education system. Since students are required to be more than academicians, there is only limited time available for the study of traditional academic subjects. Time spent in the fields and on courses dealing with Marxist-Leninist thought can be questioned. Because there is a shortage of qualified adult teachers, more advanced students are often used to instruct younger pupils, although the government is working to train new teachers. At the university level there has been a reorientation toward subjects considered to be of more practical importance. For instance, in 1957 about 65 percent of the students attending the University of Havana were majoring in medicine and law. Students now are encouraged to enter priority areas such as education, engineering, agriculture, and the health sciences. Furthermore, under communism the traditional Latin American role of the university as a center for dissent has been abrogated. Because of a refusal to tolerate any conflicting thoughts, the educational process has closed Cuba to much of the world's thinking in the social sciences, arts, and humanities. If freedom of thinking is considered an integral component of academic excellence, then that achievement has been seriously subordinated in Cuban universities.

PUBLIC HEALTH

Of all aspects of Cuban society that have been affected by the Revolution, public health has probably experienced the greatest success. The progress that has been made in this area is even more remarkable since during the early 1960s close to half of all Cuban doctors emigrated to the United States when most of their practices were nationalized.

Today, Cuban doctors work for the state, rather than owning their own practices. They receive regular salaries like most other workers, although there are a few exceptions to this generalization. A small number of doctors and dentists who stayed in Cuba after the Revolution have been allowed to remain in private practice, as a reward for not leaving the country, although they cannot own buildings or operate clinics. Even though health care is free when obtained from one of the government clinics, a citizen can elect to visit a private doctor as long as he or she is willing to pay the fee. Doctors who have been trained since 1959 at government expense do not have the option of entering private practice. To keep these newly trained physicians happy, they receive special preferential treatment. For instance, they are accorded the highest prestige of any class of workers, receive the highest salaries, and are given first priority on buying lists for scarce consumer commodities, such as automobiles and appliances.

In 1958 over half of Cuba's doctors and hospital beds were located in Havana, where less than a fourth of the population lived. Few doctors or medical facilities were found in rural areas. Since then the government has gone to great efforts to improve the quality of health care in the countryside. As a result, the percentage of the island's hospital beds that were located in Havana declined from 62 percent in 1958 to about 42 percent by the middle 1970s.

Sanitation and vaccination campaigns have experienced great success in Cuba since 1962, when they were initiated on a large scale. As a result, the island has progressed through an epidemiological transition, so that the leading causes of death have shifted from contagious diseases to degenerative factors such as heart disease, cancer, and stroke. Polio was eliminated in 1963. Malaria was virtually eradicated by 1968. There have been no reported cases of diptheria since 1971. The number of deaths due to gastroenteritis have declined from 4000 per year in the late 1950s to less than 800 today.[24] In 1982 Cuba's infant mortality rate had been reduced to 19.3 deaths per 1000 births, one of the lowest in Latin America. In addition, the life expectancy at birth for Cuban males and females combined was 73 years. As a standard of of comparison, the average American only lives one year longer, to the age of 74 years.[25]

Housing

With enactment of the Urban Reform Law of 1960 and plans to enter into a massive housing construction program, Cubans looked optimistically toward a time when their housing needs would be satisfied. As the landlord class was eliminated by the Urban Reform Law, rents were lowered so that no family was charged more than ten percent of its monthly income. Depending on the type and size of housing occupied, ownership was to be transferred to the families living in the units over a period varying from 5 to 20 years.

Despite these efforts there is evidence to suggest that Cuba's housing shortage has worsened over the years, instead of improving. In short, despite the emigration of large numbers of Cubans to the United States, housing construction has failed to keep pace with the island's population growth and much of the housing that was built before the Revolution has fallen into disrepair. In 1960 it was estimated that the country's housing deficit was approximately 655,000 units. By 1980 the shortage had increased to about 1.5 million. The problem is most severe in the urban areas. For instance, in 1978 it was estimated that 50 percent of Havana's total housing stock was in need of repair. About 30,000 units needed to be propped up to keep them from falling down, and 40,000 were declared uninhabitable.[26]

Although many large apartment buildings have been constructed in the cities as showcase examples of the efforts of the Revolution, housing remains in short supply because of policy decisions directing most of the building resources to productive investments, such as roads, factories, and power plants, as well as to the increased provision of social services. Looking for housing is a frustrating experience in Cuba. Families wanting housing are placed on waiting lists, as long as they can present evidence that they have been good citizens and support the ideals of the Revolution. It is not uncommon to wait several years before a unit becomes available.

The acute housing shortage in Cuba has affected some of the island's recent vital statistics. Research indicates that the unavailability of new housing for young couples is one factor that caused the marriage rate to drop by about 40 percent between the late 1960s and 1978. There is also evidence that the housing shortage has placed a severe strain on many marriages and has been partly responsible for the fivefold increase in the country's divorce rate since prerevolutionary times. Often housing must be shared with relatives through an extended-family arrangement. Indirectly, the housing deficit also has been one of the factors that has affected the island's declining fertility rate through delayed marriages and the growing number of divorces.[27]

URBAN AND RURAL GROWTH

As is typical for most other Latin American countries, Cuba's city system is characterized by a high level of primacy, in which one city, Havana, has traditionally dominated the urban scene. According to the 1981 census results, Havana's population was 1,924,886. This means 19.8 percent of all Cubans live in the capital city. It is almost 6 times as large as the island's second largest city, Santiago (345,298). In fact, it is larger than the combined population of Cuba's next 12 largest cities.[28]

Throughout most of the twentieth century Havana's share of the total Cuban population has increased, as most of the economic and social opportunities and other amenities were located there. In 1915, 15 percent of all Cubans lived in Havana. By 1953 the figure had risen to 21 percent. Immediately after the Castro Revolution there was a small increase, so that in 1963 the proportion living in Havana rose to a high of 22 percent. The latter increase proved to be temporary and was due to a surge in migration to the capital in response to new jobs in the recently created state enterprises and to the arrival of large numbers of scholarship students, many of whom were housed in the former residences of the departed upper and middle classes.[29]

It appears that 1962 marked a turning point in Cuba's urban history. Since that time Havana's share of the island's population has slowly declined to 20 percent in 1970 and about 19 percent today. This reversal of the processes of urban primacy is a rare experience for Latin America and has been due mainly to government policies that were initiated in the early 1960s. The Castro government has embarked on a deliberate program designed to reduce the overwhelming dominance of Havana, known as "a minimum of urbanism and a maximum of ruralism." There are two reasons for this policy. One is that, since the early 1960s, there has been a severe shortage of workers in agriculture that has been blamed for being especially significant in limiting the production of the island's major export—sugar. If more people could be convinced to remain in, or move to, the rural areas it would be easier to mobilize their labor for the peak season of production. Second, Fidel Castro had a deep ideological commitment to redress the inequalities in the living standards between cities and rural areas.[30]

As a result of this population redistribution policy, investments of all types have been kept low in Havana, while higher priority has been given to smaller cities and especially the countryside. For instance, housing construction and the building of schools have received the greatest emphasis in rural areas, as have the provision of social services such as medical facilities and economic development programs. In addition, the government has embarked on an ambitious program to resettle dispersed rural residents in modern, well-equiped small centers located throughout the agricultural regions of the island. These new rural towns consist of multi-story buildings that provide facilities for an average of 250 families. Running water, electricity, sewage disposal, new schools, and medical services are provided. The government reasons that when farmers are concentrated in these towns, instead of dispersed farmsteads, it will be easier to mobilize them for large agricultural projects and facilitate the provision of services to them. Although the investments in new towns has been large, the effect on the total population has not yet been of major consequence. In the late 1970s only about five percent of the rural population lived in these settlements.[31]

The decline in Havana's growth rate since 1962 can be related generally to the shift in government investment priorities to small cities and rural areas. More specifically, however, it is due to a number of interrelated factors, including: (1) the bad housing situation in Havana; (2) efforts to decentralize new manufacturing activities away from the city; (3) emigration to the United States and other foreign countries, which has drawn people disproportionately from the cities (especially from Havana until recently); (4) improvements in rural employment; (5) a rationing system which has helped equalize consumption in rural and urban areas; and (6) the existence of residence permits, ration books, and worker's identity cards which the government uses to either inhibit or encourage internal migration flows according to program objectives.[32]

FAMILY CHANGES

One of the most fundamental changes that has taken place within Cuban society has occurred within its family structure. Prior to the Castro Revolution the family that a person came from had a major impact on his or her political position, social behavior, and economic status. Children were pampered more by their parents and were guided closely by the family. There were sharp distinctions in the roles and accepted behavior patterns of men and women. Conversely, today it is the individual that is stressed by the new socialist codes. The family that an individual comes from is supposed to be immaterial as far as a person's worth is concerned. Children are more influenced by the state, particularly if they attend boarding schools, and are thoroughly indoctrinated with Marxist-Leninist thought and the ideology of the New Man. The roles of men and women are supposed to be more similar, with an emphasis being placed on an increase in female labor force participation and greater equality in the assignment of household chores.

Before the Revolution, the ideal female, especially among the upper and middle classes, was generally limited to the roles of wife and mother. She was preferably chaste, subservient, and sexually innocent. Most were not allowed to negotiate a business contract without their husband's permission and only a small percentage attended a university. The few activities that they participated in outside the home environment were usually voluntary in nature, such as welfare or cultural promotions. Men were dominant, uninhibited, and virile. They provided the family income and were not condemned for infidelity.

Given Fidel Castro's ideological commitment to redressing the inequalities that existed in Cuban society prior to the Revolution, it is not surprising that his government passed the Fundamental Law of 1959 as one of its earliest acts. It was designed to provide full civil liberties for women and to allow them to pursue the profession of their choice. Another goal was to increase the proportion of females in the labor force. In 1975 the Cuban Family code was enacted, which formally proscribed sex discrimination in the home. In theory, although probably not in practice, the husband and wife have equal rights and obligations, even extending to household tasks that were performed traditionally by women.

In 1960 the Cuban Women's Federation was begun as an organization to promote and raise the cultural and political participation levels of women to those of men. Over 80 percent of the island's adult females belong to the Federation. It has established daycare centers to help free women for greater participation in the labor force. Partly as a result of these efforts the number of working women has increased from 194,000 in 1958 to 800,600 in 1980. Today about 30 percent of all employed persons in Cuba are females.[33] In addition, unpaid volunteers organized by the Federation help pick the island's coffee crop, organize special education and cultural programs, and assist in carrying out vaccination drives for children. Young women now are as well educated as men. In fact, over 60 percent of Cuba's medical students are women.

Still, there are cracks within the system. It is not possible to simply erase by law sexual prejudices that have prevailed for generations. Although most Cuban men agree with the basic concept of human equality, many will not allow their wives to go out at night alone and will insist that their daughters be chaperoned while on dates. Still, there can be no doubt that progress has been made toward the ultimate goal of equality between the sexes.

RATIONING

Without doubt, the most often criticized aspect of life in Cuba is its all pervasive rationing system.[34] It was initiated in 1962 when it became obvious that there were many goods that people wanted to buy that were in short supply. Rationing was developed as a way of ensuring that the scarce items would be distributed equitably among the people, regardless of income or class. Although this goal generally has been achieved, the island's rationing system is resented by most Cubans. It is considered to be an annoyance, a waste of time, and a serious limitation on one's ability to get ahead in life. The result is a "queue culture," characterized by agonizingly long lines and seemingly endless waiting.

Every Cuban has a packet of ration books, one for each category of scarce goods. All types of items are included in the list of rationed items, such as foods, clothes, appliances, and automobiles. For instance, all foods are divided into three categories: (1) those that are strictly controlled according to amount purchased per person, price, and the frequency of allowed purchases (2) those that are controlled according to amount per person and price, but without limit on frequency of purchase, so an individual can get back in line if they want to buy more; (3) foods that are not rationed. For example, a person can buy only three-fourths of a pound of beef for each member of the family every nine days. One and a half ounces of coffee per person can be bought on a weekly basis. Only three cans of milk per capita can be obtained each month, except for children under seven years of age and adults over 60 who are entitled to one liter per day.

If individuals wish to buy a home appliance such as a washing machine, refrigerator, or television set they must attend a monthly meeting that is held where they work. During this meeting, they and others explain why the appliance is needed. After considering the levels of need, work productivity, and revolutionary spirit, a committee votes to determine whose name will be added to the list. In the case of especially scarce appliances, workers who are selected from several work centers must compete again at another meeting to have their names added to the final buying list. If a person is fortunate enough to have his or her name placed on such a list, they must then wait until it is available. Automobiles are in a special class, because it is the government, not the workers' committees, which decides who can buy them. They are usually available only to professionals, such as doctors, managers, and government leaders.

Home entertaining has been affected significantly by the rationing system. Because the amount of food is so severely limited per family member, home invitations for dinner have almost ended, unless the guests bring their own food. Restaurants have become somewhat of a safety valve for food rationing because any Cuban can eat out whenever they can afford it, and whatever the restaurant has that day can be ordered. With more than one family member working, it is usually possible to eat out once or twice a month.

Cuban leaders have tried to compensate for the scarcity of rationed goods through the creation of the "parallel market" and "peasant markets." The term parallel market refers to a situation where a work center produces more than its quota of a rationed good.The surplus is allowed to be sold at state-controlled prices which approximate the free market price. These prices are normally much higher than the state-subsidized prices for the same products when they are purchased under the quota system. The peasant markets function in a similar manner, except that food products (except beef, coffee, and tobacco) are involved rather than manufactured items.[33] In addition to these two market mechanisms, there is an active black market operating in the island. However, its prices are also high and the risks are great because people who are caught trading on the black market are subject to prison terms.

Conclusions

Cuba's history has had a major influence on the characteristics of the island today. Although the period of Spanish rule was crucial in the formation of a Cuban culture, it also would indelibly impress Cubans with the ills of political and economic colonialism. The Spaniards did not guide their Cuban subjects toward independence and a democratic form of government. Cuba was controlled under a mercantilistic system that was designed to favor Spain in every regard. It was the Spanish who introduced slavery and class distinctions.The economic system emphasized the agricultural sector with an overwhelming reliance on the sugar industry for external trade.

Just when it appeared that the 30-year rebellion against Spain would succeed, the United States entered the so-called Spanish-American War. From 1898 until 1902 the United States Army ran Cuba, and henceforth Cuban historians and politicians would always question American motives for their involvement in the island's affairs. The Platt Amendment, which was effective between 1901 and 1934, gave the United States authority to intervene in Cuban events whenever the Americans deemed it appropriate. Quickly, American corporations began to invest capital in Cuban business enterprises and extract enormous profits. Before long, Cuba's economy was dominated by the U.S. Altogether, these events led to resentment that would make the United States an easy target for anti-American propaganda.

Cuba's flirtations with democracy between 1902 and 1958 simply did not work out well. The dictatorships that prevailed during this period maintained many of the class distinctions that existed during the Spanish period. Although considerable economic growth did occur, its benefits were not equally distributed and most Cubans remained very poor, especially those living in rural areas. Given these inequalities and the failures of the first experience with democracy, Cuba was ripe for revolution. Because of the resentment that had developed toward the United States, it is not surprising that the American model of democracy and capitalism was rejected.

The socialist revolution that Fidel Castro initiated when he assumed control of Cuba's government in January 1959 was without precedent in the Western hemisphere. It should have been expected that a process of trial and error would ensue. For instance, one researcher has identified five different phases in the island's policies of economic development since Castro's government gained control.[36] As a consequence, Cuba's economy has alternately ebbed and flowed during the last 24 years. As the animosities between the United States and Cuba increased due to the appropriation of American-owned properties, the American trade embargo, the Bay of Pigs invasion, and the missile crisis, Cuba drifted more into the sphere of influence of the Soviet Union.

Many critics are quick to point out that Cuba is as economically dependent upon the Soviet Union today as it was on the United States during the 1950s. The Cuban government argues, however, that there are some important differences. The Soviets have given the Cubans easy payment terms on their loans and have extended credit when the United States withdrew its aid in a deliberate attempt to cause the island's economy to collapse. The Americans used to *own* almost all of the Cuban utility companies, many of the island's sugar mills, much of the best land, most of the banks, and the transportation system. American investors were always motivated by the hope of achieving large profits. The Soviets do not *own* anything in Cuba and their ties with Cuba represent an economic liability, rather than an asset, regardless of the political motives involved.[37]

The changes that have taken place in Cuba since 1959 have drastically altered the basic fabric of Cuban society. The undying principle behind these changes was a desire to achieve a more equitable distribution of incomes and living standards. This involved a redistribution of wealth which benefited many of the people included in the poorer classes, but at the same time worked to the disadvantage of the privileged wealthy class. It is not surprising that the Revolution would be controversial.

As is typical of communist societies, individual freedoms were suppressed and the good of society as a whole was stressed. An attempt was made to replace the profit motive with the concept of the New Man, who was viewed as being genuinely altruistic in behavior. Individuals were pressured to join mass organizations and thus conform to the new standards of the pervasive socialist philosophy. Great efforts were made in upgrading the island's education and health care systems and allowing their benefits to become more readily available to all people, rather than the privileged few. Almost all businesses were taken over by the state and wages were determined by a highly centralized government. The inequalities that formerly existed between living standards in rural and urban areas was addressed, with the result that conditions in the former improved, while those in the latter generally deteriorated. Efforts were made to redirect population growth away from Havana and toward intermediate sized cities and rural areas. Attempts also were made to alter the basic structure of the Cuban family by reducing some of the differences between males and females and to educate children in state-operated boarding schools. Finally, a strict rationing system was employed as a means of equally distributing scarce food and consumer items. These are some of the changes underlying the massive migration of Cubans to the United States that took place after Castro's government took control in 1959.

Notes

1. Several of the more important of these works are: Hugh Thomas, *Cuba: The Pursuit of Freedom* (New York: Harper and Row, 1971); Carmelo Mesa-Lago, ed., *Revolutionary Change in Cuba* (Pittsburgh: University of Pittsburgh Press, 1971); Cole Blasier and Carmelo Mesa-Lago, *Cuba in the World* (Pittsburgh: University of Pittsburgh Press, 1979); Carmelo Mesa-Lago, *The Economy of Socialist Cuba: A Two Decade Appraisal* (Albuquerque: University of New Mexico Press, 1981); and Jaime Suchlicki, *Cuba: From Columbus to Castro* (New York: Scribner's, 1975).
2. Howard K. Blutstein et al., *Area Handbook for Cuba* (Washington, D.C.: U.S. Government Printing Office, 1971), p. 27.
3. Barent Landstreet, "Cuba," in Aaron L. Segal, ed., *Population Policies in the Caribbean* (Lexington, Mass.: D.C. Heath, 1975), p. 128.
4. Blutstein, op. cit., p. 32.
5. Terrance Cannon, *Revolutionary Cuba* (New York: Thomas Y. Crowell, 1981), pp. 18–23.
6. Fred Ward, *Inside Cuba Today* (New York: Crown Publishers, 1978), p. 250.
7. Robert C. West and John P. Augelli, *Middle America: Its Lands and People* (Englewood Cliffs, N.J.: Prentice-Hall, 1976), pp. 135–139.
8. Landstreet, op. cit., p. 128.

9. Sergio Diaz-Briquets and Lisandro Perez, "Fertility Decline in Cuba: A Socioeconomic Interpretation," *Population and Development Review* 8:513–537, September 1983.
10. Ibid., p. 518.
11. Blutstein, op. cit., pp. 52–53.
12. Ward, op. cit., p. 195.
13. Cannon, op. cit., p. 225.
14. Lawrence H. Theriot, "Cuba Faces the Economic Realities of the 1980s" (a study prepared for the Joint Economic Committee, Congress of the United States, Washington, D.C.: U.S. Government Printing Office, 1982), p. 7.
15. Carmelo Mesa-Lago, "The Economy: Caution, Frugality, and Resilient Ideology," in Jorge I. Dominguez, ed., *Cuba: Internal and International Affairs* (Beverly Hills, Calif.: Sage Publications, 1982), p. 151.
16. Mesa-Lago, *The Economy of Socialist Cuba: A Two Decade Appraisal*, p. 35.
17. Arthur MacEwan, *Revolution and Economic Development in Cuba* (New York: St. Martin's Press, 1981), p. 181; and Jay Ducassi, "Cuba's Communists Offer Capitalist Work Incentives," *The Miami Herald*, January 6, 1983, p. 1A.
18. Mesa-Lago, "The Economy: Caution, Frugality, and Resilient Ideology," pp. 116–140.
19. Diaz-Briquets and Perez, op. cit., pp. 518
20. MacEwan, op. cit., pp. 42–43.
21. Most of this section draws freely from Ward, op. cit., pp. 55–80.
22. Blutstein, op. cit., p. 143.
23. Ward, op. cit., p. 112.
24. Cannon, op. cit., pp. 203–205.
25. *1982 World Population Data Sheet* (Washington, D.C.: Population Reference Bureau, April 1982).
26. Diaz-Briquets and Perez, op. cit., pp. 525–526.
27. Ibid., p. 526.
28. *The Europa Year Book 1982: A World Survey* (London: Europa Publications Limited, 1982, Vol. 2), p. 208.
29. Landstreet, op. cit., pp. 136–139.
30. Ibid.
31. Sergio Diaz-Briquets and Lisandro Perez, *Cuba Demography of Revolution* (Washington, D.C.: Population Reference Bureau, Vol. 36, No. 1, 1981), pp. 10–11.
32. Ibid., p.11; and Nelson Amaro and Carmelo Mesa-Lago, "Inequality and Classes," in Carmelo Mesa-Lago, ed., *Revolutionary Change in Cuba*, pp. 342–346.
33. Cannon, p. 233.
34. Most of this section draws freely from Ward, op. cit., pp. 18–28.
35. Mesa-Lago, "The Economy: Caution, Frugality, and Resilient Ideology," pp. 133–134.
36. Carmelo Mesa-Lago, *Cuba in the 1970s* (Albuquerque: University of New Mexico, 1978), pp. 1–29.
37. Cannon, op. cit., pp. 164–165.

3
History of Cuban Migration to the United States

The history of Cuban emigration to the United States comprises one of the more dramatic chapters in the voluminous annals of American immigration. A total of approximately 1,000,000 Cubans have migrated to the United States, representating all socioeconomic classes, ethnic groups, and regions of Cuba. The overwhelming majority has arrived since 1959 in the wake of the tumultuous revolution that propelled Fidel Castro to power and altered the basic political, social, and economic structure of the island nation.

It is only against this backdrop of sociopolitical upheaval and change, of personal suffering and discontent, that it is possible to understand the catalysts of this migration . Yet it would be incorrect to assume that all Cubans have come to America strictly to escape the often repressive socialistic regime imposed by Castro. The promise of refuge and political exile, the lure of economic opportunity, the quest for family reunification, and above all a desire for freedom have been powerful migrational "pull" forces.

For these reasons (and for others known only to the individuals concerned), Cubans continue to flee their native country, abandoning in the process the security of work, the familiarity of home, and the love of friends and relatives all in search of a new and hopefully better life in the United States. It is with compassion and respect that we should view the individual trauma of people leaving behind the lives they had built in their country of birth for a new land and a uncertain future. This central concern should not be lost in the facts and figures that are used in this chapter to document this extraordinary migration.

Cuban emigration to the United States can be broken up into seven clearly distinctive phases. The first was a trickle that began in the middle 1800s and continued until Fidel Castro assumed control in 1959. The second was a large-scale movement that occurred between 1959 and 1962 in the wake of the Revolution. The third was a hiatus, initiated by the Cuban Missile Crisis in 1962 and lasting until 1965, when Castro altered his migration policy. Emigration to the United States was renewed and lasted until 1973. This fourth phase is known as the period of the Freedom Flights. Between 1973 and 1980 there was another temporary interlude that represents the fifth phase. In 1973 Castro again closed Cuban ports for direct passage to American destinations. Unexpectedly, in April 1980 a veritable flood of Cuban migration was unleashed (as the sixth phase) through the small northern port of Mariel. Although it lasted only five months, approximately 125,000 Cubans travelled by boat to the United States during this wave. Since September 1980 emigration has declined once again. Both the Cuban and United States governments have reconsidered their migration policies, adopting seemingly stricter guidelines. This represents the seventh and current phase.

The Early Trickle

The first year for which census data are available for determining the number of Cubans in the United States is 1870 (Table 3.1). At that time a little over 5000 persons living on the United States mainland were born in Cuba. By the mid-1800s a sizable exodus of Cubans occurred in response to political turmoil on the island. Key West, Tampa, and New York City became particularly notable as places of refuge for Cuban political exiles who were plotting the overthrow of their Spanish rulers.[1] In addition, during the 1860s and 1870s several cigar manufacturers moved their operations from Havana to these three cities, thereby providing additional employment opportunities for Cuban immigrants.[2] A slow growth pattern emerged that was temporarily interrupted for short periods by World War I and the Great Depression of the 1930s. Miami did not begin to appear as a center of Cuban influence until the 1930s, when exiles fled the effects of the revolution against Gerardo Machado. Another spurt in the stream to Miami occurred from 1953 to 1959, as would-be revolutionaries fled the Batista regime.[3] From the beginning of the twentieth century until the Castro Revolution in 1959, immigration fluctuated according to changing political and economic conditions on the island.[4]

By 1959 Cubans had established a considerable historical legacy of settlement in the United States. Figures for 1930 (Table 3.1) show that almost half of the Cuban-Americans were second-generation residents. As the effects of the Castro Revolution became increasingly felt through massive emigration, this would change and a much larger percentage would become first-generation residents. Although further away from Cuba than any of the Florida urban areas, New York City clearly established a dom-

Table 3.1 Estimates of the Cuban-American Population, 1870–1981
(numbers in thousands)

Year[a]	Foreign-born	U.S.-born of Cuban parents	Total
1870	5.3	NA	NA
1880	6.9	NA	NA
1890	NA	NA	NA
1900	11.1	NA	NA
1910	15.1	NA	NA
1920	14.9	NA	NA
1930	18.5	17.0	35.5
1940	18.0	NA	NA
1950	33.7	NA	NA
1960	79.2	45.3	124.5
1970	439.0	122.0	561.0
1980[b]	NA	NA	831.0
1981[c]	NA	NA	1,000.0

NA = data not available.

[a] For the 1870 to 1970 period the figures are derived from : A. J. Jaffe, Ruth M. Cullen, and Thomas D. Boswell, *The Changing Demography of Spanish Americans* (New York: Academic Press, 1980), p. 247.

[b] The 1980 figure is for all persons who consider themselves to be of Cuban descent. It contains some individuals who were born in the United States with American-born parents. U.S. Bureau of the Census, *Current Population Reports*, Series P-20, No. 361: "Persons of Spanish Origin in the United States," March 1980 (Advance Report) (Washington, D.C.: U.S. Government Printing Office, 1981), p. 5.

[c] Estimate obtained from: Antonio Jorge and Raul Moncarz, *International Factor Movement and Complementary: Growth and Entrepreneurship Under Conditions of Cultural Variation* (The Hague, Netherlands: Research Group for European Migration Problems, R.E.M.P. Bulletin, Supplement 14, 1981), p. 4.

inant position as a home for Cubans living in the United States. Results from the 1950 Census show that there were 13,295 whites living in the state of New York who were born in Cuba, out of 29,295 for the entire country. The figure for Florida was a distant second with 7910. Thus, 72.4 percent of all those born in Cuba and living in the United States were residing in New York and Florida, with New York being the clear leader with 45.4 percent.[5] According to Jorge and Moncarz, there were approximately 40,000 Cuban-born Americans at the end of 1958, on the eve of Castro's assumption of power.[6]

The early experience of Cubans living in New York and Florida cannot be underestimated. It was crucial for the ability of future generations of Cuban immigrants to adjust to life in the United States. Cuban history books, songs, folktales, and poetry, for example, provide moving accounts of living conditions in America. The exiles who would emigrate after the introduction of communism in Cuba were at least partially aware, through these sources, of the Latin cultural concentrations in New York and Miami. Many were also familiar with the geographical and climatic similarities between Cuba and southern Florida.

Period of the "Golden Exiles"

Historically throughout the Caribbean, when one dictatorship is replaced by another, especially through use of force, the opponents of the victor become political exiles. This happened many times in Cuba before the advent of Castro. Therefore, it was not surprising that when Fidel Castro's forces overthrew the government of Fulgencio Batista in January 1959 an out-migration of backers of the ousted government occurred. The magnitude of this exodus, however, was not anticipated. During the 22-year period between 1959 and 1980 approximately 794,000 Cubans emigrated to the United States (Table 3.2). Except for Puerto Rico, no other island in the Caribbean has experienced a comparable outpouring in such a short period of time.

The key to understanding the reasons behind this remarkable exodus lies in an appreciation for the pervasiveness and speed of the societal changes that took place as Castro consolidated his power between 1959 and 1962 (see Chapter 2 for the details of these changes). In contrast to all other changes in dictatorships that have taken place in the Caribbean, Castro's efforts left no social sector untouched. The changes were, as Fagen et al. state, "cataclysmic."[7] The social structure, economic life, and political institutions were radically and rapidly altered. Those who were able and willing to adjust were welcomed into the new order. Persons who could not, or

Table 3.2 Cuban Migration to the United States, 1959–1980

Year	Number
1959[a]	26,527
1960[b]	60,224
1961	49,961
1962	78,611
1963	42,929
1964	15,616
1965	16,447
1966	46,688
1967	52,147
1968	55,945
1969	52,625
1970	49,545
1971	50,001
1972	23,977
1973	12,579
1974	13,670
1975	8,488
1976	4,515
1977[c]	4,548
1978	4,108
1979	2,644
1980	122,061
Total, January 1, 1959, to September 30, 1980	793,856
Total, April 1, 1980, to December 31, 1980	125,118

[a] For 1959 the figures are for January 1 to June 30.

[b] For 1960 through 1976 the figures are for fiscal years beginning July 1 and ending June 30.

[c] For 1977 through 1980 the figures are for fiscal years beginning October 1 and ending September 30.

Source: Sergio Diaz Briquets and Lisandro Perez, *Cuba: The Demography of Revolution* (Washington, D.C.: Population Reference Bureau, vol. 36, no. 1, April 1981), p. 26.

would not, accomodate to the system were rudely shouldered aside and often treated harshly. A considerable amount of confusion, suspicion, and uncertainty accompanied these changes. Of course there were many people, perhaps a majority, who perceived themselves as benefiting from these changes. Included would be the vast majority of the rural masses, blacks, perhaps the indoctrinated youth, and members of the new managerial and political class of elites.

More than 215,000 Cubans migrated to America between 1959 and 1962 (Table 3.2). In the beginning, the majority were members of the economic and political elite openly affiliated with the government of Batista. By the middle of 1959 members of the landholding aristocracy began to leave as an agrarian reform law was instituted in June, with the stated purpose of breaking up large landholdings. In July 1960 a law was passed authorizing the expropriation of all American-owned property. In the same year an urban reform law was enacted in October that was designed to confiscate rental property in the cities.[8] By this time the Revolution was also felt by middle-class entrepreneurs. In 1960 the number leaving had expanded to approximately 60,000.

Relations between the United States and Cuba began to cool rapidly in early 1961. On the third of January diplomatic relations with Cuba were broken by the American government. The ill-fated Bay of Pigs invasion was launched in April. Castro announced that he was a Marxist-Leninist and that Cuba was destined to become a socialist state. Severe restrictions were placed on the amount of property and money that could be taken out of the country. Finally, in October 1962, the Cuban missile crisis resulted in termination of air traffic to the United States. Legal emigration to America would remain suspended for about three years until September 1965.[9]

A study conducted in 1963 determined some of the primary reasons why Cubans immigrated to Miami between 1959 and 1962.[10] Twenty percent of those questioned stated that imprisonment or fear of imprisonment was the most significant motivating factor in their decision to leave. Another 20 percent indicated that harassment and persecution in Cuba was the most significant reason for their departure. Persons believed not to be supporters of the Castro regime were frequently exposed to abuse, both by government officials and by neighbors who were members of the infamous Committees for the Defense of the Revolution. Thirty-seven percent said they left Cuba because they generally disagreed with government activities, or took exception to communism. Surprisingly, only 6 percent said they left because of a loss of job, possessions, or sources of income. The remaining 14 percent listed miscellaneous reasons for emigrating.[11]

The 1963 motivation study also determined that 64 percent of the Miami immigrants interviewed experienced a decline in income under the

Figure 3.1 Appropriately named the Freedom Tower, this building in Miami served as the major processing center for Cuban refugees. (Photo courtesy of the Historical Association of Southern Florida.)

Castro policies before they left. Approximately 18 percent gained in income while the remaining 18 percent stayed about the same. With so many having lost income, why did only 6 percent indicate an economic reason for leaving? The authors of the study suggest three possible reasons. First, it is likely that a decrease in income did not in all cases represent a decline in purchasing power. Under socialism the cost of living was reduced through the greater provision of social services by the government, such as a reduction in rents, free health care, and free education at all levels. Second, of all the reasons for leaving, economic motives were probably the most difficult to admit. Appearing to be "materialistic" would make them seem to be less patriotic. Most emigrants considered themselves to be intensely loyal to Cuba, despite the fact that they left the island. Their complaint was not with the Cuban people per se, but with the radicalization of the Castro government along Marxist-Leninist lines. A third possible reason is that economic reasons really were simply not very important in reaching a decision to emigrate. Even among those who were destroyed economically by government expropriations and reorganization, financial losses were only one facet of a broader upheaval that divested them of power, privilege, and prestige. Thus, they saw themselves as being refugees from everything for which the communist regime stood.[12]

The 1959 to 1962 era of Cuban immigration to the United States is often referred to as the wave of "Golden Exiles." This refers to the belief that the vast majority were former members of the elite classes in Cuba. The data in Table 3.3 suggest that this concept is only partly correct. The refugees were overrepresented in the legal and white-collar professions and underrepresented in the primary occupations (such as agriculture and fishing) and in blue collar jobs.[13] However, the refugees were also a highly diverse group. Virtually all occupations were represented, making it incorrect to think of all of them as having been elites in Cuba. In fact, less than 40 percent should be so considered. Nevertheless, when considered as a whole, the refugees for the 1959 to 1962 interval were not representative of the entire Cuban population.

Data also confirm the notions of a higher level of education among Cuban emigrants, while also suggesting considerable diversity. When the education levels of the Miami refugees were compared to those of the entire Cuban population for 1953, it was found that the former were considerably better educated. Only 4 percent of the refugees had less than a fourth-grade education, compared with 52 percent for all Cubans. On the other hand, 36 percent of the refugees had completed either high school or some college whereas the comparable figure for Cuba was only 4 percent.[14]

Table 3.3 Comparison of the Occupational Structure of Cuba in 1953 with the Occupations of Cuban Refugees at the Time They Migrated to Miami Between 1959 and 1963

Occupation	1953 Cuban census	Percentage of census	1959-63 Cuban refugees	Percentage of refugees	Ratio: percentage of refugees to percentage of census
Lawyers and judges	7,858	.5	1,695	3.0	7.8
Professional and semi-professional	78,051	4.0	12,124	22.0	5.5
Managerial and executive	93,662	5.0	6,771	12.0	2.5
Clerical and sales	264,569	14.0	17,123	31.0	2.3
Domestic service, military, and police	160,406	8.0	4,801	9.0	1.1
Skilled, semi-skilled, and unskilled	526,168	27.0	11,301	20.0	.7
Agricultural and fishing	807,514	41.5	1,539	3.0	.1
Total	1,938,228		55,354		

Source: Richard R. Fagen, Richard A. Brody, and Thomas J. O'Leary, *Cubans in Exile: Disaffection and the Revolution* (Stanford, Calif.: Stanford University Press, 1968), p. 19.

The Miami Cuban refugee study also determined that a much larger than proportionate share of the emigrants were from urban origins than was the case for the 1953 Cuban population. For instance, 87 percent of the refugees lived either in Havana (62 percent) or some other large city (25 percent) in Cuba before leaving for Florida, whereas only 31 percent of Cuba's total population lived in the same areas. On the other hand, 69 percent of all Cubans resided in small towns or rural areas, while the figure for the refugees was 13 percent.[15]

Although precise figures are not available, it is apparent that more than half the Cuban emigrants to the United States were females. It was frequently the case that businessmen would send their wives and children to America, while they waited in Cuba to see if their investments and property could be saved.[16] They reasoned that if the situation became dangerous it would be easier for them to escape alone. Furthermore, they often had friends or relatives in Florida or New York who would help their family adjust to living outside Cuba.

Missile Crisis Hiatus

The missile crisis and United States military blockade of Cuba in October 1962 brought to an abrupt halt all direct legal transportation between the two countries. A hiatus in legal migration to the United States was to ensue for three years until September 1965. This would not be the only time that the Castro government would quickly reverse its position on emigration. Rather, it was a harbinger of future similar sharp reversals in emigration policy.

The Castro government has always exhibited a considerable degree of ambivalence toward out-migration. One view is labelled the "purification" theme. It suggests that the Cuban revolutionary movement will be better off without those persons who cannot or will not accomodate themselves to the new order. If those individuals wish to leave, so much the better for Cuba—let them go. A contrasting view holds that emigration is detrimental to the Cuban Revolution for two principal reasons: first, it has created a serious "brain drain," where badly needed skilled and educated manpower has been lost; second, it has created a "demonstration effect" that has injured the reputation of the communist government. Officials, as well as the general population, know that not all who fled the island were members of the elite sector during the Batista era. Many have come from those sectors that the Revolution was supposed to help the most. This has proven to be a conspicuous embarrassment, both internally and internationally.[17]

Despite the fact that direct legal transportation was stopped between Cuba and the United States, it has been estimated that close to 56,000 still managed to migrate. This includes about 6700 who were able to escape Cuba, mainly in boats and a few in planes. A little over 6000 additional persons were allowed to leave directly for the United States during this period. These were former prisoners from the Bay of Pigs expedition and members of their families. They were released in exchange for a ransom consisting of shipments of badly needed medicines and medical supplies for Cuba.[18]

The vast majority of the remaining 43,300 who were able to reach the United States from Cuba during this three-year period did so indirectly through intermediate countries, most frequently through Spain or Mexico.[19] However, this was a costly and enervating process. Persons who arrived in either New York or Miami directly from Cuba were automatically granted immediate legal entry. Yet those who sought entry from a third country were considered aliens by the United States Department of Immigration and Natualization Service, and were therefore subject to all existing immigration restrictions. Often the wait in Madrid or Mexico City was well over a year before clearance was obtained.[20]

Period of Freedom Flights

On September 28, 1965, Fidel Castro announced that he would permit Cubans with relatives living in the United States to emigrate beginning on the following October tenth.[21] The departures would take place by boat through the small port of Camarioca on the northern coast of Matanzas Province. Immediately, hundreds of boats departed from southern Florida for Cuba to pick up friends and relatives. Unfortunately, not all the crafts were seaworthy and a number of tragedies occurred. The chaos that ensued, as a result of the panicky rush and accompanying accidents, created a source of embarrassment for the Cuban government. As a consequence, United States and Cuban authorities signed a "Memorandum of Understanding" which established arrangements for an airlift between Miami and a Cuban airport located east of Havana, in the town of Varadero. The agreement was organized through the Swiss Embassy in Havana and the flights became variously known as the "Freedom Flights," "Aerial Bridge," or "Family Reunification Flights."

Air transportatiion was initiated on December 1, 1965, and continued until April 6, 1973. Normally 2 flights a day, 5 days per week, were operated between Miami and Havana, carrying 3000 to 4000 persons per month.[22] It has been estimated that 297,318 persons arrived during the seven-year airlift. In addition, 4993 came by boat during the 2-month boatlift from Camarioca. A little over 302,000 Cubans migrated directly to the United States between October 10, 1965, and April 6, 1973.[23] A few also continued to travel indirectly from Cuba via third countries, such as Mexico and Spain, to Miami and New York.

The airlift did not result in a free exodus from Cuba. Relatives of persons already living in the United States were given priority according to closeness of the family relationship. Members of nuclear families were accorded the highest preference. Males of military age (17 to 26 years old) usually were not allowed to leave. Skilled and highly trained individuals working in critical occupations often were not granted exit visas, until replacements could be found and trained. The elderly and sick also were more likely to receive clearance to leave, since there was a greater likelihood that they would be dependent on the Cuban social security system for their support. Persons who filed exit applications frequently lost their jobs and were required to perform agricultural labor until plane space became available. It was not uncommon for an adult male to spend two or three years working in agricultural fields for minimal wages before being allowed to leave.[24]

By the late 1960s, the communist regime had gained sufficient strength to consolidate its control over the remaining middle-class, private, small-business sector of the Cuban economy. In this way, the Revolution had widened to include also the vestiges of a lower-middle class composed of artisans, small businessmen, and merchants. As a result, the occupational mixture of the Cuban immigrants began to change from what it had been during the period of the "Golden Exiles" between 1959 and 1962. For instance, the percentage of arriving refugees who were working in Cuba as professional and managerial employees declined from 31 percent in 1962 to 18 percent in 1967.[25] Furthermore, the first job taken in the United States was very likely to be at a lower level, in terms of both income and skills, than the one left behind in Cuba. This was especially true for more highly trained persons in the professional and managerial occupations.[26] Gradually, the migration stream was maturing, so the immigrants were beginning to approach the occupational characteristics of the labor force in Cuba. Despite this trend, however, those migrating to the United States (considered as a group) still were characterized by higher socioeconomic status (at the time they left Cuba) than those who remained behind.[27]

During the period of the Freedom Flights the largest number of Cuban refugees who arrived in Miami and Union City-West New York came from the provinces of Havana and Las Villas. As was the case during the period of the "Golden Exiles," the majority also came from large cities, with only a very small number arriving from rural areas. In the case of Union City-West New York in 1968, less than one percent came from rural areas in Cuba.[28]

Social networks have proven to be very influential in determining where refugees finally settle in the United States. During the 1959 to 1962 period approximately 70 percent of the refugees in Miami had either relatives or close friends living in southern Florida.[29] In 1968, 93 percent of the Cubans in West New York had some family members living in the United States before they arrived.[30] The corresponding figure for Miami was almost 99 percent.[31] And generally those with relatives in Miami generally settled in Miami and those with family members in the New York metropolitan area usually settled there.

The Interlude from 1973 to 1980

Beginning in August 1971 the Cuban government started creating occasional interruptions in the Freedom Flights. Castro had decided by the end of May 1969 to stop accepting new applications for exit visas. In Septmeber 1971 he announced that the list of people who had requested permits was getting smaller and that the exodus would end soon. It was claimed that the intention of the "Memorandum of Understanding," which was to reunite separated families, had largely been fulfilled. As a result the number of airlift immigrants began to slacken toward the end of 1971 and continued to decrease throughout 1972, until the last flight was made on April 6, 1973.[32]

From July 1, 1973 to September 30, 1979, a total of just under 38,000 Cubans arrived in the United States (see Table 3.2). This was less than 13 percent of the number that arrived during the period of the Freedom Flights and the Camarioca boatlift. Those who were able to emigrate during this seven-year interlude did so primarily through third countries, just as they did during the Cuban missile crisis hiatus earlier. Again, Mexico and Spain served as the primary stepping stones on the way to the Miami or New York metropolitan areas, with smaller numbers being channeled through Jamaica and Venezuela.

There was one notable exception to the generalization that most immigrants from Cuba at this time came indirectly through intervening countries. In October 1978 Castro announced that he had reached a decision to release 3600 political prisoners held in Cuban jails, as a gesture of good will. An airlift ensued over the next seventeen months, until it was suddenly ended by Castro in March 1980 without explanation. Family members were often allowed to accompany the prisoners in their departure to the United States. Estimates are that between 10,000 and 14,000 persons took part in this bizarre exodus.[33]

The migration selectivity processes and trends that were operating in earlier phases of the Cuban emigration waves were also in effect during the 1973 to 1980 interval. Studies of Cubans living in West New York[34] and Miami[35] indicate that although the new immigrants were better off in terms of their occupational and income status than the majority left behind in Cuba, the degree of positive selection was declining. As was the case during the 1965 to 1973 period, this most recent wave was coming closer to being representative of the Cuban population. It also was becoming apparent that economic motives were beginning to play a larger role in affecting the decision to leave Cuba, certainly more so than had been the case in the early 1960s.[36]

As mentioned earlier, it was usually the case that when the refugees arrived in the United States their first jobs were at lower levels than had been the case in Cuba prior to their departure. However, it became clear in the 1970s that once they had spent a few years in the United States they begin to experience considerable upward occupational mobility.[37]

An interesting change began to clearly emerge during the 1970s with respect to the emigrants' origins in Cuba. Although Havana had dominated as the leading sender, with Las Villas Province being a distant second, by 1979 Las Villas had surpassed Havana as the leading origin for Cubans going to West New York and was apparently having more of an influence as an origin for persons going to Miami as well. Furthermore, small cities, towns, and rural areas were beginning to account for an increasingly larger proportion of the refugees. In 1968 56 percent of the Cubans living in West New York had come from large cities in Cuba. In 1979 the comparable figure had declined to 40 percent.[38] This general shift toward smaller settlements in Cuba is part of the same trend noted previously with respect to occupation and income, namely a tendency for the immigrants over time to take on characteristics more similar to the population living in Cuba.

The Flood from Mariel

In April 1980 Cuban history repeated itself, as once again mass emigration was allowed to the United States in a manner reminiscent of the boatlift from Camarioca harbor in 1965. Again the mode of transportation was by the sea and this time the place of departure selected by Castro was the small port of Mariel, located on the northern coast approximately 20 miles west of Havana. There was, however, one major difference between this exodus and the one from Camarioca that took place 15 years earlier. The Camarioca boatlift lasted for about two months and involved approximately 5,000 Cubans; the Mariel diaspora lasted for close to 5 months (April 21 to September 26, 1980) and involved 124,779 people. During the single month of May the number leaving for the United States was

86,488.[39] This was more than the number who left the island during the entire year of 1962 (78,611), which until 1980 was the year characterized by the largest outflow of Cubans to America (Table 3.2).

To understand the mechanisms behind the Mariel exodus it is necessary to go back to December 1978 when President Castro announced that he would allow Cuban-Americans to return to Cuba for one-week visits with their families.[40] Throughout 1979 and early 1980 about 100,000 persons took part in these sojourns, spending perhaps $100 million on the island. This stream of visitors has often been referred to as the "blue- jeans revolution" because returning émigrés usually brought gifts, such as designer jeans, for their relatives living in Cuba.[41] There were at least three motives for allowing these visits. First, the money spent in Cuba by the visitors would help the ailing Cuban economy. Second, by allowing the former Cuban residents to return, Castro hoped to demonstrate that his government was in firm control and that further attempts by Cuban exiles to dislodge him from power would prove futile. Third, Castro figured that his actions would improve his government's human rights image in other countries. What Castro and his advisors did not foresee was the "demonstration effect" that the returnees would have on their relatives still living in Cuba. Suddenly, 20 years of anti-American and anti-exile propaganda subsided as visitors provided tangible evidence and vivid accounts of a much better lifestyle in the United States that contrasted sharply with the austere living conditions which existed under the direction of the totalitarian government of Cuba.[42] Perhaps the tales of opportunities and material benefits of life in the United States were sometimes overstated. Nevertheless, the effect was clearly to promote, or increase, the desire among many Cubans to leave.

In addition to the effect of the "blue-jeans revolution" there were several other factors that influenced the decision by many Cubans to migrate to the United States. Cuba's economy was experiencing a serious recession. The two major export crops, sugar and tobacco, were being riddled by diseases. Inflation and unemployment were beginning to emerge as major problems.[43] There were still many family members who remained in Cuba and wished to join their relatives living in the United States but were unable to do so during the earlier Freedom Flights. Some of these were males who were obliged to participate in the military services, and others were persons working in certain skilled occupations who were not allowed to leave until replacements could be found. Also, 1979 was a year in which political dissent increased as a result of government austerity programs. When 400 Mariel immigrants in Miami were asked why they left Cuba, 79 percent said they did so for political reasons. Another 12 percent cited economic reasons for their decision to leave and 6 percent claimed that family reunification was their primary goal.[44]

On April 4, 1980, the Peruvian Embassy was suddenly opened by the Castro government to any Cubans who wished to leave the island. Within a couple of days the number seeking asylum had risen, astonishingly, to almost 11,000. At first, Castro allowed these people to exit to Peru and Costa Rica. The large-scale exodus to these two Latin American countries, and the spectacle it caused, was regarded as a major embarrassment for the Cuban government. Therefore, on April 21, 1980, it was decided to open the port of Mariel to any individuals who wished to go directly to the United States, so the emigration stream would be redirected away from Central and South America.

Over one percent of the Cuban population left for the United States during the Mariel boatlift. In the process, this partially relieved an acute housing shortage and the increasing unemployment that plagued the island at this time. It also allowed the government to rid itself of (or identify) dissidents who were not supporting the communist regime. It also provided Castro with scapegoats who could be blamed for undermining the Cuban economy and would be used to infuse more spirit into the Revolution that was showing signs of stagnation.[45] It has been estimated that more than one million additional Cubans would have left the island had Mariel not been closed to further emigration by Castro in September 1980.[46]

Once it became apparent that the number of persons who wanted to leave Cuba was going to be a lot larger than the Cuban government had originally predicted, Castro tried to turn an embarrassing situation into his advantage. He decided to force most of the captains of the boats that had been sent from Florida to pick up family members to take back to the United States many of whom Castro labelled as social undesirables. Included in this were a number of persons with criminal records, homosexuals, patients from mental institutions, and even deaf-mutes and lepers. In addition to trying to rid the island of these unwanted people, there is little doubt that the Cuban government was trying to taint the reputation of the Cuban-Americans. Approximately 26,000 of the Mariel refugees have prison records, but many had been jailed for political reasons or for minor crimes, such as stealing food or trading on the black market for a pair of blue-jeans.[47] Although estimates vary, perhaps 5,000 (or 4 percent) were hard-core criminals.

It is a fact that this criminal element has helped increase the levels of violent crime in both the Miami and New York metropolitan areas. In April 1981 it was estimated that between 30 and 40 percent of Dade County's (Miami) jail population was Latin, and most were believed to be

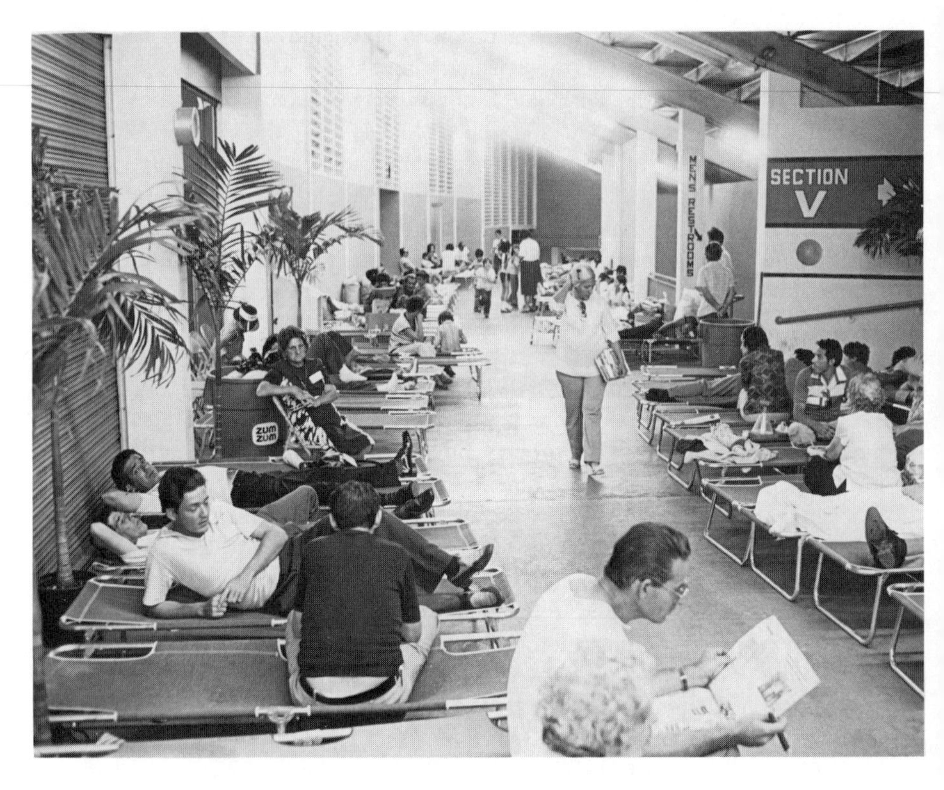

Figure 3.2 During the Mariel exodus in 1980, the Orange Bowl in Miami provided temporary shelter for Cuban refugees awaiting resettlement. (Photo courtesy of the City of Miami, Office of Information.)

"Marielitos."[48] Perhaps, half of all violent crimes in Miami in 1981 were caused by these people.[49] It is also likely that the level of criminal activity has declined in Cuba as a result of the Mariel wave.[50]

An opinion poll conducted by *The Miami Herald* in May 1980 determined that 68 percent of the non-Latin whites and 57 percent of the blacks surveyed felt that the Mariel refugees have had a largely negative impact on Dade County.[51] In addition to the perception that the Mariel sealift was being used by Castro to empty his jails and mental institutions, there are at least four other reasons why the "Marielitos" were not welcomed upon their arrival in Florida. First, the suddennes and massive size of the influx intensified problems in helping them settle. Many who did not have relatives or friends to help them adjust were temporarily housed in military camps in Florida, Arkansas, Pennsylvania, and Wisconsin. One estimate is that it has cost the United States Government close to $1 billion to

Figure 3.3 Tents were erected beneath the bypasses off Interstate 95 on the edge of downtown Miami to house Mariel refugees. The area quickly became known as "Tent City." (Photo courtesy of the City of Miami, Office of Information.)

provide for the Mariel exiles, including the budgets for the Navy and Coast Guard operations that took place during the flotilla.[52] A second reason for refugees from Mariel not being welcomed is that the United States' economy in 1980 was experiencing a recession, accompanied by inflation. In Dade County it has been estimated that the unemployment rate jumped from about 5 percent to 13 percent, primarily due to the Mariel influx. Also, the apartment vacancy rate was reduced to less than 1 percent, creating an acute housing shortage and high rents.[53]

A third reason for the cool reception given the Marielitos is that by 1980 public opinion was in favor of reducing immigration, as a result of attention given by the news media to the problems encountered during the migrations of Vietnamese, Mexicans, and Haitians to the United States.[54] A fourth factor was that between 70 and 75 percent of all the Mariel émigrés settled in southern Florida, especially in Dade County. This degree of concentration was greater than for the earlier Cuban waves and thus made their adjustment problems more visible and newsworthy. Had they been evenly dispersed throughout the 50 states, they probably would have been hardly noticed. But the three largest cities in Dade County all experienced increases in their Latin populations as a result of the Mariel flotilla. The percentage of the population of the city of Miami that was Latin increased from 56 percent to 59 percent. For Hialeah the growth was from 74 to 78 percent; while for Miami Beach the increase was from 22 to 27 percent.[55]

Unfortunately, the negative attitude toward the Marielitos expanded to many of the Cuban-Americans who arrived prior to 1980. It is now common to hear members of the Cuban Community in Miami speak in terms of "new" and "old" Cubans. The "old" Cubans are among the harshest critics of the "new" ones. This is a tendency that has been noted historically among other immigrant groups in the United States, but has been especially aggravated by the special set of circumstances that have accompanied the Mariel wave, particularly the forced inclusion by Castro of criminals.[56] Many of the old Cubans fear that the new will tarnish their reputation, just as Castro had hoped they would.

Unlike the emigrants from Cuba who preceded them, the Mariel group was not composed equally of males and females; almost 70 percent were males. There are two reasons for this. First, most of the criminals and social misfits that were included in the immigration wave were males. Second, many of the young men who were unable to travel aboard the Freedom Flights between 1965 and 1973, because of required military service, were able to leave in 1980 since they had served their military obligations.

The Marielitos also differed from earlier movements in that a larger percentage (about 20 percent) were blacks and a somewhat greater proportion arrived as single adults.[57] These are significant characteristics because the Cuban Refugee Resettlement Center has experienced the most difficulty in finding help for the settlement of single, black, adult Cuban males.

Occupationally, the Mariel flow can best be represented as a continuation of the trend previously noted during earlier Cuban emigration stages. Again, there was an increase in the representation of the working classes and a decline in the percentage of professional and managerial workers, as they came closer to being representative of the population in Cuba. Still, the Marielitos as a whole enjoyed a somewhat higher socioeconomic status than the population left behind in Cuba. It is clear that these most recent emigrants were not marginal to the Cuban economy, nor are they unemployable in the United States.[58] Despite some of the problems created by a reputation sensationalized by both the Cuban and American presses, it is the concensus of most who have studied them that the Mariel refugees will quickly and effectively accomodate themselves to life in the United States.

Summary of Historical Trends

Cuban emigration to the United States has a history that dates back to before the middle 1800s. However the flow has become significant only since 1959, when Fidel Castro assumed control of the government in Cuba. The Revolution that followed was pervasive: virtually no segment of Cuban society was able to escape its effects. Since 1959 out-migration has ebbed and flowed primarily according to dictates of the Castro government. Several thousand Cubans have been able to escape occasionally in boats (a few in planes), but they have never represented a very large share of the total emigrant population. Although the Cuban government has steadfastly denied that its emigration policies have been related to problems of population pressure,[59] there is considerable evidence to the contrary. For instance out-migration has certainly eased Cuba's acute housing shortage and unemployment problems. It also has been used as a device for ridding the country of political dissidents and others who did not fit into Castro's society. On the other hand, emigration has created a serious "brain drain" of professional and skilled workers and at times has created a source of embarrassment.

It is clear that there have been some significant changes between the types of people who moved from Cuba to the United States during the 22-year period from the time of the "Golden Exiles" to the flow of the Marielitos. Although the waves have been diverse in composition, the earliest were richer and more educated, while the later ones tended to be more representative of the population still living in Cuba.

There is also considerable evidence that the motivation for migrating from Cuba to the United States has changed over time. During the early 1960s it was clear that most were emigrating for political, social, and religious reasons. These persons were clearly refugees and therefore were accorded special immigration status upon entry into the United States. This expedited their processing by American immigration authorities and made it easier for them to receive financial and social assistance. By the 1970s, however, it began to become apparent that economic motives were beginning to replace those of political and religious persecution. As a result, the United States government enacted the 1980 Refugee Act which severely limits the number of Cubans allowed to legally enter this country. The Marielitos who arrived during this period were granted a special status known as "Entrants-Status Pending" which allowed them to enter the United States, with the details of their stay to be decided at a later date.

All other Cubans who were to seek entrance after October 1980 are required to apply in the same manner as all other nonrefugees. They must now apply for entrance on an individual basis. Those who seek refugee status must prove beyond reasonable doubt that they face political or religious persecution if they are repatriated to Cuba.[60] The effect of this change in policy has been to greatly reduce the flow of Cubans to the United States since October 1980.[61]

The migration from Cuba holds additional significance beyond the contribution of a million people to the population of the United States and the considerable impact it has had on the nation's ethnic and cultural patterns. This migration also is important for the practical and symbolic role it has played in shaping American attitudes and policies toward immigration. Cubans, in general, have been as well-received in this country as has any immigrant group in recent history. Their flight from communism and from the iron-clad rule of an apparently malevolent (though nonetheless charismatic) dictator struck a responsive chord in America. It pulled at the very heart of American patriotism and sense of justice and compassion.

In the more recent stages of the migration, now entering its third decade since the revolution, questions have been raised concerning the imposition and the effectiveness of federal immigration laws and policy. This change in attitude is a reflection of the view that our Cuban emigration policy is set not by the U.S. government, but by Fidel Castro. The history of the past twenty years of this migration has shown repeatedly the weaknesses and vulnerability of our immigration policy. Should fundamental change in our official immigration posture occur, it will be related in a significant way to the migration from Cuba.

Notes

1. Patrick Lee Gallagher, *The Cuban Exile: A Socio-Political Analysis* (New York: Arno Press, 1980), pp. 23–36.
2. A. J. Jaffe, Ruth M. Cullen, and Thomas D. Boswell, *The Changing Demography of Spanish Americans* (New York: Academic Press, 1980), pp. 246–248.
3. Gallagher, op. cit., pp. 34–35.
4. Lisandro Perez, "Cubans," in *The Harvard Encyclopedia of American Ethnic Groups* (edited by Stephan Thernstrom; Cambridge: The Belknap Press of Harvard University Press, 1980), p. 256.
5. U.S. Bureau of the Census, *U.S. Census of Population: 1950*, Vol. 4, Special Reports, Part 3, Chapter A, "Nativity and Parentage" (Washington, D.C.: U.S. Government Printing Office, 1954), pp. 71–74.
6. Antonio Jorge and Raul Moncarz, *Internation Factor Movement and Complementary Growth and Entrepreneurship Under Conditions of Cultural Variation* (The Hague, Netherlands: Research Group for European Migration Problems, R.E.M.P. Bulletin, supplement 14, 1981), p. 3.

7. Richard R. Fagen, Richard A. Brody, and Thomas J. O'Leary, *Cubans in Exile: Disaffection and the Revolution* (Stanford, Calif.: Stanford University Press, 1968), p. 100.

8. Gallagher, op. cit., pp. 37–39.

9. University of Miami, *The Cuban Immigration, 1959–1966, and Its Impact on Miami-Dade County, Florida* (Coral Gables: Research Institute for Cuba and the Caribbean, Center for Advanced International Studies, University of Miami, July 10, 1967), p. 1, Appendix A.

10. Fagen, Brody, and O'Leary, op. cit., pp. 75–98.

11. Ibid., p. 90.

12. Ibid., pp. 85–86.

13. The 1953 Cuban population census was the one that was the most recently available at the time Fagen, Brody, and O'Leary conducted their investigation.

14. Fagen, Brody, and O'Leary, op. cit., p. 19.

15. Ibid., p. 13.

16. University of Miami, op. cit., p. 11–13.

17. Fagen, Brody, and O'Leary, op. cit., p. 117.

18. Juan M. Clark, "The Exodus from Revolutionary Cuba (1959–1974): A Sociological Analysis" (Ph.D. dissertation, University of Florida, Florida, 1975), p. 75.
1975), p. 75.

19. It has been reported that 1,612 persons (638 of whom had U.S. citizenship) were transported from Havana to Miami on an American Red Cross sponsored aircraft. Virginia R. Dominguez, *From Neighbor to Stranger: The Dilemma of Caribbean Peoples in the United States* (New Haven, Conn.: Antilles Research Program, Yale University, Occasional Paper, No. 5, 1975), p. 22.

20. Gallagher, op. cit., pp. 39–42.

21. Dominguez, op. cit., p. 22.

22. Barent Landstreet, "Cuba," in *Population Policies in the Caribbean* Aaron Lee Segal, ed. (Lexington, Mass.: Lexington Books, 1975), pp. 140–141.

23. Clark, op. cit., pp. 85–98.

24. Alejandro Portes, Juan M. Clark, and Robert L. Bach, "The New Wave: A Statistical Profile of Recent Cuban Exiles to the U.S.," *Cuban Studies* 7:17, January 1977.

25. Fagen, Brody, and O'Leary, op. cit., p. 115.

26. Portes, Clark, and Bach, op. cit., pp. 19–24; and Eleanor Meyer Rogg, *The Assimilation of Cuban Exiles: The Role of Community and Class* (New York: Aberdeen Press, 1974), pp. 135, 137.

27. The 1953 Census for Cuba showed only 9.5 percent of the labor force being employed as professional and managerial workers (see Table 3.3). In Cuba 41.5 percent of all employed persons were working in agriculture and fishing; while for the refugees arriving in Miami in 1967 the corresponding figure was only 4 percent. Fagen, Brody, and O'Leary, op. cit., p. 115.

28. Portes, Clark, and Bach, op. cit., p. 11; and Rogg, op. cit., p. 27.

29. Fagen, Brody, and O'Leary, op. cit., p. 102.

30. Rogg, op. cit., pp. 28–29, 132.

31. Portes, Clark, and Bach, op. cit., p. 18.

32. Landstreet, op. cit., p. 141.

33. Clyde McCoy, Duane McBride, Bryan Page, and Diana Gonzalez, "The Post-Revolutionary Immigration—Cubans in the United States 1959–January, 1981" (unpublished manuscript, Department of Psychiatry, Medical School, University of Miami, 1982), pp. 66–67.

34. Eleanor Meyer Rogg and Rosemary Santana Cooney, *Adaptation and Adjustment of Cubans: West New York, New Jersey* (New York: Monograph No. 5, Hispanic Research Center, Fordham University, 1980), pp. 35–46.

35. Alejandro Portes, Juan M. Clark, and Manuel M. Lopez, "Six Years Later, A Profile of the Process of Incorporation of Cuban Exiles in the United States," *Cuban Studies* 11:1–24, July 1981.

36. Portes, Clark, and Bach, op. cit., pp. 2, 30–31.
37. Rogg and Cooney, op. cit., p. 37; Portes, Clark, and Bach, op. cit., p. 16; and Aida Tomas Levitan, "Hispanics in Dade County: Their Characteristics and Needs" (Miami: Latin Affairs, Office of County Manager, Metropolitan Dade County, printed report, Spring 1980), p. 14.
38. Rogg and Cooney, op. cit., pp. 18–19; and Portes, Clark, and Bach, op. cit., p. 11.
39. For a listing of the numbers of Cubans arriving in the United States by individual months during the Mariel boatlift, see: Juan M. Clark, Jose L. Lasaga, and Rose S. Reque, *The 1980 Mariel Exodus: An Assessment and Prospect* (Washington, D.C.: Council for Inter-American Security, A Special Report, 1981), p. 5.
40. Sergio Diaz-Briquets and Lisandro Perez, *Cuba: The Demography of Revolution* (Washington, D.C.: Population Reference Bureau, Vol. 36, No. 1, April 1981), p. 28.
41. Guy Gugliotta, "How a Trickle Became a Flood: Origins of the Freedom Flotilla," *The Cuban Exodus, The Miami Herald*, Special Reprint, 1980, pp. 8–10.
42. Clark, Lasaga, and Reque, op. cit., p. 2.
43. Gugliotta, op. cit., p. 10.
44. Clark, Lasaga, and Reque, op. cit., p. 9.
45. Ibid., p. 6.
46. Guillermo Martinez, "Mariel Refugees: A City Within a City," *The Miami Herald*, December 14, 1980, p. 1A.
47. Clark, Lasaga, and Reque, op. cit., p. 7.
48. "Wake from Mariel's Boats Still Washes South Florida," *The Miami Herald*, April 19, 1981, p. 16A; and Joyce Wadler, "Violent Mariel Refugees Plague New York, Too," *The Miami Herald*, December 13, 1981, p.1G.
49. "Trouble in Paradise," *Time*, November 23, 1981, p. 23.
50. Fabiola Santiago, "Has Cuba's Crime Fallen Since Mariel?" *The Miami Herald*, December 25, 1981, p. 9A.
51. Richard Morin, "Deluge Adds to Fear in Uneasy Miami," *The Cuban Exodus, The Miami Herald*, p. 11. The attitudes toward the Cuban refugees who came during the twenty years before the Mariel exodus were more favorable in the same poll. About 50 percent of the non-Latin whites and 48 percent of the blacks felt that they had a largely positive impact on Dade County.
52. Clark, Lasaga, and Reque, op. cit., p. 15.
53. Ibid., p. 12.
54. In June 1980, the Roper Poll surveyed the American public concerning its attitudes toward controlling immigration. The results showed that 80 percent agreed that the quota for legal immigration should be lowered. Furthermore, there was strong agreement among ethnic and socioeconomic groups. "What Americans Want," *The Other Side* (Newsletter of the Environmental Fund, Washington, D.C., No. 22, Spring 1981), p. 4.
55. Fredrick Tasker, "Refugees Have Revised Census Data," *The Miami Herald*, January 31, 1981, p. 1B.
56. Guillermo Martinez, "Cuban Miamians Prone to Highlight How They Contrast with Marielitos," *The Miami Herald*, May 26, 1981, p. 7A; and Zita Arocha, "Mariel's Scorned Youths Feel Sting of Rejection," *The Miami Herald*, March 23, 1981, p. 2B.
57. Guy Gugliotta, "Who Are They? Boatloads Salted With Criminals," *The Cuban Exodus, The Miami Herald*, p. 12.
58. Robert L. Bach, "The New Cuban Immigrants: Their Background and Prospects," *Monthly Labor Review* 103:39–46, October 1980.
59. Landstreet, op. cit., p. 142.
60. Liz Balmaseda, "After Two Decades, United States Is Closing 'Open Door' to Cubans," *The Miami Herald*, November 21, 1981, p. 1A.
61. Don Bohning, "Legal Cuban Entries Virtually at Standstill," *The Miami Herald*, September 12, 1981, p. 26A; and Helga Silva, "Cuban Sent Home; Move Is a First," *The Miami Herald*, January 16, 1982, p. 1A.

Much of this chapter draws extensively from the following source: Thomas D. Boswell, "Cuban-Americans," in Jesse O. McKee, ed., *Ethnicity in Contemporary America* (Dubuque, Iowa: Kendall-Hunt Publishing Co., forthcoming 1984).

4

Cuban Settlement in the United States: Patterns and Processes

It is estimated that between 85 and 90 percent of all Cubans who have emigrated since the Castro Revolution in 1959 have moved to the United States.[1] The remainder, from 111,000 to 176,000, have settled primarily in Spain, Mexico, Puerto Rico, Canada, Venezuela, Costa Rica, and Peru.

It is reasonable to ask why the United States has become the home of the vast majority of the Cuban emigrants, instead of any of the nearby Latin American countries that have more in common with Cuba in terms of language and culture. The answer is found in the cultural and economic ties that bound Cuba to the United States from the middle 1800s until 1959. There is a long tradition of migration of Cuban political exiles to cities such as New York City, Key West, Tampa, and later Miami. In addition, American entrepreneurs and businessmen played a major role in resuscitating the Cuban economy after the Spanish-American War and Cuba's subsequent independence from Spain. Between 1898 and 1959 Cuba became as economically dependent upon the United States as it is dependent today on the Soviet Union. Most of the clothing worn by urban Cubans, much of the food they ate, virtually all the cars and trucks they drove, and most of the radios they listened to came from the United States. Thus, despite language differences, many Cubans were very aware of living conditions in the United States and had acquired tastes for the American lifestyle. This was especially true of the better educated and more highly skilled immigrants, who accounted for a disproportionate share of the earliest wave of "Golden Exiles." Once these people led the way, the momentum of the stream quickly flowed in the direction of the United States.

Concentration in a Few States and Large Cities

Like virtually all immigrant groups before them, Cubans have exhibited a highly concentrated pattern of settlement in a few areas of the United

Table 4.1 Cuban-Americans Living in the United States, by Selected States, 1970 and 1980

			Percentage	
	1970	1980	1970	1980
Florida	250,406	470,250	46.0	58.5
New Jersey	68,048	80,860	12.5	10.1
New York	89,596	76,942	16.5	9.6
California	47,560	61,004	8.7	7.6
Illinois	20,796	19,063	3.8	2.4
Texas	6,963	14,124	1.3	1.8
Total for 6 states	483,369	722,243	88.8	89.9
Total for the United States	544,600	803,226	100.0	100.0

Note: These figures do not include approximately 125,000 refugees who arrived shortly after the 1980 census enumeration.

Source: U.S. Bureau of Census, *Census of Population: 1980*, Supplementary Report, PC80-S1-7, "Persons of Spanish Origin by State: 1980" (Washington, D.C.: U.S. Government Printing Office, August 1982), p. 13.

States (Figure 4.1). In 1980, before the arrival of the Marielitos, approximately 90 percent of all Cuban-Americans lived in six states (Table 4.1). Just under 60 percent lived in Florida, with the metropolitan area of Miami serving as the leading node. Another 20 percent resided collectively in the states of New Jersey and New York. A little less than 8 percent lived in California and about 2 percent lived in Illinois and Texas. Every state in the United States has at least a few residents who are of Cuban descent.[2]

The state of Florida has played a dominant role in serving as a destination for Cuban-Americans only since 1959. Earlier, New York State (more specifically New York City) was the leading recipient of Cuban immigrants, just as it had been for many earlier immigrant groups. As noted in Chapter 3, approximately 45 percent of all Cuban-Americans lived in New York in 1950, with another 27 percent residing in Florida. New York City's position as one of the leading cities of residence for Cuban exiles can be

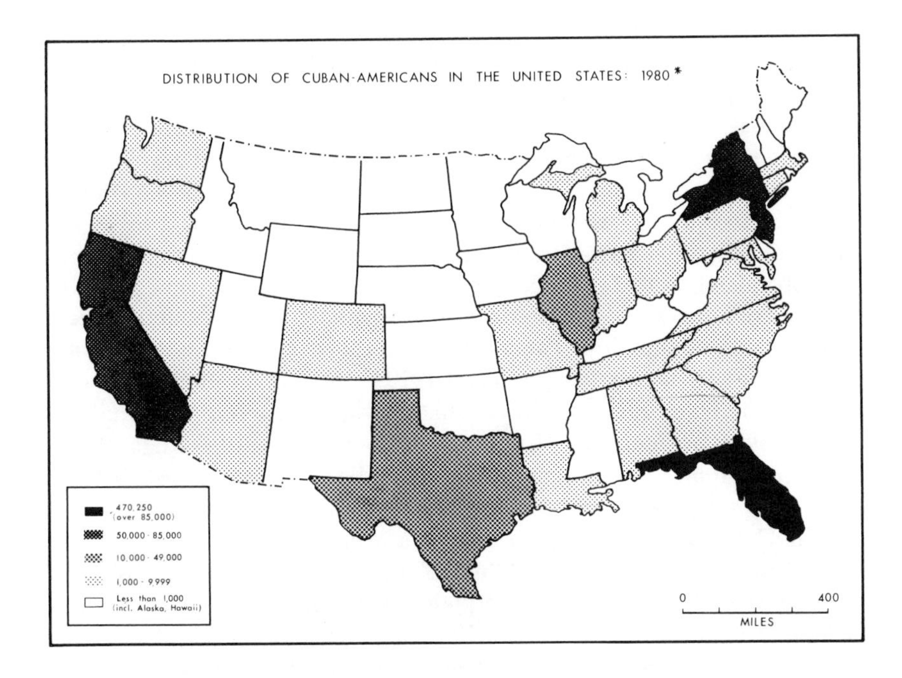

*Figure 4.1 Distribution of Cuban-Americans in the United States, 1980. These figures do not include approximately 125,000 Cuban refugees who arrived shortly after the 1980 census enumeration. (Source: U.S. Bureau of the census, (*Census of Population: 1980,*) "Persons of Spanish Origin by State: 1980," Supplementary Report, PC80-S1-7, p. 6.)*

traced back to the nineteenth century. Its history of opportunities for immigrants from other parts of the world and its reputation as a haven for political dissidents undoubtedly contributed to its attraction for Cuban exiles. Unlike the concentrations in Miami and Union City-West New York, Cubans in New York City have not formed any outstanding core of settlement. Instead, they are diffused more widely throughout the city and do not dominate any particular neighborhoods, although they often reside in sections in which other Hispanics (mainly Puerto Ricans and Dominicans) live.

During the 1960s the housing, crime, and employment situations were beginning to deteriorate in New York City, and Florida rapidly assumed a more prominent position. Many Cubans who arrived in the early 1960s believed they would be returning soon to Cuba, thinking that the Castro government would not remain in control for very long. Florida was nearby, it had a climate similar to that of Cuba, there was inexpensive housing available in an area of Miami that would become known as "Little Havana," and there was already a small community of Cubans living in Miami that could help them adjust to their new living conditions.[3]

A secondary concentration of Cuban-American settlement developed in the Union City-West New York area on the New Jersey side of the Hudson River, across from New York City. The emergence of this area as the second leading concentration of Cuban-Americans is due to a small cluster of Cuban families that lived there prior to Castro's assumption of power in Cuba. They served as an attraction for the in-migration of other Cubans coming both directly from Cuba and indirectly via a stage process through New York City during the 1960s and 1970s.[4] In addition, there were jobs available in blue-collar occupations that provided economic opportunities, since Union City and West New York are essentially centers of light industry, warehousing, and transportation. By the late 1970s two-thirds of West New York's population was comprised of persons of Cuban descent.[5]

The Cuban Refugee Program has had a major effect on the distribution of Cuban émigrés outside the state of Florida. When it was established in 1961 by President Kennedy, its purpose was to help the Cuban immigrants adjust to living conditions in the United States through job placements, temporary financial assistance, and various welfare benefits. Another of its primary goals was to lessen the burden of concentration on South Florida by redistributing "relocatable" Cuban families to areas outside the state. Individuals with higher education levels and skills, and those with some knowledge of English, were considered to be most easily resettled. If a person was offered an opportunity to relocate outside of South Florida but refused, then he or she was denied further federal government assistance and was considered to be on his or her own.[6] Of the 494,804 Cubans who registered with the Cuban Refugee Program between February 1961 and October 1981 approximately 61 percent were resettled in this manner.[7]

The vast majority (about 97%) of Cuban-Americans now live in urban areas, especially in large cities with populations in excess of 50,000 persons.[8] When compared to all families of Spanish descent and the rest of the American families that are not of Spanish origin, it is clear that Cuban families are more concentrated in large cities (Table 4.2). As was the case with many immigrants who arrived before them, Cuban-Americans have chosen to live in large urban areas because they perceive their economic opportunities as being greater there. However, it is interesting to note that although they have concentrated in metropolitan areas, less than 40 percent reside in the central cities of these areas. Almost 60 percent live outside the central cities in suburban neighborhoods, which is a much

Table 4.2 Metropolitan and Nonmetropolitan Residences for Families in the United States, March 1980
(percentages)

	Cuban origin[a]	All Spanish origin	Not of Spanish origin
Metropolitan areas[b]	96.7	83.5	65.9
(Central cities)	(39.5)	(48.2)	(25.3)
(Outside central cities)	(57.2)	(35.2)	(40.6)
Nonmetropolitan areas	3.3	16.5	34.1
Total	100.00	100.00	100.00

[a] The figures for Cubans do not include approximately 125,000 refugees who arrived shortly after the 1980 census enumeration.

[b] Metropolitan Areas = Standard Metropolitan Statistical Areas as defined by the U.S. Bureau of the Census.

Source: U.S. Bureau of the Census, *Current Population Reports*, Series P-20, No. 361, "Persons of Spanish Origin in the United States," March 1980 (Advance Report) (Washington, D.C.: U.S. Government Printing Office), p. 5.

higher percentage than for the rest of the Spanish origin population or for persons who are not of Spanish descent. This suburbanization of the Cuban-Americans is a reflection of their upward socioeconomic mobility (when compared to most other Hispanics) and is a topic that will be discussed in Chapter 5.

Since the 1980 Population Census for the United States was taken three weeks before the Mariel wave of Cuban emigration began, the Director of the Miami Division of the Cuban National Planning Council has provided estimates that are more current than the census results.[9] Although these figures are only very rough approximations, they indicate that almost all Cuban-Americans live in 14 cities (Table 4.3). The outstanding concentration in several of Florida's cities is readily apparent, with other concentrations in Union City-West New York, New York City, Los Angeles, and Chicago standing out above the rest. If there is any validity to these figures, they illustrate that the Cuban-Americans now are even more heavily

Table 4.3 Cuban-Americans by City of Residence, March 1981

	Number of Cuban-American residents in 1981
Miami	585,000
Union City–West New York	100,000
New York City	91,000
Los Angeles	30,000
Chicago	24,000
Orlando	15,000
Fort Lauderdale–Hollywood	15,000
Boston	13,000
Atlanta	10,000
Washington, D.C.	8,000
Tampa	8,000
Dallas–Fort Worth	5,000
Key West	5,000
New Orleans	2,000
Other Cities	10,000
Total	921,000

Note: These figures should be regarded as very rough estimates only. The metropolitan areas are not the same as the U.S. Census Bureau's Standard Metropolitan Statistical Areas because they are sometimes more general, including larger areas. They do, however, include estimates for most of the 125,000 refugees who arrived after the 1980 census enumeration.

Source: Guarione M. Diaz, Executive Director, Cuban National Planning Council, Miami, Florida, personal interview, March 27, 1981.

concentrated in the state of Florida then they were at the time the 1980 census was taken. Probably between 65 and 70 percent of all persons of Cuban descent living in the United States now reside in Florida.

The Return Flow to Miami

Since the late 1960s a return flow of Cubans to the Miami metropolitan area from areas outside the state of Florida has become apparent. At first it started out as a trickle,[10] but by the middle 1970s it became a major migration stream. A survey of a sample of Cuban immigrants living in Miami in 1972 determined that 27.4 percent lived elsewhere in the country before returning to Dade County. A similar survey conducted in 1977 increased that number to 34.6 percent.[11] In 1978 *The Miami Herald* commissioned a telephone survey that found that about 40 percent of Dade County's Cubans were persons who had returned from living in other parts of the country.[12] Clearly, the proportion of Dade County's Cubans that are returnees has been increasing and is likely to continue to do so, at least in the near future.

Most of the Cuban-Americans who have recently returned to Miami were settled originally in other parts of the country through the Cuban Refugee Program. Once they were able to adjust to living in the United States, save some money, and learn English they became independent of government financial assistance. Many decided to move back to Miami, their original port of entry. When questioned about their reasons for moving back to Miami, the vast majority mentioned the climate of South Florida and a desire to be near relatives and friends who were living in Dade County. Surprisingly, less than 20 percent mentioned economic opportunities as a specific motive for returning.[13]

There is a clear relationship between the states outside of Florida that received the greatest number of Cubans under the Cuban Refugee Program's resettlement efforts and the states that sent the greatest number of returnees back to Miami. For instance, between 1961 and 1981, 46.7 percent of all Cubans who resettled outside the state of Florida located in New York and New Jersey.[14] A survey conducted by the Dade County Manager's Office found that 61.1 percent of the returnees it questioned originated from these same two states.[15] Another survey undertaken by *The Miami Herald* tends to support these findings.[16] The return of Cubans from these states confirms the well-known proposition that for each major migration stream there develops a counterstream movement in the opposite direction.[17] Upon returning to Dade County most have settled in the western suburbs, rather than concentrating in the central city of Miami.[18] The years spent adjusting to American life-styles outside Florida equipped these people with abilities to live comfortably near, but not in, the major Cuban concentration of Little Havana. In addition, the skills they had developed and the money they had saved enabled them to afford suburban housing.

Ethnic Segregation

The body of literature dealing with studies of assimilation of various ethnic groups indicates that people sort themselves residentially and socially into groups that are generally homogeneous with respect to both ethnic affiliation and socioeconomic rank. This notion is known as the *ethclass* concept.[19] It will be shown in Chapter 5 that Cubans in Dade County appear to segregate themselves from one another according to socioeconomic status. A study of Cubans living in West New York alludes to a similar finding.[20] The question that remains is: To what degree are Cubans segregated residentially from the non-Cuban population?

There is considerable evidence that the Cuban population is notably segregated from other ethnic classes living in metropolitan Miami. One study has noted that Latins (most of whom are Cubans) living in Dade County are strongly segregated from blacks and Jews when considered on a census tract scale. They are also moderately segregated from non-Latin whites. For instance, in 1970, 86 percent of the black population would have needed to be redistributed to other census tracts for it to exhibit a distribution identical to that of Latins. Similarly, about 72 percent of the Jews would need to move, while between 55 and 60 percent of the Anglo whites would have to move, depending on their age class. It was further found that the differences in distribution had generally increased between 1950 and 1970.[21] A second study has further determined that Dade County's Cuban population in 1970 was notably segregated from the county's Mexican and Puerto Rican populations. It also found that there was considerable segregation within the Cuban population according to family income classes.[22] Both studies demonstrate that the concept of *ethclass* is generally applicable to the residential patterns displayed by Miami's Cuban-Americans.

The massive influx of Cubans to Dade County and the high level of segregation between Cuban-Americans and blacks, Jews, and non-Latin whites has been blamed for aggravating ethnic tensions. It has been suggested, for instance, that the expansion of neighborhoods dominated by families of Cuban origin is associated with a non-Latin white exodus from Dade County.[23] Recent estimates indicate that Dade County experienced a decline of at least 30,000 non-Latin whites between 1970 and 1980.[24] This "white flight" has had even more of an impact on the ethnic mixture of Dade County's public schools than it has on the total population. In 1974 the student population percentages in the county's public schools were 44 percent non-Latin white, 26.5 percent black, and 29.5 percent Latin. In 1982 they were 31 percent non-Latin white, 31 percent black, and 38 percent Latin.[25] It is certainly too simple to blame the immigration of Cubans as the sole cause of the exodus of whites from greater Miami. After all, Dade County had experienced major problems during the past decade. Still, the Cuban increase is frequently stated as being one of the causes radically altering the ethnic composition of metropolitan Miami.[26]

Summary and Conclusions

The people who left Cuba after Fidel Castro gained control of the government in 1959 have exhibited a clear preference for the United States as their new homeland. They chose the United States over other Latin American countries partly because of its higher general living standards but also because of the close ties that Cubans had developed with Americans between the middle 1800s and 1959. Many Cubans were familiar with the United States through personal visits, employment ties, and the purchasing of consumer goods manufactured on the mainland.

When they arrived in the United States, the Cubans almost always settled in large metropolitan areas where they perceived their economic opportunities to be at a maximum. Before the Castro Revolution more Cubans lived in New York City than any other city in the United States. However, since the Revolution, Miami and Union City-West New York have become the two metropolitan areas that have attracted the largest number of Cuban-Americans. Miami's position as the American city with the most Cuban residents is strengthening, as many former refugees who were settled in other states under the Cuban Refugee Program are returning to South Florida because of family ties, the climate, and economic opportunities for Spanish-speaking persons. Although they live within metropolitan areas, almost 60 percent of the Cuban-Americans reside in suburban neighborhoods.

Although there is considerable mixing among Cubans and other ethnic groups in the suburban areas there is still a tendency for clearly identifiable Cuban neighborhoods to develop. In metropolitan Miami the Cubans are strongly segregated residentially from Dade County's black population and are moderately segregated from the county's Jewish residents. They are least segregated from the county's Anglo population. Nevertheless, as the Latin population has increased in Dade County it has been blamed as one of the factors accounting for the exodus of approximately 30,000 non-Latin whites during the decade of the 1970s. If both the return migration of Cubans to Miami from other states and the "white flight" of Anglos continue it will not be much longer until the Hispanic population becomes Dade County's ethnic majority.

Notes

1. Barent Landstreet, "Cuba," in Aaron L. Segal, ed., *Population Policies in the Caribbean* (Lexington, Mass.: D.C. Heath, 1975), p. 141.

2. U.S. Bureau of the Census, *Census of Population: 1980*, Supplementary Report, Final Report PC80-52-7, "Persons of Spanish Origin by State: 1980" (Washington, D.C.: U.S. Government Printing Office, 1982), p. 6.

3. Thomas D. Boswell, "The Migration and Distribution of Cubans and Puerto Ricans Living in the United States," *The Journal of Geography*, forthcoming in 1984.

4. Eleanor Meyer Rogg, *The Assimilation of Cuban Exiles: The Role of Community and Class* (New York: Aberdeen Press, 1974), pp. 25–27.

5. Eleanor Meyer Rogg and Rosemary Santana Cooney, *Adaptation and Adjustment of Cubans: West New York, New Jersey* (New York: Monograph No. 5, Hispanic Research Center, Fordham University, 1980), pp. 11–14.

6. Rafael J. Projias and Lourdes Casal, *The Cuban Minority in the United States: Preliminary Report on Need Identification and Program Evaluation* (Boca Raton: Florida Atlantic University, 1973), pp. 102–117.

7. "Fact Sheet," Cuban Refugee Program, U.S. Department of Health and Human Resources, Miami, Florida, October 31, 1981.

8. U.S. Bureau of the Census, *Current Population Reports*, Series P-20, No. 361: "Persons of Spanish Origin in the United States: March 1980 (Advance Report)," May 1981 (Washington, D.C.: U.S. Government Printing Office, 1981), p. 5.

9. These estimates were provided by Guarione M. Diaz, Executive Director, Cuban National Planning Council, Miami, Florida, through a personal interview on March 27, 1981.

10. Projias and Casal, op. cit., pp. 117–120.

11. Aida Thomas Levitan, "Hispanics in Dade Country: Their Characteristics and Needs" (Miami: Latin Affairs, Office of County Manager, Metropolitan Dade County, printed report, Spring 1980), p. 43.

12. "Latins Now Are Living All Over Dade," *The Miami Herald*, July 2, 1978, p. 22A.

13. Levitan, op. cit., p. 19; and Juan M. Clark, "Los Cubanos de Miami: Cuantos Son y de Donde Provienen," *Ideal*, January 15, 1973, pp. 17–19.

14. "Fact Sheet," loc. cit.

15. Levitan, op. cit., p. 20.

16. *The Miami Herald* survey found that 56 percent of the returnees it questioned came from the New York City-New Jersey area. "Latins Now Are Living All Over Dade," p. 22A.

17. Everett S. Lee, "A Theory of Migration," *Demography* 3:47–57, 1966.

18. Levitan, op. cit., p. 18; and Dade County Planning Department, "Mobility Patterns 1964–1969 " (Miami: Dade County Planning Department, Memorandum Report, Work Element VIII, Housing in the Metropolitan Plan, April 1970), p. 43.

19. Milton M. Gordon, *Assimilation in America Life* (New York: Oxford University Press, 1964).

20. Rogg, op. cit., pp. 136–137.

21. Morton D. Winsberg, "Housing Segregation of a Predominantly Middle Class Population: Residential Patterns Developed by the Cuban Immigration Into Miami, 1950–1974," *American Journal of Economics and Sociology* 38:416, October 1979.

22. B. E. Aguirre, Kent P. Schwirian, and Anthony J. LaGreca, "The Residential Patterning of Latin American and Other Ethnic Populations in Metropolitan Miami," *Latin American Research Review* 15:56, 48–49, No. 2, 1980.

23. Morton D. Winsberg, "Housing Segregation of a Predominantly Middle-Class Population: The Case of the Miami Cubans" (unpublished paper read at the Annual Meeting of the Association of American Geographers, Los Angeles, California, April 1981).

24. Frederic Tasker, "Anglo Flight Is a Two-Way Street," *The Miami Herald*, November 16, 1980, p. 1B.

25. Jeff Golden, "Schools Hit by 'White Flight,' Enrollment Off by 8,499 in Last Year," *The Miami Herald*, January 10, 1982, p. 1B.

26. James Kelly, "Trouble in Paradise: South Florida Is Hit by a Hurricane of Crime, Drugs and Refugees," *Time* 118:22–32, November 23, 1981.

5

Miami: Cuban Capital of America

Few major cities in America have experienced a more rapid or profound transformation as a direct consequence of immigration than has Miami in the last quarter of a century. In essence, a "new," multi- ethnic urban complex has been forged since the first large wave of Cuban refugees arrived in the city in the wake of the revolution in Cuba that brought Fidel Castro to power in late 1958. The growth of the Cuban population in the greater Miami area during this short span of time has been nothing less than phenomenal. From fewer than 20,000 just prior to the revolution, there are now nearly 600,000 Cubans residing in Dade County: a 30-fold increase. This massive influx has fundamentally re-aligned the ethnic composition of the county. In 1960, for example, the county's population was approximately 81 percent non-Latin white, 15 percent black, and 4 percent Latin. Currently, in mid-1983, it is estimated that the population of non-Latin whites has declined to 44 percent, while Latins account for 39 percent, and blacks 17 percent. In the city of Miami itself, Latins now constitute approximately 60 percent of the population; the non-Latin white population has dwindled to less than 20 percent. The Miami metropolitan area has consequently emerged as one of the largest and most influential Hispanic centers in the United States. And the prospects for its continued "Latinization" show no immediate signs of abating. Indeed, the magnitude of the Cuban settlement and attendant changes in the city have served as a magnet for other Hispanic groups from Latin America and the Caribbean. It is an attraction that should become even more powerful as the population from these regions steadily increase in the area. Although over 100,000 non-Cuban Latins currently reside in Dade County, Cubans represent in excess of 80 percent of the total Hispanic population. The concentration of Cubans in Miami has grown to such a level that it now accounts for about half of the entire Cuban-descended population in the United States. This has prompted some observers to label the city "Havana North." In fact, the only city with a larger Cuban population *is* Havana. Clearly, Miami has become the "Cuban capital of America."

Beyond substantially altering Miami's ethnic composition, Cubans have had a tremendous impact on the city's social system, cultural institutions, economic base, and political structure. The schools, housing, job market, government agencies, health care facilities, language and religious patterns, and just the sense and appearance of the place have all been affected by the settlement of Cubans. But while these far-reaching changes have created a more vibrant, cosmopolitan city, dislocations and cultural conflicts have arisen. Some individuals in the Anglo and black communities, either unable or unwilling to adjust to the new social and economic order, have lashed out at the influx of Cubans and other Latins (as well as Haitian refugees). Their hostilities are most visually expressed in the form of bumper stickers, such as one that reads, "Will the Last American Leaving Miami Please Bring the Flag." The accusations and recriminations notwithstanding, the ramifications of Miami's ethnic transformation are as complex and sensitive as they are diverse. They are also perhaps to be expected in a city which has experienced such sudden and basic change.

Since Miami plays a prominent role in the overall picture of Cuban settlement and culture in the United States, many of the issues mentioned above are addressed topically in other chapters. The specific focus of this chapter is on three topics that are concerned primarily with the spatial aspects of Cuban settlement in Miami. The first section traces in chronological sequence the growth and areal expansion of the Cuban population in Dade County. An analysis of the economic enclave that Cubans have created in the metropolitan area follows. The third topic is an interpretive account of the distinctive cultural landscape of Little Havana.

Growth and Expansion of the Cuban Population

A small colony of Cubans has lived in Miami since the turn of the twentieth century. Prior to the 1950s, however, the major areas of Cuban settlement in Florida were in the cities of Key West and Tampa, while the largest concentration in the United States was in New York City. The population size and spatial distribution of Cubans living in Miami at the end of 1958, on the eve of Castro's takeover, are difficult to determine precisely. According to 1950 census data, there were approximately 20,000 Hispanics residing in Dade County, which represented about 4 percent of the total population of 495,084 (see Table 5.1). The percentage of Cubans in the Hispanic population was not revealed in the census, but was probably no more than 50 percent. In the entire state of Florida in 1950, as reported in the census, there were only 7,910 residents born in Cuba. Taking into account the Cuban settlements elsewhere in Florida, it seems unlikely that there were more than five or six thousand Cubans in Miami in 1950.

Table 5.1 Dade County Population, 1950–1980

	Total population	Percent of increase	Latin population	Percent of increase	Latin population as percentage of total
1950	495,080	—	20,000(est.)	—	4.0
1960	935,047	88.9	50,000(est.)	250.0	5.3
1970	1,267,792	35.6	299,217	598.0	23.6
1980[a]	1,625,781	28.2	581,030	94.1	35.7

[a] This figure does not include the approximately 100,000 Cuban refugees who settled in Dade County shortly after the 1980 census enumeration.

Source: U.S. Bureau of the Census, *Census of Population*, for years 1950–1980.

These early émigrés, though few in number, were crucial in the subsequent establishment of Miami as the principal center of Cuban settlement and culture in this country. Their presence, and the inroads they made in the social and economic milieu of Miami, would attract other Cubans to the area. And, like their fellow exiles who arrived following the Castro revolution, their immigration was motivated primarily by political change in Cuba. In 1933, for example, a sizeable number of Cubans sought refuge in Miami as a consequence of the ouster of Cuban president Gerardo Machado. A decade later they were joined by another group who fled the island at the end of Batista's first term in office (1940-1944). Included among these exiles were a few relatively wealthy individuals who had influential American contacts, and quickly became established in the Miami business community. Reportedly, "They invested in Florida real estate and their financial accomplishments were publicized in the local news media."[1] Again in 1952, after Batista had assumed power from Carlos Prio Socarras in a *coup d'état*, still another group of Cubans sought exile in Miami. Steadily, from 1953 through 1958, growing anti-Batista sentiments led to a stream of Cubans who came to Miami in search of asylum. Considering the increase in Cuban population in the city between 1950 and the end of 1958, it may be assumed that about 10 to 12 thousand Cubans lived in the greater Miami area just prior to the first large wave of immigration beginning in early 1959.

It is commonly thought that Miami had no Cuban quarter before the Castro revolution. Most studies, for example, conclude that the Cuban population was predominantly middle-class and scattered throughout the urban area.[2] Little Havana is most often considered to be an area of Cuban settlement that emerged in the early 1960s. In fact, there is evidence that a small colony of Cuban refugees had settled there at least as early as the overthrow of Machado in 1933. According to one Cuban-American realtor, during the early 1930s Cubans bought property in Little Havana, "mainly small apartment houses between S.W. Eighth Street and Flagler."[3] Using 1950 census tract data, Winsberg has shown that the tract with highest concentration of Latin population "was situated approximately two miles southwest of the CBD [central business district] center—and had acquired the name 'Little Havana' among the non-Latins."[4] It was also revealed in the study that 70 percent of the Latin-American-born population in metropolitan Miami "lived within a three mile semi-circle on the western side of the city's CBD—compared to only 48 percent of the white population."[5] The executive director of the Little Havana Development Authority, Wilfredo Gort, has concluded that "There were some 10,000 Cubans in the area [Little Havana] before Fidel Castro took control in Cuba."[6] Although this figure is probably an exaggeration, the point remains that Cuban settlement in Miami was perhaps more concentrated prior to the 1960s than is generally believed, especially among middle-class Cuban émigrés, and that the nucleus of Little Havana had already been established.

In the six-month period from New Year's Day 1959—Batista's fall from power—to June 30, over 26,500 Cubans poured into the United States.[7] During the following year, from July 1 to June 30, 1961, the number of Cuban immigrants exceeded 60,000. By October 1962, the Cuban Refugee Center had registered over 153,000 Cubans entering the country.[8] Less than 50,000 were initially settled outside the Miami area, and many would return at a later date. Truly, the growth of the Cuban population in Dade County during the decade of the 1960s was dramatic. In the 1960 *Census of Population*, Hispanics accounted for about 50,000 or approximately 5 percent of the total county population of 935,047, which had increased by nearly 89 percent over the preceding decade. By 1970, however, the number of Latin residents had ballooned to 299,217 (an increase of nearly 600 percent) or 23.6 percent of the county's total population of 1,267,792. The massive influx of Cubans notwithstanding, the rate of growth for the county as a whole actually declined significantly during the decennium to 35.6 percent.

Whereas prior to the 1960s Cubans had probably constituted less than 50 percent of the county's Latin population, by 1970 it had risen to over 85 percent.[9] In 1966, for example, it was estimated that 13 out of every 15 Latins residing in Dade County were Cuban.[10] This high percentage has been maintained to the present, in spite of substantial immigration from other Spanish speaking countries . The major Latin groups other than Cubans include Puerto Ricans, Dominicans, Mexicans, Nicaraguans, Panamians, Colombians, Venezuelans, and Argentinians.

The residential pattern of Cuban settlement in Miami from the beginning of 1959 through the 1960s was characterized by the development of a concentrated core community, followed by a relatively rapid rate of expansion into contiguous and selected outlying areas. The very earliest exiles who fled Cuba during this period—primarily the socioeconomic and political elite in the Batista government—were able to take money and other assets out of the country. They were, of course, in a more favorable position in respect to their residential options; many settled in the more affluent sections of the city. Quickly, however, the Castro regime imposed a ban that severely limited the amount of money that emigrants could take out of the country. Coupled with the economic reforms that were enacted subsequently (see Chapter 2), most Cuban exiles arrived in the United States without financial resources or material possessions. Some of the more fortunate were able to secure temporary shelter with relatives or friends who had previously settled in the city. Although the role of the family in this respect would become increasingly important through time as the Cuban population in Miami grew and began to prosper, for most of those who arrived during the first wave (from 1959 through the Cuban missile crisis in October 1962), other institutions were heavily relied upon for initial support. The Cuban Refugee Program and various other government, church, and civic organizations were critical, providing not only financial assistance, but also in offering housing and information regarding the location and availability of low-cost housing. Some of the earliest refugees were attracted to the low rents found in the older working class neighborhoods located northwest of downtown Miami near the garment district, such as Wynwood and Allapattah.[11] The vast majority, however, settled in Little Havana, an area roughly four square miles in size situated about two miles southwest of the central business district (see Figure 5.1).

There were a host of factors responsible for the establishment of Little Havana as the principal Cuban enclave during the 1960s. That Cubans had already settled in the area was an important historical consideration. Although clearly a minority within the neighborhood, they nonetheless formed a nucleus population. The most significant reason, however, relates to the condition of the area itself. Once a healthy, largely middle-class

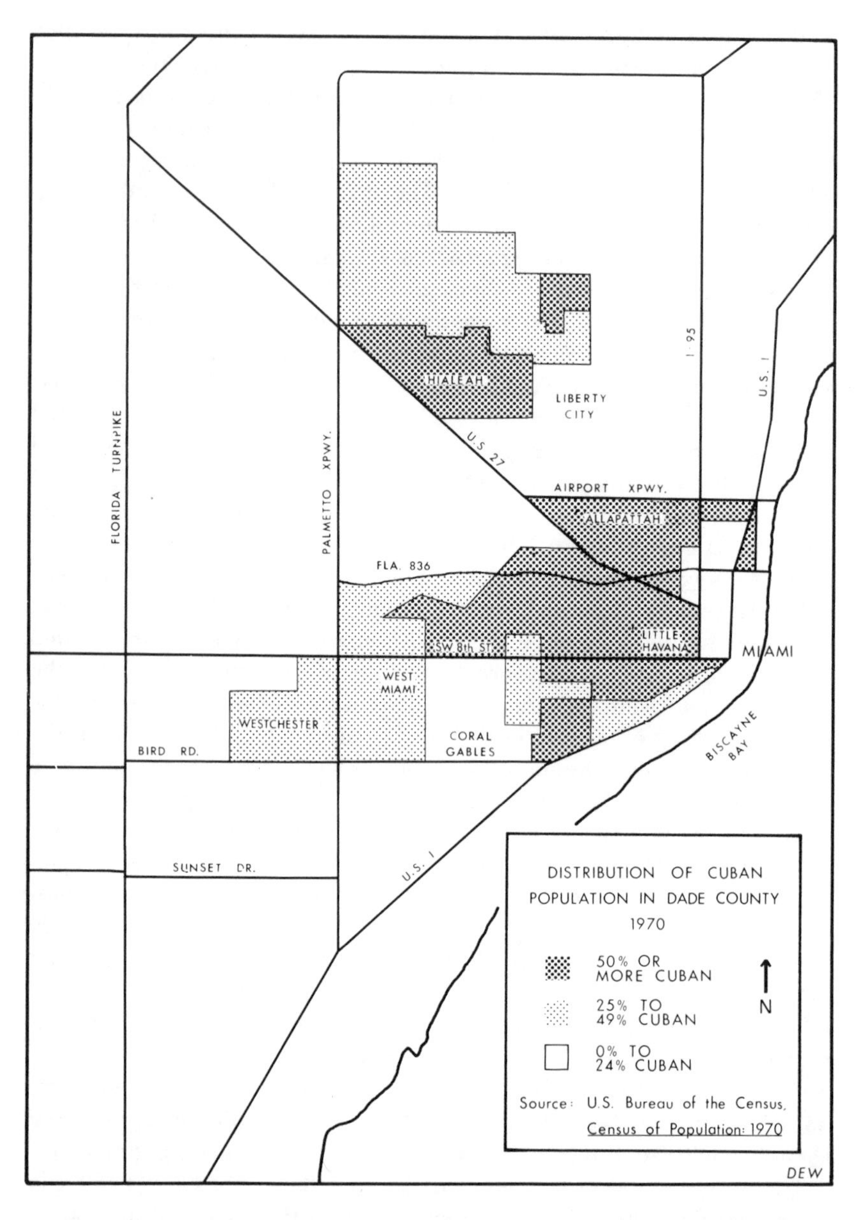

Figure 5.1 Distribution of Cuban population in Dade County, 1970. (Source: U.S. Bureau of the Census, Census Population: 1970.*)*

Anglo neighborhood developed just after the First World War, by the mid-1950s the area had become depressed and was losing population. Many of the wood-frame, single family houses and small apartment buildings of 4 to 18 units were rapidly deteriorating.[12] Properties in general were not being adequately maintained. In addition, retail trade had seriously declined and commercial vacancies were numerous. For the newly arriving Cubans this area offered available housing units, both single and multi-family, and rents were low. The vacant shops and other commercial structures along Flagler and S.W. Eighth Street likewise afforded opportunities for the establishment of businesses. The area's proximity to downtown, where social services and employment opportunities were most abundant, was also an attraction. Moreover, it was a central location and served by public transportation. There were also Catholic churches and schools in the neighborhood. Of course, once it became an established Cuban neighborhood, when Cuban restaurants, markets, drug stores, and other retail and commercial businesses had opened, it assumed an attraction of its own, independent of these other factors.[13]

During the decade of the 1960s a substantial percentage of the Cuban population in fact resided in Little Havana. By 1970, 36 percent of all Latins in the Miami Standard Metropolitan Statistical Area (SMSA) lived in the 16 census tracts that approximate the generally recognized boundaries of the area.[14] Moreover, it has been estimated that 14 percent of the total Cuban population of the United States at that time resided in the enclave.[15] Accompanying this growth was a noticeable shift in the number of people per household. Consequently, by the end of the 1960s Little Havana was among the most densely populated sections of the county, with 3 of its 16 census tracts recording in excess of 15,000 people per square mile.

Although Little Havana was clearly the center of Cuban population, the 1960s witnessed a fairly rapid expansion into adjoining and other major outlying areas. This expansion was a consequence of many factors, including the sheer magnitude of the Cuban immigration. (Again, by the end of the 1960s the Cuban population in Dade County exceeded 250,000.) It also is related to employment and housing attractions of other sections of the metropolitan area, vis-á-vis the generally crowded conditions and scarcity of rental housing in Little Havana; zoning restrictions also limited growth in certain sections of the quarter.[16] Equally as important, however, it was a positive indication of the rapidly rising socioeconomic status of many Cuban-Americans, and further suggests how quickly the process of acculturation was proceeding. This is reflected in both the rising rate of home ownership and increasing car ownership.

Between 1960 and 1970 it has been estimated that car ownership among Little Havana residents increased by 20 percent.[17]

The general direction of expansion from the core settlement in Little Havana, however, was impeded by various physical, social and economic barriers. Downtown Miami and Biscayne Bay, for example, lie only a short distance to the east. To the north the Miami River initially formed an edge, but was crossed in the early 1960s as Cubans moved steadily into Allapattah. By the end of the decade, settlement extended to the northern limits of the area, marked by the Airport Expressway. The expressway, however, stood as more than just a physical obstacle. It also was a social boundary, delimiting the southern extent of the largest predominantly black residential area in the county, centering on the community of Liberty City. It has proven to be a significant line of separation as Cubans have tended to avoid living in neighborhoods dominated by blacks (see Chapter 4). Farther west on the north side the Miami International Airport also deflected the path of expansion, either north or south. Just south of Little Havana, land values in the exclusive community of Coral Gables precluded movement in that direction, except for the most affluent Cubans. The primary effect of these barriers was to direct the thrust of settlement into the western reaches of Miami. The one major exception to this pattern of expansion was a significant stream of movement into the city of Hialeah, located northwest of the airport.

The settlement of Cubans in Hialeah (a Seminole Indian name meaning "beautiful prairie") actually began during the 1950s. In 1960, for example, Latins constituted four percent of the city's population. The second largest city in Dade County after Miami, Hialeah was incorporated in 1925 and gradually developed around its central attraction and landmark, Hialeah Park horse track.[18] From its founding, Hialeah was primarily a working class, Anglo community. For Cubans, it held many of the same locational amenities as Little Havana. Most importantly, there was abundant low-cost housing. In fact, the economic recession that plagued the region from 1959 through 1961 had led to the abandonment of a substantial number of new F.H.A.-financed single-family homes. Additionally, Hialeah was situated near several large employment centers, including most particularly Miami International Airport.[19] As a consequence of these and other attractions, the Cuban population in the city grew rapidly during the 1960s. By 1970, Latins accounted for 42 percent of the city's total population of 102,325.

In the decade of the 1970s, the Latin population of Dade County nearly doubled (94.2 percent), increasing from 299,217 to 581,030. This represented approximately 78 percent of the county's total population growth during the 10-year period, which had increased by 28.2 percent (the smallest increase in three decades). Between 1970 and 1975, it has been estimated that Latins outnumbered other new county residents by a ratio of 26 to 1.[20] The Latin proportion of the county population resultingly rose from 23.6 to 35.7 percent. Although these increases are certainly substantial, they do not include the massive immigration of Cuban and Haitian refugees into the county between the census enumeration date of April 1 and the end of calendar year 1980. Government officials in Miami estimate that during the 9-month period approximately 100,000 Cubans and nearly 22,000 Haitian refugees settled in the county.[21] Assuming these numbers are correct, the population of the county thus increased another 7.5 percent to 1,747,657, with Latins accounting for 681,030 or 39 percent (see Table 5.2).[22] Including the estimated 100,000 Cuban refugees who arrived during the Mariel exodus, it is believed that Cubans now comprise between 84 and 86 percent of the county's Latin population. (By Presidential Order, approximately 96,000 were added to the county's 1980 census population for purposes of federal aid programs, but will not be used in reapportioning congressional or state legislative seats.)

The general pattern of expansion of the Cuban population that began in the 1960s continued through the 1970s. The principal directions of movement were west and south, but with significant spread northward in the city of Hialeah. By the end of the decade the areas of concentrated Cuban settlement were in Hialeah and across a broad swath of central Dade County, located primarily between Highway 836 (the Dolphin Expressway) on the north, Bird Road on the south, and stretching westward just beyond the Florida Turnpike (see Figure 5.2). The full extent of settlement, however, was not confined to these two areas; indeed, it was far-reaching, with Latins residing in nearly all sections of the county.

Perhaps the most revealing indication of the areal extent of the Latin population in 1980 is provided by census tract data. Out of a total of 237 tracts in the county, every one had some Latin population. In fact, 124 tracts (or 52.3 percent) were 20 percent or more Latin. There were 66 tracts (or nearly 28 percent) in which the Latin population exceeded 50 percent. The expansion is also clearly reflected in the changing ethnic compositions of the 27 incorporated cities within the county (see Table 5.3). In 1970 only Miami and Hialeah had a Latin population in excess of 15 percent, whereas by 1980, 15 of the cities were at least 15 percent Latin. In fact, Latins accounted for less than 10 percent of the population in only six cities. Moreover, eight of the cities had a Latin population of 30 percent or higher, and four were in excess of 50 percent Latin, including Sweetwater (81 percent), Hialeah (74 percent), West Miami (62 percent), and Miami (56 percent). Sweetwater was once described as a "home to cowboy bars and pickup trucks with rear-window gunracks."[23] Like West

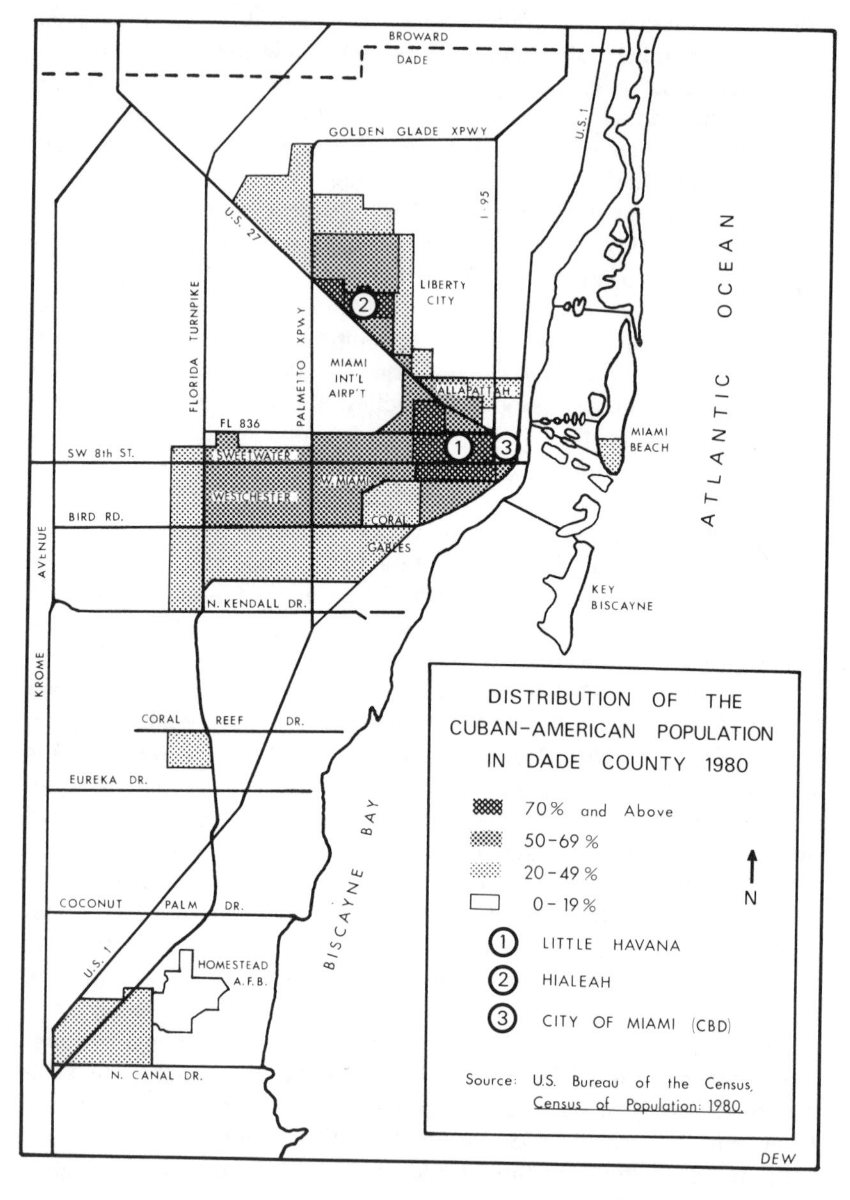

Figure 5.2 *Distribution of the Cuban-American population in Dade County, 1980. (Source: U.S. Bureau of the Census,* Census of Population: 1980.*)*

Table 5.2 1980 Cuban and Haitian Immigration to Dade County After the Federal Census

	Census pop.	Est. num. of refugees Cuban	Haitian	Pop. inc. refugees	% of increase	% Latin	Total % of Latin pop. inc. refugees
Miami	346,865	32,500	12,932	392,297	13.0	56	59
Hialeah	145,254	24,335	581	170,170	17.0	74	78
Miami Beach	96,298	7,950	700	104,948	9.0	22	27
Dade County Total	1,625,781	100,000	21,876	1,747,657	7.5	35	39

Source: Metropolitan Dade County Planning Department, "Cuban and Haitian Refugees: Miami: Standard Metropolitan Statistical Area, 1980," Miami, Florida, January 1981, pp. 14–22.

Miami, it was in the direct western path of Cuban expansion, and its ethnic transformation occurred rapidly. (In 1978 Sweetwater became the first city in the United States in which a Cuban-American [Jorge Valdés] was elected mayor;[24] Hialeah also has a Cuban-born mayor, Raúl Martínez, who was elected in the early 1980s.) The high percentages of Latin population in Miami and Hialeah rose even more as a consequence of the massive influx of Cuban refugees who arrived during the 1980 Mariel boatlift. It has been estimated that approximately 67 percent of the refugees settled in these two cities, increasing the Latin proportion of Miami's population to 59 percent and Hialeah's to 78 percent (see Table 5.2). Nearly 8,000 of the refugees settled in Miami Beach, predominantly in the deteriorated southern end of the island, which substantially increased its percentage of Latin population from 9 to 22 percent.

Although significant growth occured in the cities—all but two of the ten largest cities registered an increase of population, including Hialeah which increased by 42 percent—the greatest overall increase was in the unincorporated area.[25] During the decade of the 1970s, the population of the unincorporated area rose by 48.2 percent, compared to less than 14 percent for the 27 cities. In 1980 it had a population of 795,912 or 49 percent of the county's total number of inhabitants. Ethnically the unincorporated area was dominated by non-Latin whites, who accounted for 54 percent of the

Table 5.3 **Dade County Cities, 1980: Selected Population Characteristics**

Population Rank	City	Total population	Percent non-Latin White	Percent Latin	Percent Black	Median age
1	Miami	346,865	20	56	24	38.0
2	Hialeah	145,254	25	75	1	36.3
3	Miami Beach	96,298	77	22	1	65.8
4	Coral Gables	43,241	66	30	4	36.2
5	North Miami	42,566	81	15	4	40.6
6	North Miami Beach	36,533	85	10	5	46.1
7	Homestead	20,668	59	16	25	25.2
8	Opa-Locka	14,460	21	17	62	25.3
9	Miami Springs	12,350	79	21	0	39.4
10	South Miami	10,944	56	15	29	32.2
11	Miami Shores	9,244	91	8	1	46.1
12	Sweetwater	8,251	19	81	0	28.8
13	Florida City	6,174	31	10	59	25.0
14	West Miami	6,076	38	62	0	44.9
15	North Bay Village	4,920	86	13	1	55.2
16	Bay Harbor	4,869	93	7	0	67.4
17	Surfside	3,763	89	11	0	63.0
18	Biscayne Park	3,088	91	9	0	40.3
19	Bal Harbour	2,938	96	4	0	70.9
20	Hialeah Gardens	2,700	51	49	0	35.9
21	Virginia Gardens	2,098	62	38	0	34.1
22	El Portal	2,055	61	24	15	47.3
23	Golden Beach	612	93	7	0	53.7
24	Medley	534	70	30	0	52.2
25	Indian Creek	103	100	0	0	56.3
26	Pennsulo	15	87	13	0	*
27	Islandia	12	92	8	0	*
Unincorporated area		795,912	54	26	20	30.9
Dade County		1,625,781	48	35	17	34.8

* Data unavailable.

Source: U.S. Bureau of the Census, *Census of Population: 1980.*

population. Latins, however, were also moving into the suburbs at a rapid rate, and by 1980 constituted 26 percent of the unincorporated area's population. The suburbanization trend among Latins was most prevalent in the western area of central Dade County and was part of the general expansion of the Cuban population in that direction. The community of Westchester, bordering West Miami, experienced rapid growth during the 1970s and was well over 50 percent Cuban by the end of the decade.[26] There was also a significant movement south from Westchester into the northern and extreme western sections of Kendall, a largely middle- and upper-middle-class Anglo community. Characteristic of the process of suburbanization, these areas were settled primarily by the more socioeconomically mobile Cubans, the better educated professionals and other white collar workers, especially young couples with children.[27]

The expansion and suburbanization of Cuban settlement in Dade County can be summarized and compared to that of other American ethnic groups by examining these processes in the context of a spatial model. Jordan and Rowntree have developed a model that they suggest is applicable to the growth of most urban ethnic concentrations.[28] Typically, an ethnic area is composed of four zones. The first is a *core* that represents the original area of invasion and subsequent domination by the group. Usually, the core is located near the edge of the city's central business district and is composed of cheaper housing affordable to the poorer members of the group. Later the core will become the "port of entry" for subsequent waves of immigrants from the same country. As the earlier migrants adapt themselves to American living and working conditions, and as they become more secure financially, they begin to move away from the core by a contagious diffusion process into a *middle area* that is characterized by better quality housing and more space. The outermost contiguous sector of the ethnic area is known as the *fringe*. It represents the leading edge of the area as it expands, by a distance-decay process, into the surrounding region that is beginning to be invaded by the minority group. Typically, the fringe is occupied by a mixture of members of both the minority and the dominant groups. In most cases it contains the most upwardly mobile members of the minority class, along with better housing and higher property values. Often some of the more successful members of the ethnic group detach themselves from the ghetto and form noncontiguous *outlying clusters* of smaller ethnic concentrations. These pioneering areas often begin to develop an ethnic flavor to their landscape that is representative of the culture of the new residents.[29]

The present distribution of persons of Cuban descent by census tracts in Dade County is shown in Figure 5.2. The original *core* is located in Little Havana and provides the basic functions suggested by Jordan and Rown-

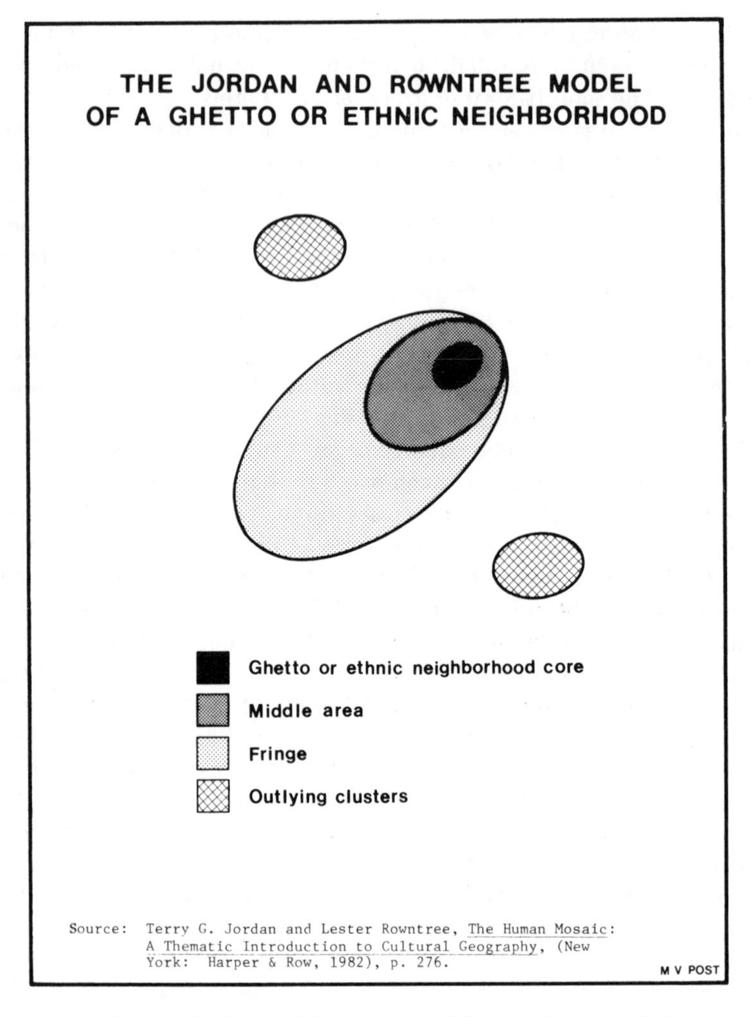

Figure 5.3 The Jordan and Rowntree model of a ghetto or ethnic neighborhood. (Source: Terry G. Jordan and Lester Rowntree, The Human Mosaic: A Thematic Introduction to Cultural Geography, *New York: Harper and Row, 1982, p. 276.)*

tree. The equivalent of their middle area is the zone 50 to 69 percent Cuban. The fringe would include the outer edges, where Cuban families are presently invading, but have not yet established numerical dominance. In this area Cubans represent 20 to 49 percent of the population. Several outlying clusters have developed as detachments from the main body of the Cuban settlement zone. The most obvious is the concentration of Cubans in Hialeah. A recent study of Miami's Little Havana supports the Jordan and Rowntree model's assumption of ghetto expansion by a contagious diffusion process.[30] Generally, the areas closest to the main Cuban concentration of settlement are the next to be encompassed by the expansion process. One exception, of course, is the Hialeah area, which was settled by a "leap-frog" or hierarchical process. Where expansion of the Cuban ethnic areas has been constrained, barriers existed, as previously discussed. Despite these barriers, it is clear that generally a distance-decay relationship exists between the distance that neighborhoods are located away from the core of Little Havana and the proportion of their population that is comprised of Cubans. Usually, the greater the distance away, the lower the percentage that is Cuban.[31]

Evidence of a suburbanization trend in the residential patterns of Cuban-Americans in Miami is provided by a recent panel study of a sample of newly arrived Cuban immigrants in Dade County. It found that in 1973, 51.7 percent of the sample lived in the central city of Miami. Six years later, in 1979, only 38.8 percent still lived in the central city. Most of the rest were living in the suburbs of Hialeah or unincorporated Dade County.[32] As suggested by the Jordan and Rowntree model, it appears likely that the core of Little Havana served as a port of entry for these exiles; later many moved out to the middle or fringe areas.

Another study found that the suburban population of metropolitan Miami has grown primarily by two types of population infusion. The first is intraurban return migration from cities outside the state of Florida to the suburbs of Dade County. Furthermore, when the socioeconomic status of suburban Dade County Cubans was compared to that of Cubans living in the central city, it was clear that (when collectively considered) the former were better off. In addition, the Cubans living in Hialeah appeared to occupy an intermediate position between the higher ranking suburban Cubans and the lower ranking Cubans who lived in Little Havana.[33] These finding also lend support to the Jordan and Rowntree model which states that the core of an ethnic area will usually be occupied by persons of lower social and economic rank, whereas the fringe and outlying clusters will normally become occupied by the more affluent members of the ethnic group.

An Economic Enclave

There are two traditional views of the ways new immigrants are incorporated into the United States labor market. The first is called the assimilationist view and assumes that immigrants start in the lower paying jobs and gradually move up the occupational ladder until they become indistinguishable, in terms of their employment characteristics, from the host population. The second perspective is termed the internal colonialist view. It holds that some ethnic groups are "unmeltable" and are, therefore, subject to exploitation in the labor market through continued employment in the lowest paying jobs with few opportunities for advancement.[34] Versions of this latter view have most often been used as an explanation for the continued disadvantaged economic position of black Americans, but have also been applied to several other traditionally disadvantaged ethnic groups, such as the Mexican-Americans and Puerto Ricans living in the United States mainland.

The labor force experiences of Cuban-Americans who live outside of metropolitan Miami most closely fit the assimilationist model. However, the Cubans living in Miami (and to a lesser extent those who live in Union City-West New York) do not appear to fit into either of the two models. A recent study of Miami suggests that Cubans have established their own economic enclave that caters particularly (but not only) to a Cuban-American and Latin market. In this enclave it is possible to transact all business negotiations in Spanish and to use Cuban business customs, thus making it easier for newly arrived immigrants to become incorporated quickly into the economic mainstream. The initial capital and entrepreneurial skills that were used to establish the enclave were provided by the earliest waves of immigrants that left Cuba in the early 1960s. The later flows of refugees sustained its growth and allowed it to reach a sufficient size for economies of scale to be developed. As the more recent waves contributed immigrants who were somewhat less educated and less skilled, they provided a cross section of laborers that would allow for a more vertically integrated local ethnic economy to develop. In this way a laboring class of Cubans was provided to work in the Cuban-owned businesses. The return migration to Miami of Cubans who had at one time settled elsewhere in the United States through assistance provided by the Cuban Refugee Program contributed additional capital and labor for further growth.[35]

The Cuban economic enclave in Miami does not exist independently of the rest of the American economy. In fact, the two are very much functionally integrated.[36] The Cuban component has had a major impact on expanding south Florida's trade with Latin America. By 1978 the U.S. Customs District, in which Miami is included, accounted for 31 percent of all the United States' trade with Latin America. Aggregate exports from this district in 1979 amounted to approximately $6 billion, of which about 80 percent went to Latin America.[37] To assist the growing number of local Cuban-American businesses that interact both with the domestic

Figure 5.4 El Guajiro is one of over twenty cigar factories located in Miami. (Photo by James R. Curtis.)

economy in south Florida and with the Latin American market, Dade County currently has no less than nine Latin Chambers of Commerce.[38]

Cuban-American–owned firms in Miami tend to concentrate on the manufacturing of textile goods, leather products, furniture, and cigar making as well as on the construction, finance, retailing, and wholesaling industries. There are more than 18,000 Cuban-owned businesses in Dade County. Cuban-Americans account for about 25,000 garment workers, 3,500 doctors, over 500 lawyers, and about half of the aircraft repair and maintenance labor force in Dade County. There are 16 Cuban-American presidents of banks and approximately 250 vice presidents. Cubans own over 60 new and used car dealerships, and about 500 supermarkets, and close to 250 drug stores. It has been estimated that the Cuban community of Dade County earns an aggregate annual income of over $2.5 million.[39]

Although the growth of Cuban-owned firms has been impressive, it should be noted that most are small scale operations. In 1977 the average Dade County business employed 14 workers, whereas the average Cuban business had only eight employees. As a result, in no major sector of the

Figure 5.5 Inside the Camacho cigar factory in Miami, a tabaquero *expertly rolls a cigar by hand. (Photo by James R. Curtis.)*

economy of Dade County do Cuban businesses employ as much as ten percent of the county's total employees. When all industrial sectors are considered, Cuban-owned firms employed only 2.2 percent of all Dade County workers.[40] Still the businesses owned by Hispanics comprise over three-fourths of all minority owned firms in the county and account for about 86 percent of the employees and 89 percent of the payrolls of such businesses. Close to three-fourths of the state of Florida's Spanish-owned businesses are found in Dade County. As a result of the Cuban influence, the Miami Standard Metropolitan Statistical Area (SMSA) had more Hispanic-owned businesses than any other metropolitan area in the United States, except for the Los Angeles-Long Beach SMSA. In addition, Hispanic-owned (mostly by Cubans) businesses in Miami rank first in the nation in terms of gross receipts per firm when compared to Spanish-owned businesses in other SMSAs.[41]

Clearly, the Cuban-American population has had a major impact on Miami's economy. Primarily as a result of their influence, Miami has developed during the last 24 years into one of the United States' most important international trade centers dealing with Latin America. Still, Cuban-owned businesses tend to be relatively small and employ few workers. As a result, the businesses they own do not play as prominent a role in the local economy as their proportion of Dade County's population might suggest. This situation, however, appears to be rapidly changing. For instance, between 1969 and 1977 the number of Hispanic-owned businesses increased by almost 140 percent. In addition, the gross receipts of these businesses grew by 469 percent.[42] As the Cuban immigrants living in Miami and their American-born children continue to be upwardly mobile through increasing accumulation of capital and higher educational attainment levels, it is almost certain that they will have even more of an impact on metropolitan Miami's economy than they do at the present time.

The Cultural Landscape of Little Havana

The *Calle Ocho* Open House is billed as "a giant Cuban street party" (Figure 5.6). Annually since 1978 it has been sponsored by the Little Havana Kiwanis Club. It is the highlight of Carnival Miami, a ten-day festival of Latin culture that has been called Miami's answer to New Orleans' Mardi Gras, but is probably closer in spirit and ambience to the Carnival in Rio de Janeiro.

On a sultry Sunday in early March 1983, a 15-block stretch of S.W. Eighth Street ("Calle Ocho"), the main commercial strip that cuts through the heart of Little Havana, has been closed to vehicular traffic in preparation for *la fiesta*. In place of the cars and buses moves a river of humanity, flowing, bobbing, strutting, and dancing to the infectious rhythms of *salsa* that fill the air. Bursting onto one of the many stages where over 40 bands will perform during the day and well into the night is the famous Cuban singer, Celia Cruz. Dressed in a bright green ruffled outfit, the "queen of *salsa*" grasps the microphone and begins to sing in a thunderous voice: "Come down, come down to Miami. Come down, come down to Miami." The audience packed around the bandstand roars its approval and instantly hands begin to clap and hips start swaying. Nearby, an old man wearing a straw hat, *guayabera* shirt, baggy pants, and Nike track shoes breaks into a solo *rumba*. Colorfully clad *comparsa* dancers prance by as *conga* lines over 50 people long snake through the crowd that fills the narrow street from sidewalk to sidewalk. At various intervals along the mile-and-a-half route are dance troups and folkloric groups from Brazil, the Bahama Islands, Colombia, Peru, and Trinidad and Tobago. On one corner the sounds of reggae blast forth as the Bahamian goombay dance group, the Sunshine Junkanoos, perform in a rainbow of *papier-mâché* cos-

Figure 5.6 Little Havana bustles with the spirit of fiesta during the Calle Ocho *Open House. (Photo courtesy of the City of Miami, Office of Information.)*

tumes. Down the street the Latin-Caribbean flavor gives way to American popular culture at the Ronald McDonald and Burger King shows. Lining the sidewalk are hundreds of exhibits and displays featuring painting and crafts, boxing and weight-lifting, cooking and karate. Most of all, there are booths offering food and drink. At one the fare is *pan con lechón* (pork sandwiches), black beans and rice, *guarapo* (sugar cane juice), and Heineken beer. At another there are hamburgers, hot dogs, Coca-Cola, and Coors beer. Next to it, a Bahamian woman sells conch fritters, pigeon peas and rice, and Budweiser beer. Estimates of the size of the crowd range from 600,000 to 750,000; the latter figure is more than twice the total population of the City of Miami. One thing about the crowd, however, is certain: most are Cuban-Americans. Overhead flies a helicopter pulling a sign that they can relate to. It reads, "Miami es para mí" (Miami is for me).

Festivals like Carnival Miami and its spirited *Calle Ocho* Open House are one aspect of the profound impact that Cuban settlement has had on the cultural life and landscape of this metropolitan area. In the predominantly Cuban sections of the city, the built environment has been modified and designed to suit the needs and tastes of its residents. It visually reflects in both vivid and subtle ways the impress of Cuban culture, and thereby graphically suggests the ethnic transformation that has occurred in these areas. Although Little Havana is now only one of many Cuban communities in Dade County, it remains in landscape and tradition the heart of Cuban Miami. If landscape is a "clue to culture," an "unwitting autobiography," as Peirce Lewis has written,[43] then nowhere is the Cuban culture in Miami more clearly manifested than in Little Havana.

In terms of authenticity, Little Havana is more Cuban than Little Italy in New York City is now Italian, and certainly more than the French Quarter in New Orleans is French. It is probably closer in this respect to Chinatown in San Francisco, though *Calle Ocho* is much less commercialized than Grant Avenue, its counterpart in Chinatown. Yet, while it is easy to stereotype Little Havana as a "foreign city within an American city," it is not as "foreign" as some writers have suggested. Rather, it is a complex, diverse community that represents an amalgam of both Cuban and American cultures. Still, for die-hard traditionalists, it is possible for a Cuban who lives in Little Havana and speaks only Spanish to shop, dine out, be medically cared for, attend church, school, shows and theaters, die and be buried without a word of English being uttered.

There are a number of public and quasi-public places in Little Havana that illustrate in different ways the nature of Cuban culture and settlement in this community. Undoubtedly, the chief public focal point in Little Havana is Domino Park, also named Antonio Maceo Minipark, in honor of one of the heros of the Cuban War of Independence. It is a small, 50 by 90 foot park located in the heart of the enclave at 15th Avenue and *Calle Ocho*. Open to the street, it is an extremely urban park. Beneath its black olive trees and two barrel-tile-roofed pavilions are tables angled to the street where games of 9-dot dominoes and to a lesser extent chess and checkers are played throughout the day and into the evening. The crowd that gathers here daily, mostly older Cuban men (women are rarely present), came to play dominoes in this spot even before the city spent $115,000 in 1976 to convert the space into a park.[44] More than just to play games, they come to discuss politics, smoke their cigars, laugh, and dream of the old days in Cuba, and maybe even their eventual return to the island. Perhaps more so than any other public place in Miami, this congested little lot is evocative of the Cuban presence in the city. Only two blocks east on *Calle Ocho*, the spirit and vitality of Domino Park are offset by the somberness surrounding another public space: the Cuban Memorial Plaza, a block-long center park dividing 13th Avenue where a monument stands in honor of the men of the Brigade 2506 who died during the Bay of Pigs invasion. It, too, is a focal point in Little Havana, especially for anti-Castro demonstrations and other political rallies.

About a mile and a half west on *Calle Ocho* is Woodlawn Memorial Park, an 80-acre cemetery founded in 1913. Though not really a public place, it nevertheless gives another perspective on the nature of Cuban settlement in Little Havana. Buried here are members of some of the founding families of Miami, including George Merrick, developer of Coral Gables, one of the first planned suburban communities in America. But here as well are the graves of former Cuban presidents Gerardo Machado and Carlos Prío Socarras, as well as ex-president of Nicaragua, Anastasio Somoza. Back at the extreme eastern boundary of Little Havana, on the edge of downtown Miami, a new public space is being created—José Martí Park. It lies beneath the massive concrete slabs of the expressway bypasses off of Interstate 95. During the Mariel exodus of 1980 it was the site of "Tent City," where hundreds of Cuban refugees were temporarily housed. Unfortunately, homeless and unemployed refugees still seek shelter in this barren place.

The commercial activities in Little Havana are concentrated along the major north-south and east-west running thoroughfares in the district, especially on Flagler Street and *Calle Ocho*. (If Little Havana was considered to be the Cuban-American world, then *Calle Ocho* would be the equator; it is the principal strip of Cuban business and culture in Miami.) The commercial landscape of Little Havana, however, does not have a unifying architectural identity. Although there are a few distinctive Art Deco and Spanish-style buildings in the area, most of the older structures are a mixture of modern styles that are rather plain and unpretentious with little

Figure 5.7 This monument in honor of the men who died in the ill-fated Bay of Pigs invasion stands in the Cuban Memorial Plaza in the heart of Little Havana. (Photo by James R. Curtis.)

or no exterior ornamentation. Some of the small shopping plazas that have been built in the district recently, however, have incorporated Spanish elements in their facades and decorative motifs. The Spanish theme has also been enhanced through a county-coordinated beautification project that included, for example, the installation of Spanish-style street lamps.[45]

Regardless of its architecture, the commercial district of Little Havana is embellished with a pronounced Cuban flavor. The advertisements, posters, and billboards are mostly in Spanish, and neon store signs flash "Joyería," "Ferretería," "Mueblería," "Farmacia," "Mercado," "Zapatería." Many of the businesses include in their names "Cuba" or "Havana" or the names of other Cuban provinces or cities. (In some cases they are named after well-known stores in Havana, and it is not uncommon that the owner also owned the original store.) Miniature Cuban flags or stickers of the flag are prominently displayed on nearly all of the shop windows. Maps of Cuba, posters of José Martí with inspirational quotes by the Cuban patriot, anti-Castro handbills, pictures of President Reagan, and campaign posters for local politicians (if they are Cuban then invariably they include the Cuban flag on the poster) are also found on many windows. Wall murals in the district depict other aspects of Cuban culture, such as the one adjacent to Domino Park of Our Lady of Charity, patron saint of Cuba. (Unlike Mexican-American or Puerto Rican communities, for example, Little Havana has almost no graffiti; the few that exist are political slogans, such as "Cuba *libre*!")

Although the shops are generally small, the range of commercial activities in Little Havana is impressive; virtually all essential (and some exotic) consumer goods and services are available. It is easy to appreciate how the enclave could function as a self-contained area for non-English speaking Cubans. In addition to the large American chain supermarkets in the enclave, which all have Spanish-speaking employees, there are numerous small, mostly family-run grocery stores (called *bodegas*) that carry a full line of Cuban food products, including meats (see Chapter 9). Fresh fruits, vegetables, and tropical tubers are sold in open-air markets located on the main commercial strips. Little Havana is also noted for its many Cuban bakeries. These formal establishments are supplemented by Cuban peddlers who sell fish, poultry, garden grown vegetables, and fruits (often peeled) out of the back of their pick-up trucks or off the hood of their cars. Pharmacies are conveniently located throughout the area, which is important for the district's many elderly residents. Virtually all of the pharmacies have signs on the window that announce, "*Envíos de Medicinas a Cuba*" (We send medicines to Cuba). Concentrated along *Calle Ocho* and Flagler Street, especially toward the eastern end, are a score of Cuban cooperative health clinics, staffed by Cuban physicians. Cuban-owned furniture stores are also clustered along *Calle Ocho*. Chairs are usually lined up along the front of these stores in keeping with an old Spanish custom.[46] Small clothing stores and shoe stores abound in the enclave, offering personalized service. For followers of *Santería*, an Afro-Cuban cult religion (see Chapter 7), there are over a dozen *botanicas* that stock an

Figure 5.8 In this clever wall mural, Charlie Brown, Alfred E. Newman, Frankenstein, and Batman are part of a "typical street scene in Little Havana." (Photo by James R. Curtis.)

utterly baffling array of items used for ritualistic purposes, including roots, herbs, oils, scents, sprays, powders, potions, and religious figurines. Beyond these stores and shops, there are in addition banks, bars, barbershops, beauty salons, book stores, car dealerships, flower shops, gift shops, jewelry stores, hardware stores, insurance offices, nightclubs, theaters, travel agencies, and even *La Casa de las Trucos* (the house of tricks). Nearly all of these businesses are Cuban-owned and cater to the Cuban population. In this respect, Little Havana is unlike most urban minority communities, where most businesses are owned by outsiders.

Perhaps more so than any other activity, Little Havana is most noted for its multitude of Cuban restaurants and *cafeterías* (see Chapter 9). For many suburban Cubans, especially younger people, they are the principal attraction that draws them to the area. There is a tremendous variety among the restaurants in respect to ambiance, price, and the cuisine itself. In restaurants like Vizcaya, Centro Vasco, or Bilbao the setting is more formal, with valet parking and tuxedoed waiters. In places like La Taxca, Lila's, Versailles (with its mirrored walls), or La Esquina de Tejas (where President Reagan dined on his visit to Little Havana in May 1983) the emphasis is on the food, while the ambiance is relaxed and friendly. A majority of the many *cafeterías* in the enclave are small, inexpensive, and usually crowded. They also typically have counters that open to the sidewalk for pedestrians to stop by for a quick cup of *café cubano* and perhaps some fresh *pasteles* (pastry). Although traditional Cuban cuisine (see Chapter 9) is the standard fare at most of the restaurants, a number combine Cuban food with Spanish, Basque, or Oriental cuisines. Little Havana's restaurants, with their distinctive aroma of simmering garlic and onions, their mixture of architectural styles, and their hearty food, greatly contribute to the area's sense of place.

Compared to the bustling street life of the commercial strips, the residential areas of Little Havana are relatively quiet and subdued. Although the housing areas have been greatly improved for the most part and changed as a consequence of the Cuban settlement, the residential landscape is not nearly as "Latinized" as the commercial district. Still, a number of characteristically Cuban (and other Hispanic) influences are apparent. Fences, for example, now enclose many, if not most, front yards. Wrought iron grill work over windows and decorative Spanish tiles also embellish many homes. Certainly one of the more distinctive features of the residential district is the large number of yard shrines, literally hundreds, that grace the area (see Chapter 7). A vast majority of the shrines are erected in honor of Catholic saints, especially Santa Barbara, Our Lady of Charity, and Saint Lazarus. The various neighborhoods within Little Havana, however, are far from uniform in terms of landscape elements or the quality of housing. Though most of the areas are essentially middle class, there are sections which are greatly overcrowded and housing is near or at substandard levels. Certainly the poorest neighborhood is East Little Havana, on the edge of downtown Miami, which has declined seriously since the Mariel boatlift in 1980 brought thousands of refugees who settled here.[47] There is fear that it may become Little Havana's first "slum," though the community is intent on seeing that it does not happen, and steps to improve the situation are being taken.[48]

The cultural landscape of Little Havana is rich and varied. It fully reflects the impress of Cuban culture on the area. Though the district has been significantly transformed, there are still many elements of American culture.[49] And, perhaps, that is appropriate for a community that is Cuban-American.

Figure 5.9 Yard shrines are common features in the cultural landscape of most Cuban residential areas in Miami, especially in Little Havana. (Photo by James R. Curtis.)

Notes

1. Clyde McCoy, Duane McBride, Bryan Page, and Diana Gonzalez, "The Ethnography of Drug Use Among Cubans in Miami" (unpublished report submitted to the National Institute of Drug Administration, 1981), p. 33.
2. The Research Institute for Cuba and the Caribbean, Center for Advanced International Studies, University of Miami, *The Cuban Immigration, 1959–1966: Its Impact on Miami-Dade County, Florida* (Coral Gables: University of Miami Press, 1967), p. 5.
3. Ivan A. Castro, "Little Havana," in Pat Morrissey, ed., *Miami's Neighborhoods* (Miami News, 1982), pp. 79–80.
4. Morton D. Winsberg, "Housing Segregation of a Predominantly Middle Class Population: Residential Patterns Developed by the Cuban Immigration Into Miami, 1950–1974," *American Journal of Economics and Sociology* 38:409, October 1979.
5. Ibid.
6. Castro, op. cit., p. 80.
7. Sergio Diaz Briquets and Lisandro Perez, *Cuba: The Demography of Revolution* (Washington, D.C.: Population Reference Bureau, Vol. 36, No. 1, April 1981), p. 26.
8. Cuban Refugee Program, Social and Rehabilitation Service, U.S. Department of Health, Education and Welfare, "Fact Sheet," Miami, Florida, December 1, 1969.
9. Carlos Arboleya, "Banker Arboleya Looks at Community," *The Miami Herald*, June 30, 1972, p. 8G.
10. The Research Institute for Cuban and the Caribbean, op. cit., p. 8.
11. Frederic Tasker and Helga Silva, "Latin Centers Spread, Transforming County," *The Miami Herald*, February 14, 1982, p. 2B.
12. Office of Community Development, Metropolitan Dade County, "Impact of the Community Development Program of Private Sector Involvement in the Commercial Rehabilitation of the 'Little Havana' Neighborhood," Miami, Florida, 1978, p. 2.
13. James R. Curtis, "Miami's Little Havana: Yard Shrines, Cult Religion, and Landscape," *Journal of Cultural Geography* 1:2, Fall-Winter 1980.
14. F. Peirce Eichelberger, "The Cubans in Miami: Residential Movement and Ethnic Group Differentiation" (M.A. thesis, University of Cincinnati, 1974), p. 49.
15. Ibid.
16. Winsberg, op. cit., p. 415.
17. Office of Community Development, op. cit., p. 3.
18. Ivan A. Castro, "Hialeah," in Morrissey, op. cit., pp. 52–54.
19. David B. Longbrake and Woodrow W. Nichols, *Sunshine and Shadows in Metropolitan Miami* (Cambridge, Mass.: Ballinger Publications, 1976), pp. 38–40.
20. William Francis Mackey and Von Nieda Beebe, *Bilingual Schools for a Bicultural Community: Miami's Adaptation to the Cuban Refugees* (Rowley, Mass.: Newbury House Publishers, 1977), p. 28.
21. Metropolitan Dade County Planning Department, *Cuban and Haitian Refugees: Miami Standard Metropolitan Statistical Area, 1980*, Miami, Florida, January 1981.
22. Frederic Tasker, "Refugee Influx Badly Outdates '80 Census Data," *The Miami Herald*, January 31, 1982, p. 1B.
23. Tasker and Silva, op. cit., p. 28.
24. Bill Gjebre, "Sweetwater," in Morrissey, op. cit., p. 137.
25. Frederic Tasker, "Dade Gets Younger, More Mixed," *The Miami Herald*, January 17, 1982, p. 1B.
26. Ana Veliana-Suarez, "Westchester," in Morrissey, op. cit., p. 146.
27. Metropolitan Dade County, Office of the County Manager, Division of Latin Affairs, "Hispanic Dade County: Their Characteristics and Needs," Miami, Florida, Spring 1980.
28. Terry G. Jordan and Lester Rowntree, *The Human Mosaic: A Thematic Introduction to Cultural Geography* (New York: Harper and Row, 1982), pp. 276–278.
29. Patrick Lee Gallagher, *The Cuban Exile: A Socio-Political Analysis* (New York: Arno Press, 1980), pp. 48–51; and Curtis, op. cit., pp. 2–10.

30. Kimball D. Woodbury, "The Spatial Diffusion of the Cuban Community in Dade County, Florida" (M.S. thesis, University of Florida, 1978), pp. 67–69.

31. Thomas D. Boswell, Afolabi A. Adelibu, and Kimberly J. Zokoski, "Spatial Attributes of Social Areas Dimensions in Miami, Florida SMSA: 1970," *The Florida Geographer* 14:7–10, February 1980.

32. Alejandro Portes, Juan Clark, and Manuel M. Lopez, "Six Years Later, A Profile of the Process of Incorporation of Cuban Exiles in the United States," *Cuban Studies*, July 1981.

33. Eichelberger, op. cit., pp. 67–93.

34. Kenneth L. Wilson and Alejandro Portes, "Immigrant Cubans in Miami," *American Journal of Sociology* 86:295–319, September 1980.

35. The Cuban Refugee Program has spent approximately $1.6 billion on its assistance for Cuban refugees. Antonio Jorge and Rual Moncarz, *International Factor Movement and Complementarity: Growth and Entrepreneurship Under Conditions of European Cultural Variation* (The Hague, Netherlands: Research Group for European Migration Problems, R.E.M.P. Bulletin, supplement 14, 1981), pp. 14–17.

36. Antonio Jorge and Rual Moncarz, *The Future of the Hispanic Market: The Cuban Entrepreneur and the Economic Development of the Miami Standard Metropolitan Statistical Area* (Miami: Discussion Paper No. 6, International Banking Center and Department of Economics, Florida International University, June 1982).

37. Jorge and Moncarz, *International Factor Movement and Complementarity: Growth and Entrepreneurship Under Conditions of Cultural Variation*, op. cit., pp. 21–25, 56.

38. Barbara Gutierrez, "Many Voices Speak for Latin Businesses," *The Miami Herald*, May 9, 1983, Business Monday Section, p. 14.

39. Carlos J. Arboleya, "The Cuban Community 1980: Coming of Age, As History Repeats Itself" (self-published letter by the President and Chief Operating Officer of Barnett Bank, Miami, Florida, 1980).

40. Jorge and Moncarz, *International Factor Movement and Complementarity: Growth and Entrepreneurship Under Conditions of Cultural Variation*, op. cit., pp. 27, 31.

41. Ibid., pp. 7–8.

42. Ibid., pp. 17, 19.

43. Peirce F. Lewis, "Axioms for Reading the Landscape: Some Guides to the American Scene," in D.W. Meinig, ed., *The Interpretation of Ordinary Landscapes* (New York: Oxford University Press, 1979), pp. 13, 15.

44. Beth Dunlop, "Don't Fence in Little Havana's Domino Park," *The Miami Herald*, May 30, 1982, p. 3L.

45. Office of Community Development, op. cit., pp. 5–14.

46. Christine Brown Arnold, "Anglo's Guide to Little Havana," *The Miami Herald*, December 2, 1977, p. 1D.

47. Ana Veciana-Suarez, "Boatlift Helps Sink East Little Havana," *The Miami Herald*, February 13, 1983, p. 1B.

48. Fabiola Santiago, "East Little Havana Fights Slum Label," *The Miami Herald*, June 12, 1983, p. 4B.

49. Liz Balmaseda, "Anglo Ocho," *The Miami Herald*, March 7, 1981, p. 2B.

6

A Demographic Profile of the Cuban-American Populations

To a considerable extent, the present demographic characteristics of an ethnic group provide a mirror of past historical tendencies. The present characteristics of Cuban-Americans have been particularly influenced by the recent history of their migration to the United States. Both the emigration policies of the Cuban government and the natural selectivity of the types of Cubans who would be most likely to participate in the exodus were to prove crucial in this regard. This chapter will provide a profile of the demographic characteristics of the persons of Cuban descent living in the United States. Two perspectives will be used. First, Cuban-Americans will be compared to the Spanish-American and non-Spanish American populations; second, Cuban-Americans in Florida will be compared with (1) those living in both New York and New Jersey, and (2) those residing in the remaining 47 states.[1]

Cuban-Americans, Spanish-Americans, and Non-Spanish Americans

A comparison of Cubans living in the United States with all Hispanic-Americans and the rest of the United States population that is not of Spanish descent will provide a basis for understanding of the context in which Cuban-Americans find themselves while living in this country. This analysis will focus on the following components of these three populations: (1) age and sex composition, (2) racial characteristics, (3) employment, occupation, and income characteristics, (4) educational attainment, and (5) fertility levels.

AGE AND SEX COMPOSITION

When the age structure of the Cuban descent population is compared to those of the total Spanish origin and non-Spanish origin populations, some significant differences become immediately apparent (Table 6.1). The median age for the Cubans is over eleven years higher than for the total Spanish-descent population and almost three years higher than for non-Spanish-descent persons. Despite the fact that most have lived for a relatively short period in the United States, the age composition of the Cuban-Americans more closely resembles that of non-Spanish persons than it does the Spanish descent population. The fact that the Cuban origin population is considerably older than the total Spanish-American population is related to two primary factors.[2] The first is the very low fertility patterns exhibited by the Cubans, when compared with most other ethnic components of the United States population. More will be said regarding this important tendency later in this chapter. Suffice it to say that lower birthrates tend to depress proportional representation in the lower age classes. As a result, the population appears to age with declining fertility.

The second factor that helps account for the older character of the Cuban-Americans has to do with the selectivity of the migrants who moved from Cuba to the United States. The Castro government was unwilling to allow many young adult males to leave the island until they had satisfied their military obligation, especially during the Freedom Flights between 1965 and 1973. This helps to explain why the Cuban population in Table 6.1 has smaller percentages in the 21-to-24 and 25-to-34 age classes, when compared to either the Spanish-origin or non-Spanish populations. It was also stated previously that elderly persons were allowed to leave more freely because it was believed that many would become dependent upon the state if they remained in Cuba.[3] This helps account for the fact that close to 10 percent of the Cuban-Americans are 65 years of age or older, whereas less than 5 percent of the total Spanish-Americans fall in this age class.

A higher proportion of females in comparison with males is the norm for populations of most Western societies, owing to the greater longevity of women. For the total United States population, approximately 51.5 percent are females. For all Hispanic-Americans the comparable figure is 50.2 percent. However, populations that are largely composed of immigrants,. such as the Cuban-Americans, are more often characterized by a slight surplus of males, unless the receiving country has an immigration policy that favors females. Prior to the Mariel boatlift in 1980, a slight majority (50.2 percent) of persons of Cuban descent living in the United States were female.[4] This very minor predominance of females also (like their age structure) was related to the migration policies of the Cuban government, rather than to those of the United States. Castro's reluctance to allow males of military age to leave during the Aerial Bridge of 1965 to 1973 had an affect, as did the greater freedom for the elderly to emigrate.[5]

Table 6.1 Age of Cuban-Americans Compared to the Total Spanish Origin and Non-Spanish Origin Populations in the United States, 1980 (in percent)

	Cuban-Americans	Total Spanish origin[a]	U.S. non-Spanish origin
Under 5	7.2	12.9	6.9
5 to 9	7.7	11.3	7.2
10 to 17	14.8	17.0	13.5
18 to 20	5.0	6.5	5.6
21 to 24	5.9	7.7	7.2
25 to 34	11.1	16.5	16.1
35 to 44	16.8	11.1	11.7
45 to 54	14.1	7.9	10.5
55 to 64	7.6	4.8	9.9
65 and over	9.7	4.2	11.3
Median age	33.5	22.1	30.7

[a] Includes persons of Cuban origin.

Source: U.S. Bureau of the Census, *Current Population Reports*, Series P-20, No. 361: "Persons of Spanish Origin in the United States: March 1980 (Advanced Report)," (Washington, D.C.: U.S. Government Printing Office, 1981), p. 5.

Since women usually live longer, it is reasonable that they would be over-represented in the oldest age classes. Since the Mariel exodus was heavily dominated by males, it is apparent that the balance now has swung in the direction of a male predominance. Although there are no official figures available from the United States Census Bureau, it can be estimated that males currently represent somewhere between 50 and 55 percent of the total Cuban-American population.[6]

Racial Characteristics

The vast majority of Cubans living in the United States are considered to be white. The most recent year for which racial data are available for

Cuban-Americans is 1970. In that year, 96.0 percent were classified as white, 3.1 percent black, and the remaining 0.9 percent were categorized as other. When all persons of Hispanic origin are considered, the comparable figures were 93.3, 5.0 and 1.6 percent, respectively.[7] For the entire population of the United States, a little over 11 percent is black. The overwhelming proportion of the Cuban-Americans that are white is not representative of the population remaining in Cuba. For instance, the 1953 Population Census for Cuba shows that about 27 percent of the island's population was black or mulatto at that time. This is about 9 times the percentage for the Cubans living in the United States.[8]

Five reasons have been suggested for explaining why a much smaller proportion of the Cuban-American population is composed of blacks than is the population living in Cuba.[9] First, the Castro revolution was designed primarily to benefit the poorer classes of Cuban society. Since blacks were more concentrated among the poor, presumably a larger percentage of them were able to take advantage of opportunities offered by the new government. Second, the Castro government has expended major efforts to depict the United States as a racist society, as part of its anti-American propaganda program. Third, as stated in Chapter 3, much of the Cuban migration to the United States has been promoted and assisted through family ties with relatives already living in the United States. Fewer Cuban blacks have moved to the United States because a smaller proportion of them have relatives living in America on whom they can rely for assistance. Fourth, the immigration policy of the United States since 1965 has generally favored the legal immigration of Cubans who have close family members already residing on American soil. Thus, not only were the kinship networks of whites not as readily available to them, but Cuban blacks also found that it was harder to gain entry through the American council in Havana because of this scarcity of American relatives. Fifth, there is evidence that some resentment exists among a minority of the white Cuban-American exiles living in the United States toward black Cubans because of a feeling that many of the blacks welcomed the Castro revolution. Evidence in support of this hypothesis is manifested in Miami's Little Havana, where the four census tracts that had the highest percentage of Cuban residents had a combined population that was less than three percent black in 1980.[10]

A recent comparative study of Cubans living in the metropolitan areas of Miami and Union City—West New York found that a slightly larger proportion of the latter's population was black. This difference was attributed to differing perceived levels of discrimination.[11] It has been noted in the literature that the majority of Cuban nonwhites live in the northeastern United States, where the reputation for racial tolerance is better than in the South.[12]

In Chapter 3 it was noted that approximately 20 percent of the Cubans who immigrated via the Mariel boatlift in 1980 were black. This represents a proportion that is about seven times higher than has been characteristic of past Cuban migration waves. But even this new figure is only about three-fourths of the percentage of the population in Cuba. Nevertheless, the fact that a larger proportion of blacks left Cuba during this last exodus than ever before has been heralded by some as being a sign that the policies of the Castro government are beginning to wear thin, even with the people it was supposed to benefit the most.

EMPLOYMENT, OCCUPATION, AND INCOME CHARACTERISTICS

When the working force and income characteristics of Cuban-Americans are compared with those of the total Spanish-American population (Table 6.2), it is clear that the Cubans have achieved a remarkably high socioeconomic level. This is particularly noteworthy considering their relatively short length of residence in the United States. In terms of occupational distribution, employment levels, and income, they are considerably better off than most other persons of Hispanic origin living in America. In fact, their economic achievements approach those of the non-Spanish descent population. Currently Cuban-Americans are represented by an intermediate position in terms of their socioeconomic status, between the Spanish-Americans and non-Spanish populations. When compared to Puerto Ricans and Mexican-Americans within the Spanish-descent class, it is clear that the Cubans are much better off economically.[13]

Although the figures displayed in Table 6.2 have been derived from the most recent available data, they present the characteristics of Cuban-Americans as they existed immediatly prior to the wave of Mariel immigrants which arrived in South Florida between April and September, 1980. If the characteristics of the Marielitos were added to these figures, they would dampen somewhat the economic position of the persons of Cuban origin because of their higher unemployment rates and lower skill levels. However, even with this impact, Cuban-Americans still would occupy an intermediate position between all Spanish-Americans and Americans who are not of Spanish descent.

The current occupational composition of Cuban-Americans is a product of four major trends that have characterized the labor force history of these émigrés. The first has been the tendency for persons with higher education levels and skills to be overrepresented in migration flows to the United States. Second, there has been a tendency for this selection process to decline over time, so that the most recent Cuban immigrants are more similar to the population left behind in Cuba than was the case of the ear-

Table 6.2 Occupation, Employment, and Income Characteristics of Cuban-Americans Compared to the Total Spanish Origin and Non-Spanish Origin Populations in the United States
(Persons 16 Years Old or Over)

	Cuban-Americans (percent)	Total Spanish origin (percent)	U.S. non-Spanish origin (percent)
Professional, technical and kindred workers	12.4	8.5	16.8
Managers and administors, except farm	9.0	6.6	11.4
Sales workers	5.9	3.8	6.3
Clerical and kindred workers	14.4	16.1	18.9
Craft and kindred workers	12.4	14.0	12.7
Operatives, including transport	28.4	23.7	13.7
Laborers, excluding farm	6.1	7.9	4.3
Farmers and farm managers	0.2	0.3	1.5
Farm laborers and supervisors	0.0	3.0	0.9
Service workers	11.3	16.2	13.4
Percent unemployed, 1980	5.0	8.9	6.5
Percent of males in labor force, 1979	83.3	80.5	76.0
Percent of females in labor force, 1979	53.1	47.4	50.9
Median family income, 1979	$17,538	$14,569	$19,965
Median personal income, 1978	$6,352	$5,893	$6,864

Sources: U.S. Bureau of the Census, *Current Population Reports*, series P-20, No. 361: "Persons of Spanish Origin in the United States: March 1980 (Advanced Report)," (Washington, D.C.: U.S. Government Printing Office, 1981), p. 5.

U.S. Bureau of the Census, *Current Population Reports*, series P-20, No. 354: "Persons of Spanish Origin in the United States: March 1979" (Washington, D.C.: U.S. Government Printing Office, 1980), pp. 10 and 29.

lier migrants. There are a couple of reasons for the decline in the proportion of professionals among the later emigration waves. Many of the better educated and more highly skilled persons who wanted to leave had already done so by the late 1960s. Thus, there were fewer remaining in Cuba to supply future streams to the United States. In addition, because the Cuban government is reluctant to see them leave, the remaining professionals have been accorded a privileged position in the socialist society of the island and there is less incentive for them to emigrate now.[14]

A third trend that has affected the occupational characteristics of Cuban-Americans has been the tendency for most to experience a decline in status with their first job in the United States. Often they have had to take whatever type of work was available when they first arrived. Their lack of facility with English was a major factor that affected their employment opportunities. In addition, many professional occupations require citizenship or formal licensing procedures that can take years to satisfy.

A fourth factor has been a tendency toward upward mobility as length of residence in the United States increases.[15] A study of Cubans living in the city of West New York found that although the last job held in Cuba prior to emigration had very little influence on the first job obtained in the United States, it did affect the potential for eventual upward mobility. Those who had higher status jobs in Cuba were more likely to become upwardly mobile. Younger migrants and those who were better educated have also exhibited more success in climbing the occupational ladder.[16]

EDUCATIONAL ATTAINMENT LEVELS

When the educational levels of Cuban-Americans are compared to those of the total Spanish-origin population and to Americans who are not of Spanish descent (Table 6.3), the results tend to corroborate the generalizations stated with respect to employment, occupation, and income. Clearly, persons of Cuban descent have not attained as high an educational level as those who are not of Spanish origin. On the other hand, the Cubans are better educated than the total Spanish-American population. They tend to occupy an intermediate position between this country's Hispanics and non-Hispanics. It is also worth noting that the Cubans are more similar to the non-Spanish in their achieved education levels then they are to the Hispanics.[17]

A closer inspection of the figures in Table 6.3 reveals another distinction. Not only are Cuban-Americans intermediate between the United States Spanish and non-Spanish populations, but they also occupy an intermediate position within the total Hispanic population. The Cubans are much better educated than are the persons of either Mexican or Puerto Ri-

Table 6.3 Population 25 Years Old and Over by Years of Completed Schooling, March 1979

	Less than 5 years of schooling (percent)	4 years of high school or more (percent)	4 years of college or more (percent)
Total Spanish origin	17.6	42.0	6.7
Mexican origin	23.9	34.9	3.9
Puerto Rican origin	14.4	38.6	4.1
Cuban origin	6.9	50.4	12.0
Other Spanish origin	6.7	60.8	13.8
Not of Spanish origin	2.8	68.9	16.9

Source: U.S. Bureau of the Census, *Current Population Reports,* Series P-20, No. 354, "Persons of Spanish Origin in the United States: March 1979," (Washington, D.C.: U.S. Government Printing Office, 1980), p. 5.

can origin, but they are not quite as well educated as the persons of "other Spanish origin." The "other Spanish origin" class is largely (but not totally) composed of middle- and upper-class persons who have immigrated to the United States from countries located in Central and South American and from the Dominican Republic and Spain.[18]

FERTILITY LEVELS

A number of fertility studies have found that middle class families in western societies tend to have smaller numbers of children than either the poor or wealthy classes. Apparently wealthy couples can comfortably afford to have as many children as they want, whereas the standard of living for the very poor is not likely to be altered much through the addition of another child.[19] Given the fact that most Cuban-American families are middle class, it is reasonable to find that they have characteristically exhibited very low fertility patterns while living in the United States. In fact, a very low birthrate exists also in Cuba today, due partly to the effects of the Castro revolution, and to some of the processes of modernization initiated before the Castro takeover in 1959.[20]

A recent study comparing various demographic characteristics of the Spanish-American population found that persons of Cuban descent have exceptionally low birthrates.[21] The number of births per 1000 population for the Cuban-Americans was found to be 16. For the white population it was 17, whereas for Mexican-Americans and Puerto Ricans living in the United States it was 27 and 30, respectively. When controlled to take into consideration such factors as the Cuban-Americans' older age structure, higher education levels, and higher female labor force participation rates, the differences became even more pronounced. When thus standardized, women of Cuban descent exhibited a fertility rate that was 23 percent lower than that of non-Spanish white women living in the United States. When compared to Mexican-American and Puerto Rican women living in the United States, the rate for Cuban women was 47 and 28 percentage points lower, respectively.[22]

Florida, New Jersey, New York, and Other Origins

In Chapter 4 it was noted that in 1980 just under 60 percent of all Cuban-Americans lived in the state of Florida and about 20 percent resided in New Jersey and New York. In fact, this population is even more concentrated than the state figures alone indicate, since about 87 percent of Florida's Cuban-Americans live in Dade County (Greater Miami) and close to 90 percent of New York's and New Jersey's Cubans live in the greater metropolitan area of New York City and adjacent portions of New Jersey. The remaining 20 percent of the Cubans who live in the other 47 states can be regarded as being a dispersed population. This distribution suggests several interesting questions. To what degree are these three populations of Cuban-Americans different in terms of their socioeconomic characteristics? Do the heavy concentrations in South Florida and eastern New Jersey retard the development of the Cuban populations that live there? Conversely, does the dispersed character of the Cubans who live outside the states of Florida, New Jersey, and New York promote their assimilation, so that their socioeconomic characteristics reflect higher status? If the answer to these questions is yes, then can it be assumed that the Cubans who live in New Jersey and New York occupy an intermediate level of status because their magnitude of concentration is less than Florida but more than for the other states? These questions will be investigated first by considering some of the social characteristics of the three Cuban populations, and second by describing their economic distinctions.

Whenever possible in this section 1980 data have been used;[23] but where 1980 figures are not available, data from the 1970 population census are used.[24] Also, the figures for 1980 for the "other states" category include only California, Illinois, and Texas because data were not available for Cubans living in all 50 states. These three states, however, contained in 1980 half of the 20 percent of the Cuban-Americans who lived outside of Florida,

New Jersey, and New York. The 1980 figures do not include the Cuban refugees who arrived from Mariel between April and December of 1980.)

SOCIAL CHARACTERISTICS OF THE THREE CUBAN-AMERICAN POPULATIONS

The figures presented in Table 6.4 indicate that there is very little difference in the age structures of the Cuban-Americans living in Florida and those living in New Jersey–New York. The Florida Cubans have a median age that is approximately half a year older. However, the Cubans living in the three states of California, Illinois, and Texas are on the average about six years younger. The higher age of the Florida and New Jersey–New York Cubans is related to the fact that a somewhat larger percentage of their Cuban populations are foreign born (mostly in Cuba) than is the case for the other states. For instance, 84 percent of Florida's Cubans were foreign born in 1970, whereas only about 77 percent of the "other states" Cubans were born outside the United States. Given the short history of their heavy immigration to this country, it is clear that the foreign-born Cubans are older than Cubans who were born in the United States. The foreign-born Cubans are also more likely to remain in the metropolitan areas of Miami or New Jersey–New York because they find it more comfortable to live among other Cubans with whom they share a similar cultural background.

In terms of their sex structure and type of residence there is virtually no difference between Cuban-Americans living in Florida, New Jersey–New York, and the other states. Slightly more than half are females and almost all live in urban areas, especially in large cities. On the other hand, there are some significant differences when educational levels are considered. The Cubans living in the "other states" category have the highest percentage of males who have completed high school and college, while Florida has the lowest percentage. It is somewhat surprising, therefore, to find that Florida Cubans have the lowest fertility levels of the three Cuban populations, since fertility and education are usually inversely correlated. This is explained by the fact that Cuban females living in Florida have higher labor force participation rates than those living in New Jersey–New York and the other states. A recent study has determined that the degree of female labor force participation is more important as a factor affecting the fertility of Cuban-Americans than educational attainment.[25]

ECONOMIC CHARACTERISTICS OF THE THREE CUBAN-AMERICAN POPULATIONS

The occupational and income characteristics of the three Cuban-American populations for 1970 are presented in Table 6.5. Males and females are

Table 6.4 Selected Social Characteristics of Cuban-Americans by State of Residence, 1970, 1980

		State of Residence	
	Florida	New Jersey/ New York	Other states[a]
Age classes (1980)			
Percent under 20 years old	25.0	25.6	28.5
Percent 20–59 years old	55.6	58.6	57.5
Percent 60 years old or over	19.4	15.5	14.0
Median age	39.8	39.3	33.5
Percent female (1980)	52.9	52.5	51.2
Type of residence (1980)			
Percent urban	99.1	98.8	98.1
Percent in urbanized areas	97.5	98.2	95.8
Percent rural	0.9	1.2	1.9
Percent foreign born (1970)	84.0	81.0	77.0
Education for males 25–34 years of age (1970)			
Percent completed high school	54.0	57.0	64.0
Percent completed college	9.0	14.0	20.0
Number of children under 5 years of age per 100 women aged 15–44 years	27	33	38

[a] The "other states" category includes California, Illinois, and Texas when 1980 data are used, and the other 47 states when 1970 figures are used.

Source: U.S. Bureau of the Census, *Census of Population: 1980,* Final Report PC80-1-B, "General Population Characteristics," for the states of California, Florida, Illinois, New Jersey, New York, and Texas (Washington, D.C.: U.S. Government Printing Office, 1982), Tables 16 and 23; and A.J. Jaffe, Ruth M. Cullen, and Thomas D. Boswell, *The Changing Demography of Spanish Americans* (New York: Academic Press, 1980), p. 269.

Table 6.5 Occupation and Income of Cuban-Americans, 1970

	Men			*Women*		
	Florida	New Jersey and New York	All other states	Florida	New Jersey and New York	All other states
Professional, technical, and kindred workers	10.0	11.5	20.2	5.9	8.8	13.9
Managers and administrators, excluding farm	8.2	7.3	6.2	1.5	1.1	1.2
Sales workers	7.1	4.4	4.1	6.4	3.7	3.8
Clerical and kindred workers	10.3	11.5	10.5	25.0	26.5	28.2
Craftsmen, foremen and kindred workers	20.8	15.1	16.5	2.4	2.8	2.8
Operatives, excluding transport workers	21.4	27.9	24.9	43.7	45.8	37.0
Laborers, excluding farm	7.7	5.3	4.3	0.9	0.6	1.2
All service workers	13.7	16.9	12.8	13.8	10.6	11.8
Farmers and farm managers	0.3	0.0	0.2	0.0	0.0	0.0
Farm laborers	0.6	0.1	0.3	0.5	0.1	0.2
Mean personal income for persons 16 years and older for 1969	$5,420	$6,440	$6,970	$2,680	$3,360	$3,460

Source: A.J. Jaffe, Ruth M. Cullen, and Thomas D. Boswell, *The Changing Demography of Spanish Americans* (New York: Academic Press, 1980), pp. 274, 276.

shown separately because they are usually employed in different occupations and are paid different wages. It is clear that when the occupations of either males or females are considered, the Florida and New Jersey–New York Cubans are quite similar, while the Cubans living in the other states have achieved higher status. As a way of summarizing these occupational characteristics Jaffe, et al. have calculated a set of socioeconomic status (SES) scores for the three areas.[26] For males they found that Cuban men living in Florida and in New Jersey–New York had an identical SES score of 56, whereas men in the other states had a score of 60. The SES score for women living in Florida was 55, while for New Jersey–New York women it was 56, and for women in the other states it was 59.

Income data indicate about the same results as the occupational data, except that there is a clearer distinction between the Florida and New Jersey–New York Cuban-Americans, with the latter having the higher incomes. Again, the Cubans living in the other states enjoy the highest incomes, while the Florida Cubans have the lowest.

Summary and Conclusions

When Cuban-Americans are compared to all Spanish-Americans and the American population not of Spanish descent, it is clear that on the average the Cubans occupy an intermediate position in terms of their socioeconomic status. They have higher paying jobs, higher incomes, and lower fertility rates than the total Spanish origin population, but they are not quite as well off as non-Spanish origin persons. The Cubans are, however, more similar to the latter than they are to the former. Demographically, they are rapidly approaching the characteristics of the Anglo majority, to the extent that in the near future they will probably become indistinguishable from the white, non-Spanish American population. To what extent they will retain their separate cultural identity is another matter, but in terms of their population characteristics they are quickly converging toward American norms.

On the other hand, the Cubans also occupy an intermediate position within the Hispanic-American population. They enjoy higher socioeconomic status than either the mainland Puerto Ricans or the Mexican-Americans, but are not quite as well off as persons who either immigrated or descended from other Hispanic countries. Still, the demographic characteristics of Cuban-Americans are more similar to those of the "other Spanish" than they are to the Puerto Ricans or the Mexican-Americans, who are much more disadvantaged.

Whether measured by educational achievement, occupational structure, or income levels, the Cubans who live in the Florida are characterized by the lowest socioeconomic status when compared to those living in New Jersey–New York and the other states. Those residing in the other states have achieved the highest status. The Cubans who live in New Jersey–New York occupy an intermediate position, but are more similar to those who live in Florida.

There are at least four factors that are related to the comparatively low status of Cubans living in Florida. First, the Cuban Refugee Program most strongly encouraged those Cubans with the highest educational and skill levels to settle outside of Florida, as an attempt to lessen the burden of receiving the large mass of immigrants who suddenly arrived in southern Florida during the 1960s. It was felt that these people would possess characteristics that would make it easier for them to adjust to living conditions among non-Hispanics. Second, the return flow to Florida of Cubans who originally settled in other states probably was selective of persons who were less economically motivated than those who remained outside of Florida. Third, the second-generation Cuban-Americans have exhibited the strongest tendency to leave Florida and New Jersey–New York. In 1970, 30 percent of the American born Cubans who were living in the other states were born outside their present state of residence. For Florida and New Jersey–New York the comparable figures were 17 and 12 percent, respectively.[26] The significance of this fact is that the second generation generally enjoys more upward economic mobility than their immigrant parents because they have been able to benefit from an American education and are more fluent in English. A fourth factor that is associated with the lower status of Florida's Cubans is related to the concept that geographic dispersion facilitates acculturation and assimilation.[27] When an ethnic group is concentrated in a small area, as Cubans are in the metropolitan areas of Miami and New York, it is easier for them to retain their traditional ways, thus slowing their economic development and rate of adoption of the dominant culture. It is possible that the increasing concentration of Cubans in the state of Florida that was witnessed during the decade of the 1970s will slow the rate of assimilation of these Cubans into American society, especially if it continues. Still, the trend toward demographic convergence has established its own momentum that appears to be irreversible in the long run.

Notes

1. Several sections in this chapter draw heavily from the following source: Thomas D. Boswell, "Cuban-Americans," in Jesse O. McKee, ed., *Ethnicity in Contemporary America* (Dubuque, Iowa: Kendall-Hunt Publishing Co., forthcoming in 1984).

2. Thomas D. Boswell, Guarione M. Diaz, and Lisandro Perez, "The Socioeconomic Context of the Cuban American Population," *The Journal of Cultural Geography* 3:29–41, Fall 1982.

3. Sergio Diaz-Briquets and Lisandro Perez, *Cuba: The Demography of Revolution* (Washington, D.C.: Population Reference Bureau, Vol. 36, No. 1, April 1981), pp. 30–31.

4. U.S. Bureau of the Census, *Current Population Reports*, Series P–20, No. 361, "Persons of Spanish Origin in the United States: March 1980 (Advanced Report)," May 1981 (Washington, D.C.: U.S. Government Printing Office, 1981), p. 5.

5. Diaz-Briquets and Perez, op. cit., pp. 31–32.

6. The most recent published U.S. Census Bureau figures for Cuban-Americans by sex are for March 1980. At that time (before the Mariel boatlift) it was estimated that there were 414,000 males and 417,000 females in this population. If there were 125,000 Cubans in the Mariel exodus, and if (as reported earlier) 70 percent were male and 30 percent were female, the appropriate number of males (87,500) and females (37,500) can be added to the Census Bureau's 1980 figures to obtain a figure of 52.5 percent for males and 47.5 percent for females.

7. U.S. Bureau of the Census, *Census of Population: 1970*, Subject Reports, Final Report PC(2)-1C, "Persons of Spanish Origin " (Washington, D.C.: U.S. Government Printing Office, 1973), p. X.

8. Benigno E. Aguirre, "Differential Migration of Cuban Social Races," *Latin American Research Review* 11:104, 1976.

9. Ibid., pp. 103–124.

10. Metropolitan Dade County Planning Department, "1980 U.S. Census for Dade County, Florida, Persons by Sex, Race, and Hispanic Origin " (Miami: Metropolitan Dade County Planning Department, printed report, January 28, 1982), p. 3.

11. Boswell, Diaz, and Perez, op. cit., pp. 35–37.

12. Aguirre, op. cit., p. 115.

13. A. J. Jaffe, Ruth M. Cullen, and Thomas D. Boswell, *The Changing Demography of Spanish Americans* (New York: Academic Press, 1980), pp. 51–62.

14. Guy Gugliotta, "Who Are They? Boatloads Salted With Criminals," *The Cuban Exodus, The Miami Herald*, Special Reprint, 1980, p. 12.

15. Alejandro Pórtes, Juan M. Clark, and Manuel M. Lopez, "Six Years Later, a Profile of the Process of Incorporation of Cuban Exiles in the United States," *Cuban Studies* 12:15–57, July 1981.

16. Eleanor Meyer Rogg and Rosemary Santana Cooney, *Adoptation and Adjustment of Cubans: West New York, New Jersey* (New York: Monograph No. 5, Hispanic Research Center, Fordham University, 1980), pp. 46, 70–72.

17. U.S. Bureau of the Census, *Current Population Reports*, Series P-20, No. 354, "Persons of Spanish Origin in the United States: March 1979," (Washington, D.C.: U.S. Government Printing Office, 1980), p. 5.

18. Jaffe, Cullen, and Boswell, op. cit., pp. 279–308.

19. William Petersen, *Population* (New York: Macmillian, 1975), pp. 528–530.

20. Diaz-Briquets and Perez, op. cit., pp. 12–24; in 1981 Cuba's Crude Birthrate was 15 births per 1000 persons, which was tied with that of Canada as being the lowest in the Western Hemisphere. *1981 World Population Data Sheet* (Washington, D.C.: Population Reference Bureau, April 1981).

21. Jaffe, Cullen, and Boswell, op. cit., pp. 40–51, 252–254.

22. Ibid., pp. 40–41.

23. U.S. Bureau of the Census, *Census of Population: 1980*, Final Report PC80-1-B, "General Population Characteristics," for the states of California, Florida, Illinois, New Jersey, New York, and Texas (Washington, D.C.: U.S. Government Printing Office, 1982), Tables 16 and 23.

24. U.S. Bureau of the Census, *Census of Population: 1970*, "Persons of Spanish Origin," op. cit.

25. Jaffe, Cullen, and Boswell, op. cit., p. 253.

26. Ibid., p. 269.

27. Ibid., p. 277.

7
Language and Religion

Among the set of cultural traits and traditions that Cuban immigrants brought with them to the United States, language and religion clearly rank as two of the most important. During a period of personal crisis and confusion for many Cuban-Americans, both have offered a measure of comfort and security, while reinforcing a shared feeling of belonging. The network of interactions and associations among Cuban-Americans that emerged as the result of language and religion have served to strengthen their social system. In this fashion, both have helped foster and perpetuate a sense of ethnic identity that transcends ties of kinship and community boundaries. Yet, when language and religious preferences differ from those of the host society, they accentuate not only an internal sense of distinctiveness, but also an external perception of that distinctiveness; they increase their visibility, which more readily identifies them as a minority. Certainly for language, and to a lesser extent religion, this has been the case for Cuban-Americans. The degree to which these language and religious patterns are maintained is often an important indicator of acculturation and assimilation.

Language

More than just a means of communication, in many respects language is the embodiment of a culture, a vehicle for the transmission of shared attitudes and perceptions. In both a symbolic and a functional way, language serves as a cohesive force that tends to encourage cooperation and interaction, which greatly helps maintain group relations, as well as nurturing a feeling of cultural compatibility. For ethnic groups in the United States, it may also become a source of pride which further enhances their sense of identity, and perhaps even exclusiveness. Yet, these positive attributes aside, if loyalty to the mother tongue persists to the point of retarding the rate at which English is learned, serious social and economic problems may arise. An immigrant's network of friends, lifestyle alternatives, and daily activity patterns may be restricted. Most importantly, occupational and employment opportunities are often severely limited, making upward socioeconomic mobility more difficult. Though notable exceptions exist, generally by the third generation many of the adjustment problems faced by earlier generations are negated as English emerges as the principal language through the unrelenting process of acculturation.

LANGUAGE USE AND PREFERENCE

Virtually all first-generation Cubans living in the United States speak Spanish as their mother tongue. And, like most other immigrant groups who have come to America, it is common for first-generation Cuban-Americans to teach their native language to their children. This is particularly true when both parents are of Cuban origin, or when one parent is from Cuba and their spouse is an immigrant from another Spanish speaking country. A number of scholarly studies, however, have concluded that language use and preference patterns tend to vary by activity, and in some cases by education attainment.

Overwhelmingly, Spanish remains the language spoken most frequently in Cuban-American homes. In fact, Spanish is used at home more often than in any other setting, or during any other activity. The findings of various investigations into language use patterns among Cuban-Americans and other Hispanic groups support this conclusion, including a study conducted in early 1980 (before the mass immigration from Mariel) by the Cuban National Planning Council (CNPC), which surveyed a sample population of over 3500 households in Miami and Union City, New Jersey.[1] The survey revealed that approximately 92 percent of the respondents in Miami and 85 percent in Union City spoke "only Spanish" at home.[2] This high percentage is related to the fact that a vast majority were first- and second-generation immigrants. That Spanish is spoken more frequently at home than in other settings supports the belief that home is the most intimate of all social environments, a place where one's sense of kinship and personal security are greatest. It is only natural, then, that conversation at home would be in the native language.

There is evidence, however, that the frequency with which Spanish is spoken at home varies by level of education, but only when the schooling is received in the United States. In the survey by the CNPC, 94 percent of the respondents in Miami who had completed the eighth grade in this country spoke only Spanish at home, compared to 81 percent who had completed sixteen grades in American institutions. Among those educated in Cuba, however, the number of grades completed was a negligible factor, with approximately 94 percent of the respondents from all grades using "Spanish only" at home. Unlike other Hispanic groups, there seems to be little difference in Spanish preference patterns at home based on income levels. This may be only a transitional phenomenon.

Away from the home environment, the exclusive use of Spanish among Cuban-Americans declines significantly, but still considerably less than for other Hispanic groups. At work, for example, in the study cited above it was found that approximately 34 percent in Miami and 39 percent in Union City spoke Spanish exclusively, whereas 23 percent and 17 percent in the two study areas spoke "mostly Spanish."[3] The use of English, therefore, still remained comparatively low, with only 17 percent in Miami and 23 percent in Union City speaking "mostly" or "only English" at work. These data seem to suggest that proficiency in English for a majority of Cuban-Americans, at least in the two metropolitan areas of Miami and Union City, is not requisite for employment. And yet its consequences for the long run are not encouraging.[4]

In a recent study conducted by Ross Stolzenberg for the Rand Corporation, it was concluded that the difference in salary between Cubans who are fluent in English and those who can barely speak the language is insignificant.[5] This is in sharp contrast to other Hispanic groups living in states other than Florida. In California, for example, Mexican-Americans who speak English fluently earn approximately 30 percent more than those who are not competent in the language. In a similar study published in 1982 by the National Commision for Employment Policy (NCEP), it was concluded that only 18 percent of Cuban-born Americans consider English to be their dominant language, compared to nearly one-third for Mexican-Americans and Puerto Ricans born on the island.[6] Yet, in spite of these figures, Cuban-American men have the highest medium income of all Hispanic groups. (It is still lower, however, than incomes for white males in the United States.) This is largely a consequence of the economic enclave that Cubans have created in south Florida, which is directly related to the extraordinary nature of the Cuban immigration to this country.

The earliest waves of immigrants who fled Cuba in the wake of the Castro revolution were primarily from the professional and managerial classes. They subsequently formed the core of a Cuban-American economic base that expanded with the growth in population, which in turn, provided employment opportunities for the greater Cuban-American community. In this specialized niche, the dominant language of business was Spanish, not English. But while this situation has provided many Cuban-Americans with an opportunity to gain employment without learning English, it nonetheless has retarded the rate with which they might have otherwise learned the language because of economic necessity. On the positive side, according to the NCEP study, approximately two-thirds of all second-generation Cuban-Americans speak English as their dominant language. This suggests that in the future the Cuban-American populations should have greater flexibility in terms of its employment opportunities and earning capacity.

The changing language-use patterns among second-generation and schoolage first-generation Cuban-Americans is further documented by results from the CNPC survey. The survey revealed that English is clearly the dominant language used in school by Cuban-American students, with over 75 percent of the effected respondents in Miami and 60 percent in Union City using "mostly" or "only English" while in school; English is used more frequently in the school environment than in any other setting.[7] Certainly English will be used increasingly in other settings as this population becomes competent with the language and moves out into the labor force.

Perhaps one of the best indicators of language preference among Cuban-Americans is the frequency with which they choose Spanish-language television, radio, or newspapers and magazines. Among the three media categories, a number of scholarly studies have concluded that Spanish is the preferred language in all but television. In a seven-year study of a sample population of 590 Cuban male émigrés who arrived in Miami in 1972 and 1973, Portes, Clark, and Lopez found that in 1979 approximately 70 percent of those responding to their follow-up interview listened exclusively to Spanish-language radio stations and read Spanish newspapers, compared to only 26 percent who watched Spanish-language television programs.[8] In the CNPC survey, over 60 percent of the respondents in both Miami and Union City listened only or mostly to Spanish radio stations and read Spanish newspapers, while approximately 35 percent in Miami and 45 percent in Union City watched television programs exclusively or mostly in Spanish.[9]

These results are supported by the findings of Rogg and Cooney, who compared television and reading language usage in the years 1968 and 1979 in their study of Cubans living in West New York. In respect to television viewing habits, they found that in 1968 nearly 67 percent watched Spanish-language television programs mostly or all the time, compared to only 17 percent who watched English language programs as often.[10] By 1979, however, those percentages had changed dramatically. Spanish television programs were watched exclusively or most of the time by only 26 percent, whereas approximately 50 percent now watched English language programs mostly or all the time. The percentage who watched both Spanish and English programming also increased from 11 percent to 23 percent in 1979. Language patterns based on reading materials, however, changed very little between the two years. In 1968, 64 percent relied on Spanish language materials exclusively or most of the time, and by 1979 this had declined only to 59 percent. The percentage who read English language materials mostly or all the time remained constant at about 18 percent. The most statistically significant change was an increase from 9 to 21 percent who read both Spanish and English materials. The authors attribute the faster rates of change for television viewing to the belief that "for many people it is easier to understand the spoken rather than the written word.[11] This contention is supported by their finding that in 1979 about 64 percent of the Cubans they surveyed in West New York felt that their command of English was "average or better" when they try to understand the spoken word, whereas only 50 percent felt they were as proficient when attempting to read English. Other explanations have been offered. The Cuban National Planning Council survey, for example, concluded that "the lower preference for Spanish television programs reflects the more restricted variety of television programming in Spanish."[12]

Certainly a contributing factor in explaining language media preferences among Cuban-Americans in the metropolitan areas of Miami and Union City–West New York is the number and variety of radio stations, newspapers, and magazines available in Spanish. In Miami, for instance, there are currently eight AM and FM radio stations broadcasting exclusively in Spanish—more than any other city in the country.[13] These stations offer the gamut in radio entertainment, from music to news and sports to talk shows and commentary (usually of a political nature dealing with Cuba). Some of the stations have nicknames, like WQBA, "*La Cubanisima*" ("the most Cuban"). The major local Spanish language newspaper is *El Herald*, a version of *The Miami Herald*, which has a daily circulation in excess of 60,000. Another daily with a large circulation is *Diario Las Americas*.[14] In addition, there are over 30 Spanish weeklies published in Miami—known locally in the Latin community as *los periodiquitos*, "little papers," because of their tabloid size and limited circulation—which together account for over 250,000 copies published each week.[15] They are usually distributed free of charge in Cuban markets (*bodegas*), drug stores, barber shops, and in *cafeterias*. Some of the titles include *Patria* (Country), *La Verdad* (The Truth), *La Nación*, and *El Impartial* (Impartial). Though often biased, they nonetheless are read. The many newstands in Little Havana and downtown Miami also stock a large complement of daily newspapers from all over Latin America. There are as well Spanish editions of a number of popular magazines, such as *Cosmopolitan* and *Playboy*, and local Spanish-language magazines like *Miami Mensual* and *Vandidades Continental*. By comparison, there is only one Spanish-language television station in Miami available to all viewers (WLTV, Channel 23), plus one pay subscription cable channel offering Spanish-language movies (GALA-TV).

Although competency in the English language remains comparatively low among the Cuban-American community as a whole, evidence suggests that levels of information about American society may in fact be relatively high. In the study by Portes, Clark, and Lopez, for example, their 1979 questionnaire of Cuban émigrés included an objective information index consisting of ten items aimed at measuring recognition of United States political figures (vice-president, governor of the state), institutions (AFL-CIO), processes (inflation), and practical matters (years to citizenship, interest rates, and taxes). The results showed that nearly 50 percent of the respondents demonstrated "moderate" or "extensive" knowledge of American society, as determined by correctly answering six or more of the ten questions. The authors attribute these levels of information to relatively high mass media exposure, though mainly "'filtered' through the local Spanish-language media."[16]

LANGUAGE PROBLEMS

The inability to communicate fully in the language of the host culture has, of course, presented considerable problems for many, if not most, Cuban-Americans. When asked what the most important problems are that they face with living in the United States, first-generation Cubans most frequently cite the language barrier. Their lack of facility with English hinders their employment opportunities and affects their abilities to obtaining government services. Since first-generation immigrants still comprise a majority of Cuban-Americans, the language problem is magnified. A survey of Hispanics living in Dade County in 1978 determined that 43.2 percent judged their English speaking ability as being poor or nonexistent.[17] In the study by Portes, Clark, and Lopez, it was found that the need to learn English was a major and persistent problem facing their respondents in adjusting to life in the United States. At the time of the first interview in 1972, the three principal problems stated were transportation (18.3 percent), economic difficulties and unemployment (16.3 percent), and learning English (16.1 percent).[18] Six years later, in 1979, language was considered to be the major problem (27.1 percent), followed by economic difficulties (11.1 percent), and health (9.5 percent), while transportation was a problem for less than 1 percent of the respondents.

Where Cuban-Americans are heavily concentrated, as in metropolitan Miami and Union City, speaking Spanish can become an emotional issue in the community. According to a recent survey conducted by *The Miami Herald*, it was found that language was clearly the main obstacle to harmony between Anglos and Cubans living in Dade County.[19] The Anglos felt that it was becoming necessary to be bilingual, in Spanish and English, to be in a position to compete for local jobs, especially for employment in the service sector, which is the mainstay of the local economy. They were afraid that second-generation Cubans were in a more favorable position because of their knowledge of both languages. It was widely believed that Spanish was being forced upon the Anglos by the large number of first-generation Cubans who, they felt, where not making a serious effort to learn English. The survey found that 79 percent of the non-Latins questioned agreed that students in Dade County schools should not be required to become proficient in Spanish.[20] On the other hand, 70 percent of the Latins felt that proficiency in Spanish should be required. The opinions of blacks, however, differed from other non-Latins, with 43 percent agreeing that students in the public schools should be required to become proficient in Spanish.[21]

Other language issues addressed in the survey revealed similar differences in attitudes between Latins and non-Latins. On the question of whether every traffic sign in the county should display its message in both Spanish and English, 81 percent of the Latins agreed, compared to only 39 percent of the non-Latins. Opinions were also widely divided on the question of whether every store in the county should have Spanish and English speaking employees to help customers, with 92 percent of the Latins and only 51 percent of the non-Latins agreeing. On this issue as well, blacks were more positively inclined than whites, with 77 percent agreeing with the question. Nearly all Latins (96 percent) and a clear majority of non-Latins (68 percent) agreed that every government agency should have both Spanish- and English-speaking people to serve the public.

These sharp differences in attitudes toward the use of Spanish have, on occasion, directly affected official government policy in Miami, which could have negative economic ramifications for the area. In 1973, the Dade County Commissioners, in recognition of the large and growing proportion of Spanish-speaking Latins in the county, passed an ordinance that officially declared the county to be bilingual. Yet only seven years later, in November 1980 (immediately after the Mariel exodus), the electorate of Dade County, following an emotional and divisive election campaign, repealed the ordinance in a referendum by a voting ratio of three to two. The new ordinance stipulates that public funds are not to be used to teach languages other than English or "promote a culture other than the culture of the United States." Many Miami businessmen and government officials fear that this action may have a damaging effect on south Florida's lucrative trade with Latin America, as well as reducing the volume of tourism from that region. Moreover, in 1983 the ordinance forced the Dade County Council of Arts to deny public funding to support the programs of several Hispanic cultural organizations.[22]

"SPANGLISH"

Although nearly all second-generation Cuban-Americans speak Spanish, their command of the language is often very elementary, more functional than complete. This is also true for many first-generation immigrants who arrived in this country at an early age and received their formal education in English-speaking schools. Mixed marriages that involve an immigrant spouse and a native Anglo seldom produce children who are truly fluent in Spanish. (An exception to this generalization is sometimes encountered when the mother works outside of the home and the children are raised by a Spanish-speaking relative, usually a grandmother or aunt.) Although Spanish may be the language used most often or even exclusively at home, when this group converses with friends or siblings it usually is in a mixture of both Spanish and English, called "Spanglish."

Spanglish freely borrows, jumbles, and combines words, phrases, and expressions of both languages to create a linguistic synthesis that is unique and somewhat particular to the area in which it is spoken. Among those raised speaking Spanglish, the flow of conversation is just as fluid and natural as in any other language or dialect. For most Cuban-American youths, Spanglish is an accepted aspect of their lives, one of the many ways in which they have shaped a pattern of existence that reflects both their Cuban heritage and their American environment.[23] At the same time, speaking Spanglish helps foster an internal sense of subcultural identity and distinctiveness, while reinforcing an external perception of that distinctiveness. The ease with which Spanglish speakers move from one language to another, usually in the same sentence, creates some interesting results. One might hear, for example, a Cuban-American teenager say to another, "*tenga un* nice day," or "*Vamos de* shopping." In other cases, even expressions spoken just in Spanish have American meanings, such as in a telephone conversation in which one says to another, "*Te llamo para atrás*," meaning "I will call you back," but using "back" in the sense of "behind." Spanglish is not confined, however, exclusively to Cuban-American youths; its usage has begun to slip into the everyday Spanish spoken and read by older, first-generation Cubans as well. A sign on a store window in Little Havana might announce, for instance, a "*Gran* Sale." In part, this change is related to the creation of new English-sounding verbs as substitutes for traditional Spanish verbs, such as *taipear* (to type), rather than the longer *mecanografiar* or *escribir a máquina* (see Table 7.1). Of course, some new verbs, like *xeroxear*, have come into use because of technological inventions. Frequently, English words are used for nouns of a technical nature, such as *el* muffler, or when an electrician might tell a customer, "*Tu necesitas un* three-way switch."

Table 7.1 Anglicisms in Spanish Spoken by Cubans in the United States

bacon	frigidaire	ring
bar	futbol	rosbif
bar (*mueble*)	handicap	round
bakdet (ball)	high fidelity	sandwich
biste	hit	shwal
bell boy	home	shock
blues	homerun	show
block	inning	smoking
boy (*corte a lo*)	jet	slide
bridge	left field	sprey
bridge	marketing	standard
cake	mitin	strapless
catcher	monorail	subway
cawboys (*películas de*)	night club	sueter
center field	okey	test
clergyman	out	ticket
coctel	ponche	vanity
ferry	retirado	yipi
file	right field	zipper

Source: Roberto G. Fernandez, "El Cuento Cubano Del Exilio: Un Enforque" (Ph.D. dissertation, The Florida State University, 1977), pp.143–144.

A professor of foreign languages at a community college in Miami has concluded that Cuban children in the local area have a vocabulary in Spanish of only about 500 words; just enough to function in the language around the home and in other informal settings.[24] The relatively limited and poor quality of Spanish they learn may serve as a source of embarrassment for themselves and for their parents. Another problem encountered by some Cuban-American youths who grew up speaking Spanglish in Miami and then moved to another city is that they have found themselves unable to converse comfortably, or perhaps even at all, with Spanish speakers from other places. To help remedy this situation, there are now Spanish courses being offered at colleges in Miami for native speakers.

LINGUISTIC ASSIMILATION?

Since by far the majority of Cuban-Americans are still members of the first and second generation, it is somewhat speculative to predict the language abilities of the third generation and beyond. In this regard, scholarly evidence has shown that Spanish is the most persistent of all foreign languages in the United States, and the one, according to Fishman and Hofman, "with the greatest prospects of survival."[25] In the southwestern United States, for example, Spanish has survived for over 200 years, though a large and continuing immigration from Mexico has certainly been a critical factor in its persistence.[26] Research on language loyalty among Cuban-Americans, however, is limited and hence opinions vary widely. Enrique Rosa, a professor of foreign languages at Miami-Dade Community College, has been quoted as saying that, "In twenty-five years Spanish will be dead in Miami as a first language."[27] Sister Frances Aid, a professor at Florida International University in Miami, takes the opposite view. She has stated that in Miami "there is a middle-class [Cuban] community with an established economy and social structure. That is one reason the language will survive. Another is trade and Latin American commerce."[28]

Whether the undisputed changes occuring in the Spanish spoken in the Cuban-American community will ultimately lead to linguistic assimilation will only be determined in time. Regardless, there are still many young first- and second-generation Spanish-speaking persons of Cuban descent residing in Miami, Union City, and New York City who have many years to live. And even if the Cuban-American population was to become linguistically assimilated, it would take at least four or five more decades. This process, of course, would be delayed even longer by any future large-scale immigration waves from Cuba.

Religion

Religion is one of the elements of culture that immigrant groups in the United States are *not* expected to change. Whereas tremendous pressures to conform linguistically have been and continue to be placed on non-English speaking immigrants, freedom of religious expression is one of the basic rights that Americans cherish most. Thus religion often persists among immigrant groups while other cultural traits and traditions may decline in importance or vanish completely. For many first- and second-generation immigrants, religion has offered them both spiritual support and a sense of belonging. At a community level, the church has historically been an important ethnic institution, a focal point of activity and organization that is often as social and practical in purpose as it is theological.

Religion is an important aspect of the Cuban-American experience. Though Roman Catholicism is clearly the dominant religion, a sizable number of Cuban-Americans belong to various Protestant denominations and sects, plus a lesser number of Jews, as well as a significant number who are followers of *Santería*, an Afro-Cuban cult religion.

ROMAN CATHOLICISM

Most Cuban-Americans are at least nominally Roman Catholics. Like immigrants from other Latin American countries, their identification with and practice of the Catholic faith, as well as their general perception of themselves as being religious, tends to be more personal or communal than institutional. This is not to suggest that organized religion is not important, but rather that their affiliation with the Catholic church, their participation in its associations, and their identification with its formal structure are often different than those of other Catholics in the United States, especially non-Hispanics. This is largely a consequence of the role played by the Catholic church in Spanish colonial policy in Latin America and the Caribbean. It is also related to the persistent influences of Amerindian and particularly African religious beliefs and rites on the practice of Catholicism in that region. The personalistic character of religious practice that evolved in Cuba, as elsewhere in Latin America, is most evident in the devotion and attention directed toward the saints, and to a lesser extent the Virgin Mary and representations of Jesus. An individual's relationship with the saints is seen as personal, even intimate; they are perceived as close friends to confide in and offer comfort, yet still worshipped for their help and protection. This personal relationship takes place, however, as Joseph Fitzpatrick has stated, "quite outside the organized structure of the Church . . . if the organized Church should be shut down, the relationship would go on as usual."[29] Adherence to the Catholic church is thus often tenuous, which partially explains why church attendance was relatively low in pre-Castro Cuba. Though estimates vary, it is generally believed that as little as 10 percent of the population attended mass on a regular basis.[30]

The nature of religious practice and attendance patterns aside, the arrival since 1959 of hundreds of thousands of Cuban émigrés has had a tremendous impact on the membership of Catholic churches in the areas of concentrated settlement, especially the Catholic Archdiocese of Miami. And, unquestionably, for many first-generation Cuban-Americans, the

Catholic church has served as an important spiritual foundation, offering emotional security and a sense of identity during a period of considerable trauma and confusion. For still others, the church has functioned as an adaptive institution that has provided assistance and support, either directly or indirectly, through its various agencies and sponsored programs. From the standpoint of the church, the sudden and massive influx of Catholic, Spanish-speaking Cuban refugees demanded a response on its part. The immediacy of this concern became apparent in Miami within three years of the arrival of the initial waves of immigrants from Cuba following the Castro revolution, when in 1962 the number of baptized Catholics in the metropolitan area suddenly doubled to over 300,000.[31]

Practically, as well as philosophically, the Catholic church in the United States has encountered this situation many times before. During the nineteenth and early twentieth centuries, the church tended to favor the establishment of national or language parishes to meet the massive immigration from predominantly Catholic countries, especially from southern and eastern Europe. Although national parishes were successful in fulfilling the religious needs of first- and second-generation immigrants, by the third-generation problems arose.[32] In general membership declined as the process of acculturation took effect, and the population began moving away from the older, established core of the ethnic community, leaving church buildings often under-used. Yet, change was resisted because of the symbolic value of the buildings to the ethnic group. Since World War II, the establishment of national parishes has been avoided. Integrated parishes have been encouraged in some locations. This is where attempts are made to integrate an immigrant group into an existing parish. If its language is different from that of the parish population, then, in most cases, special masses and services are held by clergy who are fluent in the language. Recently, existing parishes have been asked to maintain flexibility; in other words, to adapt to the particular situation they may face. In the Miami Archdiocese a pragmatic approach has been followed. Though parishes are technically territorial, in fact many are overwhelmingly Hispanic, especially Cuban, and services are usually conducted in Spanish.

The degree of success these parishes enjoy is often predicated on the availability of Hispanic clergy. After 1964, following the introduction of the vernacular in the liturgy, the need for Spanish-speaking priests became even more critical. The Catholic church in Miami was fortunate in this respect, since many of the priests who were expelled from Cuba in 1961 joined the clergy of the Archdiocese, including Agustín Román, now an auxiliary bishop. At the present time, out of 610 priests in the greater Miami area, 118 are Hispanic, composing nearly one-third of the pastors.[33] To help increase the number of Spanish-speaking clergy, the church has established a bilingual, bicultural seminary in Miami. Although estimates of the total Catholic population in the metropolitan area ranges from 550,000 to 950,000, it is believed that Hispanics account for over 60 percent.

Since the early 1960s, the Catholic church in Miami has taken an activist, and at times controversial, role regarding refugee policy and settlement. In the Archdiocese, there are a number of agencies and organizations geared specifically toward assisting refugees, including the Office of Refugee Resettlement, Office of Immigration Services, Migration and Refugee Services, and the *Centro Hispano Católico*. In addition, the growth of lay apostolic movements has been encouraged as another means of reaching out to the immigrant population, particularly new arrivals. In the Cuban community, these movements range from the *Agrupación Católica Universitaria* to the *Cursillo* Movement to the *Coral Cubana*, a youth choir dedicated to church music.

The church also has been active in providing educational opportunities and alternatives to meet the needs and wishes of the immigrant community. Many Cuban-American parents prefer that their children attend Catholic school. This was particularly true of the earliest, more affluent immigration waves during the 1960s. In part this is related to the fact that in Cuba the public school system was geared primarily toward education of the lower socioeconomic classes. It also reflects a generally negative impression that many Cuban-Americans have of the public school system in the United States, both in terms of the quality of instruction and the school environment itself.[34] The schools are often perceived as undisciplined and plagued by crime, drug abuse, and immorality. In response to this situation, and as existing Catholic schools quickly filled to capacity, several Catholic religious orders established new parochial schools. This pattern continues to the present day, and demand for additional schools shows no signs of abating. During the 1982/83 school year, Hispanics (mostly Cubans) accounted for over 65 percent of the more than 19,000 students enrolled in the 30 primary and 8 secondary Catholic schools in Dade County. In spite of the fact that tuition ranges as high as $1450 per year in the secondary schools, some schools reportedly have waiting lists of over 600 names. Monsignor Bryan O. Walsh of the Miami Archdiocese has stated that, "We could double the enrollment today if we could build the schools fast enough . . . the inability to meet the demand for additional schools is one of the major problems we face."[35]

There is some evidence that the domination of Roman Catholicism has been declining among Cuban-Americans. Between 1968 and 1979 the percentage of Cubans in West New York, for example, who expressed a preference for the Catholic faith decreased from 91.5 percent to 78.3 percent; those with no particular religious preference increased from 1.2 percent to 11.3 percent.[36] In addition, attendance rates dropped. The proportion who attended church at least once a month went from 79 percent to 47.1 percent. Those who never attended increased from 5 percent to 19.6 percent. Importantly, however, in spite of these declining attendance rates, almost three-fourths of those surveyed in 1979 indicated that religion was still a very important part of their life. This is compared to only 56 percent of the total United States population. An explanation for the apparent decreasing religious participation ratios of Cuban-Americans is necessarily speculative, but three possible factors are worth mentioning. First, it is possible that they are being influenced by the lower participation levels of non-Spanish Americans. Second, the percentage of practicing Catholics has declined as the Cuban-American population has become more representative of the total population of Cuba. Although only about 10 percent of the population in pre-Castro Cuba attended mass regularly, the percentage of practicing Catholics was over-represented in the first waves of immigration after the 1959 revolution. It has been estimated that as many as 80 percent of the first 100,000 Cubans arriving in 1960–61 were practicing Catholics.[37] The percentage in each successive wave has decreased. Three, Castro's efforts to purge Cuba of religion may have reduced the religiosity of some Cuban immigrants, especially those who are recent arrivals. Among the Mariel refugees, for example, it has been estimated by church officials in Miami that only 2 percent of the nearly 125,000 are practicing Catholics.[38]

The cultural landscape of Cuban-American communities often conspicuously reflects the influence of the Catholic religion in the form of church buildings, schools, and yard shrines. Yard shrines in particular are a common landscape element in most Cuban-American neighborhoods. In the predominately Cuban sections of Miami, especially in Little Havana, there are literally thousands of shrines gracing the front yards of Cuban homes, as well as commercial areas.[39] Most of the shrines are erected in honor of the saints. By far, the three saints that are most frequently enshrined in Miami are Santa Barbara, Our Lady of Charity (patron saint of Cuba), and Saint Lazarus. This phenomenon graphically illustrates the personalized nature of the Catholic religion to many Cuban-Americans, in particular their extraordinary devotion to the saints. Although most of the shrines are built by Catholics, usually in gratitude for prayers answered or just for good luck, some are erected by followers of an Afro-Cuban cult known as *Santería* (discussed more fully later in this chapter).

There are also a number of religious celebrations that have special significance for Cuban. Christmas eve, for example, is *Noche Buena*. The celebration is highlighted by a traditional meal of roast suckling pig (*lechón asado*). January 6th is the day of *Los Tres Reyes Magos*, or Three Kings Day. Traditionally this is the day that parents give their children gifts, although Christmas day has also become an occasion for exchanging gifts. In Miami, *Los Tres Reyes Magos* is celebrated with a parade down *Calle Ocho* in the heart of Little Havana. In 1983 the parade had over 3,000 participants, including 14 school bands and more than 40 floats, and drew in excess of 200,000 spectators. The parade was organized in the early 1970s in response to Castro's cancellation of Christmas celebrations in Cuba because they interfered with the sugar harvest. Certainly one of the most important religious celebrations is held on September 8th in honor of *Nuestra Señora de la Caridad* (Our Lady of Charity), who is the patron saint of Cuba. In Miami a procession is held at the Miami Marine Stadium where the saint is brought in by boat and a mass is celebrated. Afterward followers throw flowers to the saint on the stage. The birthdays of other popular saints are also commemorated, such as Santa Barbara (on December 4th), and collectively on All Saints Day on November 1st.

PROTESTANT FAITHS

Lacking scholarly studies or other documentation on the subject, the extent of membership among Cuban-Americans in Protestant denominations is difficult to determine. It is probably safe to assume, however, that less than 10 percent of the Cuban-American population belongs to Protestant faiths. One indication is provided in the study conducted by Rogg and Cooney of Cubans living in West New York, New Jersey. In 1968 and in 1979, they found 6.9 percent and 6.1 percent of their respondents, respectively, expressed a preference for Protestant religions.[40]

Protestantism was introduced into Cuba in the end of the nineteenth century and gradually expanded until the revolution in 1959. It is estimated that about 40 Protestant denominations established missions on the island.[41] They catered to the middle and lower classes, chiefly in the urban areas. The largest denominations were Southern Baptist, Methodist, and Presbyterian. A number of Holiness and Pentecostal sects, especially Jehovah's Witnesses, were also active. In addition, Episcopalians established several churches. Most of the Protestant churches were strongly oriented toward the United States and were theologically conservative. It has been estimated that the total Protestant population in Cuba in 1959 was about 250,000.

In the United States, Cuban Protestants appear to be widely distributed among several denominations and evangelical sects. One rough indication is suggested by the number of non-Catholic "Spanish" churches in Miami listed in the 1982/83 *Church and Synagogue Directory* of the Metropolitan Fellowship of Churches. Of a total of 67 churches identified by name as being Spanish and with a pastor with a Spanish surname, there were 25 Baptist, 11 Assemblies of God, 9 Methodist, and 5 Pentecostal, with the rest scattered among 12 other denominations.[42]

It has been speculated that some Cuban-Americans who join Protestant faiths, as well as evangelical sects, are attracted by the smaller congregations and the informal and personalized nature of worship services and religious expression.

CUBAN JEWS

Another distinctive, though numerically smaller religious minority within the Cuban-American community, are Cuban Jews. Jews have lived in Cuba, especially in Havana, since the beginning of the colonial period, when they were known as *Marranos*. Yet, their total population, mostly Ashkenazim, never exceeded 15,000. There were five Jewish congregations that existed in Havana before the revolution of 1959.[43] While it is impossible to determine the exact number who have emigrated to the United States, current estimates range from 7,000 to 10,000. According to statistics compiled by the National Council of Jewish Women and the Hebrew Immigrant Aid Society (HIAS), approximately 4,500 Cuban Jews registered with the Cuban refugee program in Miami, and another 2,500 migrated to south Florida from other cities in the United States, or entered by way of a third country, including Israel.[44] Between 1961 and 1967, HIAS resettled over 3,000 Cuban Jews outside of south Florida, including 1,600 in New York City.

Overwhelmingly, the two largest concentrations are in the metropolitan areas of Miami and New York City. In south Florida, where an estimated 3,500 to 4,500 reside, Miami Beach is clearly the favored residential community, especially the North Shore area for the more affluent and the South Beach district for those with lower incomes. Although many Cuban Jews in Miami have integrated into the American Jewish community, a majority has not, preferring instead to establish their own separate organizations, including both Ashkenazim and Sephardim. The *Círculo Cubano Hebreo* in south Miami Beach, for example, has emerged as an important religious and social institution among Ashkenazim. The Cuban Sephardi Hebrew congregation is smaller, but more traditional in religious practice. Among young Cuban Jews, however, the division between Ashkenazim and Sephardim appears to be diminishing in importance as they increasingly interact at school and in other social settings.

Just as among the Cuban-American community in general, Spanish remains the dominant language spoken in the home. In interviews conducted by Liebman, it was found that Cuban Jewish parents wanted their children to speak Spanish. He notes that, "In several homes, where Yiddish had been the main language before emigration, it now was Spanish."[45] This, Liebman suggests, was not necessarily to increase participation in Cuban-American cultural life. Rather, "The most plausible explanation of their devotion to Spanish in their new home may be found in what immigrants generally considered the most agreeable aspect of life in Cuba, namely their acceptance as equals by Cubans."[46]

SANTERÍA

Certainly one of the more unique religions practiced by some Cuban-Americans is *Santería*, a syncretic Afro-Cuban cult faith that combines elements of Roman Catholicism and other European influences with ancient Yoruba tribal beliefs and practices. In the popular media, *Santería* is most commonly portrayed as a Cuban version of voodoò or witchcraft. Stories tend to stress its more sensational, if not bizarre, aspects, such as animal sacrifice and ceremonial spirit possession. Although these elements are part of the folk religious complex, *Santería* also includes theological beliefs, magical and medical practices, has a detailed system of rituals, and a recognized cadre of priests, known as *santeros*. Like other Afro-Cuban syncretic cults, *Santería* (or *Regla Lucumi*, as it is also known) evolved in colonial Cuba as a consequence of slavery. Through their exposure to the Catholic faith, the Yoruba-speaking slaves eventually came to associate their African deities (called *orishas*) with the images of Catholic saints; the *orishas* then became *santos* ("saints"). *Santería* means, literally, the worship of saints, though many other Catholic elements, African religious practices, and secular European contributions are incorporated into the religious complex.[47] Unlike most religions, one of the attractions of *Santería* for its followers is that it is present-oriented and practical. Cult members, as well as uninitiated clients (who usually profess to be Catholic), may call upon a *santero* whenever they wish to invoke, placate, or thwart the supernatural, seek assistance in curing an illness, help in finding a job, or perhaps exorcise an evil spirit.

In response to social pressures, the followers of *Santería* have traditionally sought anonymity in cult houses which operate under the independent guidance of a *santero/a*, who is free to interpret the belief system, conduct ceremonies, and perform other functions based on his (or her) own training, experience, and the needs of the clients. In Miami, as elsewhere in the United States where Cubans have settled in large numbers, cult houses display considerable heterogeneity; the degree to which either Catholic or African elements are stressed typically follows racial lines.[48]

Figure 7.1 Inside this botanica *in Miami the shelves are lined with items used for ritualistic purposes in the Santeŕia cult religion. (Photo by James R. Curtis.)*

Although it is virtually impossible to ascertain the number of active (or occasional) followers of *Santeŕia*, it is widely believed that it is becoming increasingly popular among certain segments of the Cuban community, as well as other Latin groups. The reason most frequently cited for its apparent growth is the fear that some Cuban-Americans have of losing their cultural identity through acculturation to the American way of life.[49] In this respect, *Santeŕia* is seen as being a link to the past and hence a means of coping with many of the adjustment pressures imposed by the new social, economic, and political order. Disenchantment with the Catholic faith is another reason often mentioned as contributing to the expansion of *Santeŕia*. Specifically, the Catholic church's questioning of the historical validity of certain saints who were popular in Cuba (such as Saint Lazarus), the elimination of many religious rituals practiced in Cuba, and just the size and institutionalized nature of the Catholic religion have prompted some Cuban-Americans to seek out alternative religious associations, including *Santería*. Moreover, the adaptive nature of *Santería* has likewise been suggested as another internal factor in its apparent growth. Anthropologist Mercedes Sandoval, for example, concludes that, "Its intrinsic flexibility, eclecticism and heterogeneity have been advantages in helping ensure functional, dogmatic and ritual changes which enable it to meet the different needs of its many followers."[50] For some, *Santería* may well represent a belief of last resort. In a survey of Cubans living in Miami and Union City, for example, it was found that whereas only 1.2 percent of the households reported practicing *Santería*, 7.1 percent of the respondents in Miami and 23.5 percent of the Union City respondents said they would use a *santero* if they felt they needed help.[51] Reportedly one of its more attractive aspects in this regard is its function as a mental health care system.

Beyond these suggested reasons for its expansion, one indicator of its presence is the existence in Miami of over two dozen retail outlets that cater to the *Santería* trade, called *botánicas*, which stock roots, herbs, beads, oils, scents, sprays, powders, potions, and other paraphernalia used in *Santería* rituals and ceremonies. Whether the interest in this cult is a transitional phenomenon that will subside as the process of acculturation speeds ahead, remains a question that will only be determined in time. But for now, it very definitely is an aspect of the religious experience of many Cuban-Americans.

Notes

1. Guarione M. Diaz, ed., *Evaluation and Identification of Policy Issues in the Cuban Community* (Miami: Cuban National Planning Council, 1980).
2. Ibid., p. 74.
3. Ibid., p. 48.
4. Guillermo Martinez, "The Language of Cuban Success," *The Miami Herald*, October 7, 1982, p. 29A.
5. Ross M. Stolzenburg, *Occupational Differences Between Hispanics and Non-Hispanics* (Santa Monica: The Rand Corporation, 1982).
6. National Commission for Employment Policy, *Hispanics and Jobs: Barriers to Progress*, Report No. 14, September 1982, p. 27.
7. Diaz, op. cit., p. 49.
8. Alejandro Portes, Juan M. Clark, and Manuel M. Lopez, "Six Years Later, a Profile of the Process of Incorporation of Cuban Exiles in the United States," *Cuban Studies* 11:6–7, July 1981.
9. Diaz, op. cit., pp. 49–50.
10. Eleanor Meyer Rogg and Rosemary Santana Cooney, *Adaptation and Adjustment of Cubans: West New York, New Jersey* (New York: Monograph No. 5, Hispanic Research Center, Fordham University, 1980), p. 31.
11. Ibid., p. 32.
12. Diaz, op. cit., p. 47.

13. Mimi Whitefield, "Miami's Spanish Radio Stations: Sedate They're Not," *The Miami Herald*, February 2, 1981, Business Week Section, pp. 20–21.

14. Marcia C. Garcia, "Diario's Man of the Americas," *The Miami Herald*, May 15, 1983, p. 1C.

15. Jay Ducassi, "Cuban Papers Brash, Biased, and Read," *The Miami Herald*, May 2, 1982, p. 1D.

16. Portes, Clark, and Lopez, op. cit., p. 10.

17. Aida Thomas Levitan, "Hispanics in Dade County: Their Characteristics and Needs," (Miami: Latin American Affairs, Office of the County Manager, Metropolitan Dade County, printed report, Spring 1980), pp. 25–29, 33–36.

18. Portes, Clark, and Lopez, op. cit., p. 9.

19. Sam Jacobs, "Language: Main Obstacle to Harmony," *The Miami Herald*, July 13, 1978, p. 1A.

20. Ibid., p. 14A.

21. Morris S. Thompson, "Poll: Blacks Tolerant of Latins, Resent Job Threat," *The Miami Herald*, July 5, 1978, p. 20A.

22. Laurie Horn, "Hispanics Denied Dade Arts Grants," *The Miami Herald*, May 5, 1983, p. 10B.

23. John Dorschner, "Growing Up Spanglish in Miami," *The Miami Herald*, September 11, 1977, Tropic Section, p. 6.

24. William D. Montalbano, "Spanglish Spoken Here," *The Miami Herald*, April 1, 1979, Tropic Section, p. 32.

25. Joshua A. Fishman and John E. Hofman, "Mother Tongue and Nativity in the American Population," in Joshua A. Fishman et al. eds., *Language Loyalty in the United States* (The Hague: Mounton, 1966), p. 37.

26. Leo Grebber, Joan W. Moore, and Ralph C. Guzman, *The Mexican-American People: The Nation's Second Largest Minority* (New York: The Free Press, 1970), pp. 428–432.

27. Montalbano, op. cit., p. 32.

28. Ibid., p. 33.

29. Joseph P. Fitzpatrick, *Puerto Rican Americans: The Meaning of Migration to the Mainland* (Englewood Cliffs, N.J.: Prentice-Hall, 1971), p. 116.

30. Howard I. Blutstein et al, *Area Handbook for Cuba* (Washington, D.C.: U.S. Government Printing Office, 1971), p. 188.

31. Bryan O. Walsh, "The Catholic Church and the City: The Miami Experience," *Catholic World* 225:108, May-June 1982.

32. Fitzpatrick, op. cit., pp. 123–127.

33. Compiled from Marjorie L. Donohue, *The Archdiocese of Miami: Directory 1982–1984* (Miami: The Archdiocese of Miami, 1982)

34. Maria C. Garcia, "Quest for the Best: The Private School Explosion," *The Miami Herald*, April 18, 1982, p. 1G

35. Bryan O. Walsh, personal communication, February 28, 1983.

36. Rogg and Cooney, op. cit., p. 26.

37. Walsh, "The Church and the City," p. 108.

38. Ibid.

39. James R. Curtis, "Miami's Little Havana: Yard Shrines, Cult Religion, and Landscape," *Journal of Cultural Geography*, 1:1–15, Fall-Winter 1980.

40. Rogg and Cooney, op. cit., p. 26.

41. Blutstein, op. cit., p. 189.

42. Compiled from *Church and Synagogue Directory of Greater Miami, Florida: 1982–1983* (Coral Gables: The Metropolitan Fellowship of Churches, 1982).

43. Blutstein, op. cit., p. 191.

44. Seymour B. Liebman, "Cuban Jewish Community in South Florida," in Abraham D. Lavender, ed., *A Coat of Many Colors: Jewish Subcommunities in the United States* (Westport, Conn.: Greenwood Press, 1977), p. 300.

45. Ibid., p. 303.

46. Ibid.

47. Migene Gonzalez-Whippler, *Santería: African Magic in Latin America* (New York: The Julian Press, 1973).
48. James R. Curtis, *Santería*: Persistence and Change in an Afro-Cuban Cult Religion," in Ray B. Browne, ed., *Objects of Special Devotion: Fetishes and Fetishism in Popular Culture* (Bowling Green, Ohio: Bowling Green State University's Popular Press, 1982), pp. 336–351.
49. Curtis, "Miami's Little Havana," pp. 14–15.
50. Mercedes C. Sandoval, "Santeria as a Mental Health Care System: An Historical Overview," *Social Science and Medicine* 12:137, April 1979.
51. Diaz, op. cit., pp. 123–124.

8
Cuban-American Artistic Expression

Artistic expression both contributes to culture and is a reflection of it. The artist seeks in words, sounds, and images to heighten human awareness, increase our sensitivity, and to illuminate experiences. In this sense, art is a mirror held up to society. It speculates on reality and stimulates the imagination about the nature of existence from a personal perspective. The value of art is decidedly aesthetic; it is intended to enrich the quality of our lives. But, at another level, it also is a cultural achievement that serves as a source of group pride, and is a means of enhancing group consciousness and identity. This role is particularly important for immigrant groups in the United States who value their heritage, but who must at the same time struggle to maintain their ethnicity in the face of acculturation.

Although Cuban-Americans have been extraordinarily successful in adapting to life in this country, they remain, as a group, extremely committed to preserving their own ethnic culture. In Cuba the arts were important, and they are equally as important in the Cuban-American culture today, and supported by the exile community. In fact, the revolution and the exile experience have stimulated artistic production. Similarly, the arts are evolving in the United States—new forms and expressions are emerging—as a consequence of the changes that Cuban-Americans have experienced.

Music

Music is an important aspect of Cuban-American culture and life. Like other elements in the cultural baggage that Cuban immigrants brought with them to the United States, many traditional forms of Cuban music persist in the exile community. They are heard on Spanish language radio stations, played on home stereo units, and danced to at social gatherings, ceremonies, and festivals. Among many of the older first-generation Cuban-Americans, the music of their homeland and youth may be the only music that is listened to, or appreciated. In this context, it should be stressed that traditional Cuban music endures in the Cuban-American community for reasons beyond its aesthetic qualities and the enjoyment it offers. Just as the maintenance of religion, language, cuisine, and other cultural practices help foster and perpetuate a sense of ethnic identity and group consciousness, so too does music.

Yet, largely as consequence of the Cuban-American experience, new musical forms, part-Cuban, part-American, have emerged in the United States. This fusion of traditional Cuban and other Latin musical influences with popular North American musical idioms began at least by the turn of the century. In the process, Cuban music and musicians have had a significant effect on commercial musical styles in the United States. One noted ethnomusicologist has stated that of all Latin influences on the music of this country, "the impact of Cuban music . . . has been much the greatest, most varied, and most long lasting."[1]

TRADITIONAL CUBAN MUSIC

The musical heritage that Cuban immigrants transported with them to the United States is rich and varied. It represents in essence a complex blending of both African and European, especially Iberian, musical components, including rhythmic, melodic, and harmonic techniques, as well as instrumentation.[2] The most important African-derived elements include drumming styles, plus chants and melodies, typically sung in call-and-response patterns (often using Yoruba words and phrases).[3] These features are preserved in their purest form in Afro-Cuban cult religions, such as *Santería*, in which music, particularly rendered on the sacred *batá* drums, serves as a critical organizing aspect of most rituals and ceremonies.[4] The longest lasting European contributions include guitar-backed vocal music based on country melodies from southern Spain. The brass band and dance music of nineteenth century Europe has also been very important and enduring.

Euro-Cuban and Afro-Cuban music, however, did not begin to merge until the end of the nineteenth century. Prior to that time, Euro-Cuban music was confined to the white population in rural areas and to the urban upper class. It was based primarily on Spanish melodies and forms such as the *bolero*, although the tempo of the *bolero* was reduced, the meter changed from 3/4 to 2/4, and became known as the Cuban *bolero*, of which the *habanera* was one of the more popular rhythms and dance. Afro-Cuban music was initially reserved for religious ceremonies. But by the nineteenth century, it had developed a secular function and was performed in public, especially during religious holidays such as the pre-Lenten carnival celebrations. After independence, and with the increasing movement of blacks into the urban centers, the two musical traditions began to fuse.[5]

The basic foundation of popular Cuban music in the twentieth century is the *clave* rhythmic pattern. The *clave* is an African-derived, off-beat, syncopated rhythmic structure. It typically incorporates the African-style call-and-response structure by emphasizing the first part, followed by an "answering" second part. Emilio Grenet, a Cuban musicologist, states that to play out of *clave* "produces such a notorious discrepancy between the melody and the rhythm that it becomes unbearable to ears accustomed to our music."[6] The *clave*, however, is extremely variable and may accommodate different accents and tempos played simultaneously on a number of percussion instruments. The role of percussion in creating this infectious, polyrhythmic foundation is central. Among the many percussion instruments used in Cuban music, the most important include the *bongo* (two small attached single-headed drums held between the knees), *conga* or *tumbadora* (a single-headed drum with a tapered barrel shape), *claves* (resonant wooden sticks), *cencerro* (a hand-held cowbell played with a stick), *maracas* (a tuned pair of rattles), *güiro* (a notched gourd that is scraped with a stick), and *timbales* (a fixed percussion set-up consisting of metal drums, cowbells, frequently a cymbal, and other features), which are a recent addition to the ensemble.[7] The rhythmic structure created by these and other percussion instruments is extremely important not only as framework for the music itself, but also as a foundation for dancing. At its core, Cuban music is dance music. This is vitally important to a culture in which people of all ages and social classes dance as a matter of course.

Improvisation is another common feature of popular Cuban music. The musical structure of many songs frequently includes a *montuno* section, which is based on a two-, three-, or four-chord pattern that allows for either instrumental improvisation or for the lead singer to improvise against the refrains of a two- or three-voice chorus.[8] This adds a lively, spontaneous feeling to the music which is particularly effective when performed before an audience.

There are three distinct types of traditional popular musical groups, each of which specialized in a substyle of Cuban music. A *septeto*, which is the oldest form, is a trumpet-led string ensemble that generally includes a guitar, a *tres* (a guitar-like nine-stringed instrument), a bass instrument, percussion, and voices. *Septetos* are identified with an Afro-Cuban musical form called *son*.[9] Beginning in the rural areas of Cuba among blacks, the *son* was continually modified as it moved from the countryside to the city and was exposed to the white population. In the urban areas the *son* combined African-based rhythms with the structure, melody and text (usually romantic) of Spanish-derived country music most often associated with

Cuban farmers, called *guajiros*. It became very popular in Havana during the 1920s and formed the basis for the *rumba* craze in the United States in the 1930s.

A second group is the *conjunto* ("combo"), which evolved in the 1930s from black carnival parade bands; this is similar in process to the emergence of Dixieland jazz in New Orleans.[10] Typically, *conjuntos* emphasize a brassy, upbeat, spirited sound and consist of a lead singer (called a *sonero*) and a small chorus, backed by trumpets, trombones and percussion, especially *conga* drums. When performing indoors, piano and bass are usually added.

A third group is the *charanga*, a more formal dance orchestra, which was strongly influenced by European elements. In the *charangas*, the musical lead is provided by a flute, accompanied by violins and percussion, especially the *timbales*. Unlike the *septetos* or *conjuntos*, the vocals are characteristically rendered by two voices singing in harmony. There are, of course, many variations of these three basic groups, both in terms of styles and instrumentation. Yet, while they have changed through time and have influenced each other, they remain distinct. The *conjunto* in particular is still an extremely important grouping and style, especially in the contemporary Latin *salsa* sound.

CUBAN MUSIC IN THE UNITED STATES

Since the early 1930s, a sequence of Cuban musical forms introduced to the United States—primarily by Cuban émigrés—have become commercially popular. In most cases, however, the success enjoyed was short-lived, and the sound was often diluted or "Americanized" to enhance market appeal. The progression began with the introduction of the *rumba* in the 1920s, and was followed by the *mambo* in the 1940s and early fifties, and the *chachachá* in the mid-1950s. The continuous fusion of Cuban musical elements with other Latin and North American musical idioms, including rock and jazz, gave rise in the 1960s to a sound known as Latin *bugalú*, which was followed in the 1970s by *salsa*, a New York-based form of contemporary Latin dance music.

The *rumba* was perhaps the first example of Cuban dance music most Americans of the time had heard.[11] It was seen by Americans as a lighthearted, exotic sound and a curiously romantic dance. The *rumba* craze that swept the nation in the 1930s was sparked by the success of one tune, "El Manicero" ("The Peanut Vendor") by Eliseo Grenet.[12] "El Manicero" was recorded in 1921 by celebrated Cuban bandleader Don Azpiazu and his Havana Casino Orchestra. The *rumba* was an authentic form of the Cuban *son*. But in the wake of the success following release of "The

Peanut Vendor" on the RCA Victor label, it was quickly polished and simplified for Anglo audiences, especially by the big bands of the period such as Xavier Cugat's dance band. Although the popularity of the *rumba* had greatly diminished by the end of the decade, it had nevertheless offered Americans (and Europeans) with an opportunity to hear and dance to Cuban music, as well as provided recognition and employment for Cuban musicians.

During the 1940s, the big band *mambo* sound, which would become immensely popular in the early fifties, was taking shape. Certainly a critical factor in the rise of the *mambo* was the formation of a group widely recognized as one of the most important Latin bands ever in the United States, namely Machito and His Afro-Cubans. Cuban-born Machito (Frank Grillo), who is considered "the Basie of Latin music," combined elements of American jazz with the traditional rhythms, vocal, and instrumental styles and structure of Cuban music.[13] The most characteristic feature of the sound was a *mambo* section of contrasting brass and saxophone riffs, often backing instrumental or vocal solos. As the *mambo* fad emerged, Machito, Jose Curbelo, and other noted Cuban-American musicians worked the bigger New York nightclubs, and established the city as the center of Latin music in the United States, a position it still holds. The greatest commercial success, however, was enjoyed by another Cuban-born musician, Pérez Prado, who is associated with a West Coast version of the *mambo,* which is generally considered to be be a less authentic style. Prado's simplified, brassy *mambos* were tailored for a non-Latin market. Prado's "Cerezo Rosa" ("Cherry Pink and Apple Blossom White") and "Patricia" each sold over four million worldwide.

The popularity (and commercialization) of the *mambo* was exceeded in the mid-1950s by the *chachachá* mania. Originating in Cuba in the early 1950s, the catchy *chachachá* rhythm (based on a triple fourth beat) was initially designed for the flute-and-violin *charanga* groups. Less complex than the *mambo,* the beat and melody lines of the *chachachá* were easily diluted, and the dance was relatively simple and fun to perform.

After the demise of the *chachachá*, Cuban-American music slipped out of the commercial limelight, replaced by a reaffirmation of traditional Cuban elements. The fusion with jazz, however, continued unabatedly. In the early 1960s a return to the *charanga* sound occured as part of a revival of the *tipico* (or characteristic) music of Cuba. This was related in part to the revolution and the consequent arrival of Cuban refugees seeking exile. Later in the 1960s a new fusion occurred: Cuban with American black "soul" music. This blend gave rise to a substyle called Latin *bugalú*. It was characterized by Latin rhythms and piano *montunos*, fused with rhythm and blues and jazz elements. Lyrics often moved easily between Spanish and English. One of the most popular songs of this genre, for example, was Joe Cuba's "Bang, Bang."

Since the early 1970s the term *salsa* has been widely used to describe a generally uptempo, "hot" Latin dance music. Although the literal meaning is sauce," the connotation is one of feeling. It has been said that *salsa* is to Latins as "soul" is to blacks.[14] *Salsa* is characterized by a variety of musical forms associated with a number of Latin culture groups, including Cuban-Americans. Most Latin musicians claim that *salsa* is not really new, at least musically.[15] Machito, for example, has said that "*Salsa* is a replica of what we've been doing for at least fifty years."[16] In general, however, mainstream *salsa* is most closely associated with the New York Latin community where it represents a fusion of Afro-Latin-Caribbean musical forms, especially Cuban and Puerto Rican, with elements of jazz. It is typically played by *conjunto* groups.

A regional variation of *salsa* has emerged in south Florida since the mid-1970s. Known locally and increasingly in the music industry as the "Miami Sound," it represents a fusion of traditional and contemporary Latin musical influences with American popular formats and elements.[17] It is perhaps best described as a mellow form of *salsa*, in which commercial American rock and jazz elements are emphasized, more so than in New York–based *salsa*. In fact, the music of the Miami Sound Machine, one of the more popular groups, was recently characterized in *Billboard* as a fusion of "disco, samba, salsa, pop and rock."[18]

All of these musical forms, from the most traditional to the contemporary, are heard within the Cuban-American community. This illustrates how elements of Cuban culture have not only persisted in the United States, but also have adapted and changed in response to new influences.

The Visual Arts

Cuban émigré art has flourished and evolved in the United States. In the nearly two and a half decades since the revolution, a relatively large number of Cuban painters and sculptors, including some of the country's most distinguished, have sought exile in America. They represent various generations and work in a variety of styles, from the older realms of realism and impressionism to expressionism, abstraction, and fantasy in the modern idiom. In their individual approach to the visual arts, they range along a continuum from traditionalists to innovators. This diverse and productive group is the heart of the Cuban exile arts community. In recent years, it has been joined by an active younger generation of Cuban-American artists who have drawn from both Latin and American influences and traditions to produce works that are highly individualistic and unique. The dynamic variety of Cuban artistic production in the United States thus defies easy classification. It also is a subject that, unfortunately, has received little academic or critical review, either in this country or abroad.

COMMON THEMES

In spite of the individuality and diversity characterizing Cuban art production, there remain certain underlying elements of commonality. In general, Cuban visual arts are noted for their vibrant, colorful and rhythmic qualities.[19] One of the distinguishing features of Cuban painting, for example, is the bold use of color. José Gómez-Sicre, a leading authority on Latin American art, has stated that "What Cuba seems to have given her artists, both historical and contemporary, is a richness of color and intensity of light that infuses . . . a spontaneity."[20] The tropical exuberance and exotic mixtures of color together with a certain baroqueness, often imparts as well a sensuality and a sense of drama. In addition to color, others have noted that "the modern idiom in Cuban painting is based on a thoroughgoing discipline in drawing and a sustained interest in classical composition."[21]

In respect to subject matter, certain unifying themes are also evident, particularly in the work of older Cuban artists. There is an established *criollo* group, for example, that draws inspiration from vestiges of the Spanish colonial tenure in Cuba. Colonial architecture is a particularly popular subject. It is frequently depicted in a variety of styles with people set in a lush, tropical, idealized landscape. A continuing interest in, and demand for, *criollo* paintings persist in the Cuban-American community, especially those executed in impressionist styles. This perhaps comes from the feeling of nostalgia they evoke in the eyes of some émigrés. Selected aspects of Afro-Cuban life and culture form another traditional subject, especially the colorful imagery and symbolism associated with various cult rites and practices.[22] The Afro-Cuban theme, however, has declined in importance in the United States, particularly among younger artists.

Though certainly a universal subject, there has been an extraordinary interest among modern Cuban artists in the human form as an artistic motif. Cuban-American art critic, Ricardo Pau-Llosa, convincingly argues this point. He concludes that, "Whether the emphasis is on projecting the whole of the human figure in a new way, breaking it up into organic components and constructing a new anatomy with the components, or isolating the organic fragments for their particular formal value, the human form and its wide parameters of subordinate forms is perhaps the one element on which a Cuban national style can be grounded. It is a factor that recurs intensely in the different generations of modern artists."[23] Pau-Llosa speculates that the human figure probably occupies its special place in Cuban art due to "the fact that Victor Manuel, the man who fathered Cuba's modern art movement in the twenties, concentrated most of his effort on representing the human face in a more direct, simplified manner than the ways to which his academic predecesors subscribed."[24] Within these broad thematic areas, however, there is a wide range of individual interpretation and stylistic presentation.

ESTABLISHED ARTISTS

At the creative center of the Cuban-American arts community is a group of older generation artists who brought with them into exile established reputations and a fully mature artistic expression. Many were graduates of the prestigious San Alejandro Academy of Arts in Havana, and had often studied and exhibited abroad. They were, and continue to be, instrumental in the development of the modern idiom in Cuban art. The modern movement that emerged in the 1920s was largely a reaction against the rigid academicism imposed by the San Alejandro Academy which had institutionally dominated the arts, and had followed Spanish and eighteenth-century French models.[25] This group of second- and third-generation modern artists have built on the foundation laid by the leaders of that movement, including most notably Víctor Manuel, Amelia Peláez, Fidelio Ponce, Eduardo Abela, and Carlos Enríquez. Although this established group of exile artists share a common national origin and are products of the same era, their creative efforts are more dissimilar than uniform. Their originality is illustrated in the work of four of the more prominent modern Cuban artists currently living in the United States, including José Maria Mijares, Rafael Soriano, Osvaldo Gutiérrez, and Enrique Riverón.

José Maria Mijares is one of the leading modern Cuban painters. Born in 1922 in Havana, Mijares studied at the San Alejandro Academy. In 1944 and again in 1950 he won national first prizes in Cuba for his paintings. His work has been widely exhibited, including showings in Paris, Venice, Tokyo, Sao Paulo, Caracas, San Juan and in major American cities. His unique style exemplifies the highly personal nature of the creative arts. Like many of his fellow artists, he has progressed through a series of distinct stages, from two-dimensional abstracts to his current focus on abstracts that project a colorful and sensual organic quality, based on recognizable but complex human figures. "My art," he once said, "is a tropical landscape of the subconscious."[26] When asked how being in exile had affected his work, he replied, "I miss Cuba enormously; I want to be

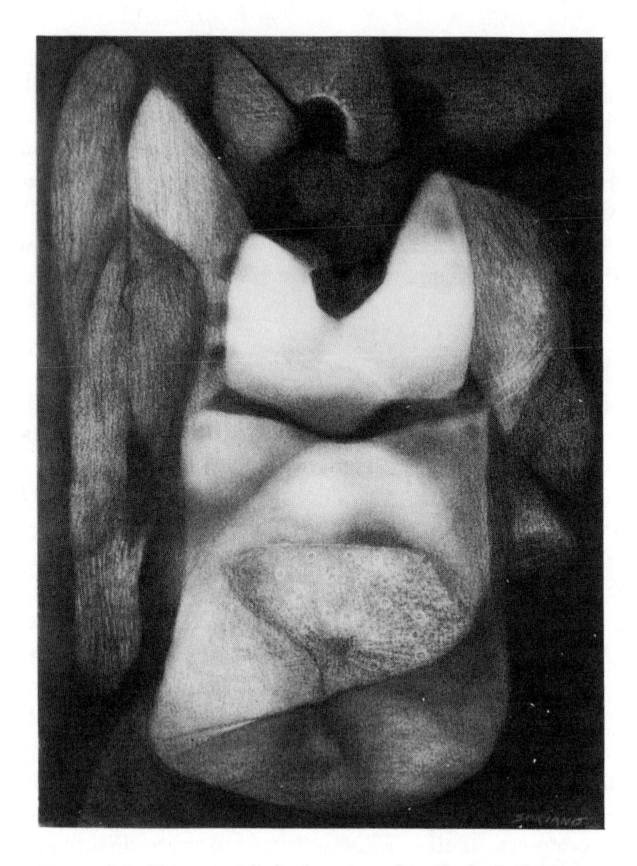

Figure 8.1 This untitled drawing by Rafael Soriano shows the artist's extraordinary use of light. (Photo courtesy of the Bacardi Art Gallery Miami, Florida.)

over there. In respect to my creativity, in all honesty, the experience of exile has not affected me. In fact, what I am doing now is of a better quality than what I was doing before. Though I don't think this has anything to do with having had to leave Cuba."[27]

Rafael Soriano is considered by many to be one of the true masters of modern Cuban painting. He was born in Matanzas, Cuba, in 1920 and studied at the San Alejandro Academy. From 1952 to 1955 he was Director of the School of Fine Arts in Matanzas. Like Mijares, he now resides in Miami. His abstract creations are noted for their mysticism and an extraordinary luminosity that seems to emit a strange and powerful irridescent glow. Pau-Llosa has stated that "no one in Cuban art has attained the spiritual grandeur and universality" of Soriano.[28] Soriano has described his work in these terms: "I try to express in all my painting the intangible dimensions of my interior world."[29]

Osvaldo Gutiérrez was born in Cuba in 1917. He has exhibited widely in Latin America, Europe, and the United States. Now a resident of Miami, Gutiérrez's art has changed from a focus on impressionistic urban landscapes to bright color abstractions in which interlined elements give the illusion of geometric planes. He describes his work as "expressing the intimate contents of my spirit in the simple things of life, in magical and vibrant form."[30]

Enrique Riverón was born in Cienfuegos, Cuba, in 1906. He has studied and worked in a number of countries in Europe and Latin America, but has resided in the United States for over four decades. His early career was as illustrator and cartoonist, but since the 1940s he has concentrated on painting and sculpture. Riverón was the first Cuban artist to approach abstraction.[31] In his distinguished career, he has focused on various styles and experimented with many techniques. Recently he has concentrated on paintings that emphasize sharp-edged geometric lines. His work is best known for its purity of color and use of space. Riverón feels that "Art is creation and invention. Each work is an adventure."[32]

These prominent artists represent only a small sample of the many established artists who remain active and influential in the Cuban-American arts community. Others in this generation include Hugo Consuegra, Augustín Fernández, Roberto Estopiñán, Emilio Sánchez, Fernando Luis, Rudolfo Tardo, Tomás Oliva, Tony López, Eladio González, Thorvald Sánchez, Dionisio Perkins, Raquel Lázaro, Miguel Jorge, and Daniel Serra-Badue. This group is joined by a number of renowned Cuban artists who live in exile in other countries or outside of the United States mainland, but who often exhibit their work in this country and have many personal and artistic ties with the Cuban-American arts community. This group includes: Mario Carreño in Santiago, Chile; Cundo Bermúdez, Rolando López Dirube, Alfredo Lozano in San Juan; and Baruj Salinas in Barcelona; and Jorge Camacho and Jorge Castaño in Paris.

YOUNGER ARTISTS

Besides this older group of established artists, there is an intermediate and younger generation of Cuban painters and sculptors living in the United States. Although most were born in Cuba, they have spent much or all of their adult lives in this country, and this experience is often reflected in their work. Typically, they blend Cuban and American artistic traditions,

Figure 8.2 *This imaginative work by Enrique Riverón illustrates the extraordinary interest among modern Cuban artists in the human form as an artistic motif. (Photo courtesy of the Forma Gallery, Coral Gables, Florida.)*

yet in a highly individualistic fashion. Likewise, their subjects are frequently drawn from both cultures, as well as a mixture of the two. It is a unique and experimental art that tends to be expressed in inventive idioms rather than in established modes; the Cuban masters are more admired than followed. One art critic has observed, for example, that their "American education, layered onto a rich patrimony of religious and cultural symbolism, has engendered a new art that defies categorization by nationality."[33] The work of four Cuban-American artists in their thirties—Emilio Falero, Juan González. María Brito-Avellana, and César Trasobares—suggests the tremendous diversity and creativity of this younger generation.

Emilio Falero was born in Sagua La Grande, Cuba, in 1947. A resident of Miami, he studied at local colleges and has exhibited widely in south Florida. Falero's style has been characterized as "a realism which acquires surreal connotations."[34] He is perhaps best known for his work concerned with the theme of "art over art," in which time and cultures are bridged by combining the styles and themes of famous artists. One of Falero's creations, for example, was described in these terms: "Velasquez is combined with Picasso, is superimposed on Miro, becomes a self-portrait with El Greco to show the disparity as well as the link between art epochs."[35]

Juan González is one of the more acclaimed younger Cuban-American artists. He was born in 1945 in Camaguey, Cuba, and left the island in 1962. His graduate studies were conducted at the University of Miami, where he received a Master of Fine Arts degree. Currently a resident of New York, González is most noted for his impeccable, surreal pencil drawings. "My art," he has said, "is a dialogue of symbols and associations."[36]

María Brito-Avellana is a sculptor who was born in Havana in 1947. After early work with clay, she now combines both man-made and natural materials to create total settings of large symbolic furniture, often complete with movable segments. One critic has said that her "wonderful spontaneous imagination gives fresh life to old, surrealist ideas."[37]

César Trasobares was born in Holguin, Cuba, in 1949. A resident of Miami, Trasobares received his master's degree in art from Florida State University. He is best known for his conceptual art, especially his boxed, mixed media constructions that focus in a satiric way on the rituals and ceremonies of both Cuban and American cultures.[38]

Other talented younger Cuban-American artists whose works are regularly exhibited in Miami or in New York include Humberto Calzada, Ramón Carulla, Rafael Vadía, Pablo Cano, Julio Fernández Larraz, Juan René Lezcano, Francisco Méndez Diez, Fernando García, Roberto Montes de Oca, Ricardo Viera, Ramón Alejandro, Vicente Dopico, Humberto Figueras, and Ana Mendieta.

Figure 8.3 This painting by Emilio Falero illustrates the theme he developed of "art over art." (Photo courtesy of the Forma Gallery, Coral Gables, Florida.)

COMMUNITY SUPPORT

Miami is undisputedly the center of the Cuban-American arts community. It is home for a majority of the artists, and is the site where numerous one-person and group exhibits of Cuban art are regularly held. There are a variety of galleries within the metropolitan area that specialize in showing the work of Cuban and other Latin artists, including most prominently the Forma, de Armas, and the Bacardi Art Galleries. The Miami-Dade Public

Figure 8.4 "The Sparrow and the Maiden" is a colored pencil drawing by Juan Gonzalez, executed in 1975. (Photo courtesy of the Nancy Hoffman Gallery, New York City.)

Library, the Cuban Museum of Art and Culture, the New World Center Campus of Miami-Dade Community College, and the University of Miami's Koubec Center have also actively promoted and exhibited the work of both established and novice Cuban-American artists. Two particularly important local art festivals co-sponsored by the public library system and the Cuban Museum of Art and Culture that have brought together the works of numerous Cuban and other Latin artists are the *Re-Encuentro Cubano* and annual exhibits in honor of Hispanic Heritage Week.[39] The Little Havana Arts Center is another important community institution that serves as a resource and instructional center for local artists.

Community support for local Cuban artists in the metropolitan area of Union City–West New York, New Jersey, however, has not been as well developed as in Miami. Ileana Fuentes-Pérez, director for Hispanic Arts of the Mason Gross School of the Arts at Rutgers University, suggests that this is related to a general lack of awareness and exposure to the large pool of artistic talent that resides in the community.[40] Consequently, New York City continues to be the focus for Cuban art in the greater region.

Cuban art in the United States continues to prosper and evolve. One important source of financial support is the Cintas Foundation. Instituted in honor of Oscar B. Cintas, a prominent Cuban industrialist and former ambassador to the United States, the foundation awards fellowships to professional artists of Cuban birth or lineage. The work of many established and promising artists has been greatly aided by this program. The continuing immigration of artists from the island to the United States, such as those who came during the Mariel exodus—including Víctor Gómez, Pedro Damán, Juan Abreu Felippe, Luis Interian, Eduardo Michaelsen, Carlos Alfonso, Juan Boza, Andrés Valerio, Gilberto Ruz, and José Orbein Pérez—serves as an important periodic source of revitalization that contributes to the evolution of Cuban art in the United States.[41] In early summer of 1982, for example, an exhibit at the Intar Latin American Gallery in New York City, entitled "10 Out of Cuba," featured the work of recent Cuban émigré artists, including 9 who arrived in 1980 via Mariel. In his foreword to the exhibit catalogue, Cuban poet Heberto Padilla (who also emigrated in 1980) notes how the works of the artists have changed. "In the new paintings of these artists known to me in Cuba, stages are skipped and connections are made with unimaginable dimensions. The paintings of each one are now different."[42] Although the works of Cuban artists who go into exile are not officially recognized by the Castro government, and their names are erased from the pages of history, it is clear that Cuban art in exile is striving.[43] As José Gómez-Sicre has said, "Cuban art in exile may be a document of nostalgia, but it is a nostalgia with humor and with faith, with security in a future that has to be better."[44]

Creative Literature

A relatively large body of prose fiction and poetry has been produced since the Castro revolution by Cubans living in the United States. Most of the published authors and poets were born and educated in Cuba, and Cuban literary traditions are clearly evident in a majority of their works—both stylistically and thematically. In *Cuban Consciousness in Literature*, de Armas and Steele conclude that Cuban literature in exile is similar to literary production in Cuba in at least two ways. "First, it contains the hermetism, lyricism and existential anguish. Second, humor—at times bitter and ironic—is also cultivated."[45] Consequently, in light of these and other similarities, a truly distinctive genre of Cuban-American literature has not yet evolved.

LITERATURE AND THE REVOLUTION

The trauma of the revolution, coupled with the strains and adjustments imposed by life in a new country, however, provided subject matter and a perspective that have dominated the literature, while serving as a cause and catalyst for literary expression. In fact, most of the literature has been written by non-professional authors—teachers, lawyers, journalists—who were moved by their experiences and feelings to undertake their first literary efforts. Although some well-known authors and poets emigrated to the United States in the first years following the revolution, including Lydia Cabrera, Carlos Montenegro, Lino Novás Calvo, Enrique Labrador Ruíz, and by the mid-1960s Julio Matas and Luis Ricardo Alonso, as a group they were relatively inactive or continued to publish the same kind of literature written before the revolution. In addition, a number of important Cuban authors who defected sought exile in Europe or Latin America, such as Juan Arcocha, Calvert Casey, Nivaria Tejera, Severo Sardy, Ramón Ferreira, and most notably Guillermo Cabrera Infante, author of the critically acclaimed novel *Tres tristes tigres*. In spite of the defection of these prominent writers, a majority of Cuban authors elected to remain in their native country after the revolution, at least temporarily.

Literature in Cuba has historically been perceived not only as a vehicle for artistic and intellectual expression, but also as a medium for addressing social and ethical issues. That artists should strive in their creations to achieve more than art for art's sake is a widely held philosophy. Cuban national hero and poet José Martí (1853–95), who proclaimed "the moral power and transcendental purpose of beauty," greatly promoted this philosophy.[46] Prior to the revolution, for example, many authors held views that were anti-government and ran contrary to popular attitudes toward such social issues as race, class, and foreign domination. They often wrote a proletarian literature that focused on Afro-Cuban themes, hailing the rights of oppressed workers and rural peasants against the government.[47] Largely because of these sentiments, the revolution was generally supported by the literati, and relatively few sought exile during the first years of the Castro regime. Over the past two decades, however, a number of celebrated authors, having grown disenchanted with the revolution and its negative impact on their work, have joined the exile literary community, including most recently authors such as Reinaldo Arenas and Heberto Padilla who arrived in 1980.

In the years immediately following the revolution, relatively few novels were written by Cubans in exile, although the first appeared as early as 1960 with publication of *Enterrado vivo* by Andrés Collado.[48] During this period numerous short stories and poetry were published in periodicals or in collections. Poetry in particular, which was a popular literary form in Cuba (in part because of the influence of Martí), allowed artists an opportunity to express in an economy of words their innermost feelings and thoughts.[49] Though passionate and well-intended, most of the literary works produced at this early stage, especially the novels, were criticized as polemic and lacking in literary value. In 1966, for example, a Cuban-American academic reviewer wrote, "As for the Cubans in exile, they have written few novels, and these have been, as novels, inadequate, missing the tragic, humorous, dramatic, human experiences that exiles undergo. As documents, some have been openly reactionary."[50] Similar criticism was voiced by Seymour Menton, author of the highly regarded *Prose Fiction of the Cuban Revolution*, who concluded that most of the novels written by Cubans in exile "are anticommunist diatribes with scarce literary merit."[51] Of course, the fact that a majority of the literature was written by novice authors greatly contributed to the criticism that was leveled in the 1960s and through much of the 1970s. The fervent anti-revolutionary,anti-Castro orientation characterizing a substantial body of the literature written in exile has generated criticism as well. These works were interpreted more as political harangues than examples of serious literature.

LITERARY THEMES

Certainly one of the dominant themes in the literature has, in fact, been political-ideological, usually directed toward the revolution. Communism is routinely portrayed as evil and Castro is vilified. The loss of personal liberty and religious freedom, breakdown of the family, and dehumanization of mankind in general are also common topics. The Bay of Pigs invasion, the Cuban missile crisis, and the escape from Cuba (usually dramatic) also play prominent roles. Some of the representative novels and short story collections of this theme have been identified by Mention, including: Raoul A. Fowler y Cabrera, *En las garras de la paloma*; Salvador Díaz-Verson, . . . *Ya el mundo oscurece*; Miguel Márquez y de la Cerra, *El gallo cantó*; Pablo A. López, *Ayer sin mañana*; Luis Ricardo Alonso, *Territorio libre*; and Beltrán de Quirós, *Los unos, los otros . . . y el seibó*.[52]

Another component of the political-ideological theme concerns the Cuban exile experience in the United States, especially in Miami. The problems and often humorous aspects of adjusting to life in a new environment, as well as criticism of the perceived negative elements of American society (i.e. drug abuse, sexual immorality, materialism), have been popular topics. According to Mention, and de Armas and Steele, the following works are good examples of this subtheme: *Los primos* and *La soledad es una amiga que vendrá* by Celedonio González; *El cielo será nuestro* by Manuel Cobo Sausa; *Los desposeídos* by Ramiro Gómez Kemp; *Refugiados* by Angel A. Castro; and especially José Sánchez-Boudy's *Lilayando*.[53] In *Lilayando*, for example, which Mention suggests "is a very shortened Miami version of *Tres tristes tigres*, the picturesque vernacular of the Cuban exiles . . . is definitely the protagonist, with emphasis on puns, [although] the contents of the dialogues—social gossip and problems of acculturation—do provide sociological insight into the character of the speakers and society in which they live.[54]

A second major theme appearing in much of the literature is an expression of nostalgia; a longing for life before the revolution, coupled with a passionate, sentimental love of country as recalled in memories. Concerning this theme, de Armas and Steele write that it is"very similar stylistically speaking to the revolutionary literature within Cuba in which the subject matter consists of recollections of Cuba previous to Castro with nostalgia for what is no more—what was—with a strong and deep patriotism, often ill-defined, and a great love for Cuba, its countryside, its nightlife, its women, its sunshine, in short, a literature of nostalgic reminiscence, even suffering."[55] These fond recollections are often juxtaposed and elicited in the literature by the despair and frustration that various characters harbor about the changes that have taken place in their lives since the revolution. Among the many examples of this theme, Roberto Fernández has singled out the following two short story collections as being particularly illustrative: *Las pirañas y otros cuentos cubanos* by Asela Gutiérrez Kann; and *La mas fermosa* by Concepción T. Alzola.[56]

A universal or cosmopolitan theme, in which the Cuban experience is examined in a broader context, is also evident in a number of literary works. Though criticized by some as escapist, it is a genre that has a long and established tradition in Cuban literature. Afro-Cuban cult religions, such as *Santería*, are popular subjects for expressing the universal theme.

The writings of Lydia Cabrera, Julio Matas, José Sánchez-Boudy, Matias Montes Huidobro, Pura del Prado, and Carlos Alberto Montaner (who now lives in Spain) are prominent in the universal genre. Lydia Cabrera, for example, whose *Cuentos negros de Cuba* (1940) and *Por qué* (1948) are considered among the best examples of Afro-Cuban literature, in 1971 published in Miami another collection of nineteen Afro-Cuban short stories entitled *Ayapá: Cuentos de Jicotea*. Julio Matas in 1971 published *Erinia*, an anthology of stories (some which had been first published in Cuba in the early 1960s) in the escapist mode of his earlier works. Yet, based on Carlos Alberto Montaner's novel *Perromundo*, Mention suggests that a new trend among younger exiles may be emerging by rejecting both rabid anti-communism and escapism and by applying some of the techniques of the new Latin American novel and a short story to themes that are relevant for Cubans and, at the same time, have universal appeal.[57]

The creative literature produced by Cuban-Americans is yearly growing in volume and degree of literary sophistication. In addition to the continuing arrival of established Cuban authors, new writers educated in the United States and with fresh perspectives and experiences to share are emerging. As a consequence, the literature is evolving to reflect these changes. More literary works are being written in English, while Spanish-language versions are increasingly being translated into English to appeal to a broader market (including younger Cuban-Americans who are often more competent in reading English or unable to read Spanish at all). New Cuban-American literary journals are also being published, such as *Termino, Unveiling Cuba, Mariel,* and *Linden Lane Magazine*. The Cuban literary community in Miami, for example, is active in keeping Cuban literary traditions alive in the United States by encouraging and promoting the efforts of both established and novice authors, and by offering public lectures, seminars, and literary "salons" on various aspects of Cuban literature.[58] In addition, there are now a number of publishing outlets and bookstores in the city that specialize in Cuban and other Spanish language literature. Although complaints have been lodged by some that works by Cuban authors in the United States have been unfairly criticized or ignored altogether because of political reasons, it is clear that Cuban-Americans are greatly contributing to the body of American ethnic literature.[59]

Theater and Dance

Cuban theater and dance traditions have also been preserved and developed in the United States. Most of the theatrical companies and dance groups are located in Miami. In 1983, for example, there were seven

Cuban playhouses, two ballet companies, and one light opera group operating in the city. In addition, there are a number of smaller dance companies that range from folkloric to modern.

The playhouses are typically small, seating between 50 and 200 people, and generally open just on the weekends. Some of the performances, however, are staged in larger facilities, such as the Dade County Auditorium. Most of the actors pursue their avocation on a part-time basis, and are usually involved in all phases of the production. A number of well-known Cuban and Spanish actors, however, are regular performers.

Since the theatrical companies, such as *Grateli*, are self-supporting, the number of plays and musical productions presented each year are limited by financial considerations. The performances are in Spanish and usually of traditional Cuban or Spanish operettas and plays. In recent years, a variety of original plays and musicals have been staged, as well as popular American productions. Comedies are especially popular, particularly those concerned with political satire or the humorous aspects of life encountered by Cuban émigrés in the United States, such as Ivan Acosta's award-winning play and film, *El Super*.

Notes

1. John Storm Roberts, *The Latin Tinge: The Impact of Latin American Music on the United States* (New York: Oxford University Press, 1979), p. 4. This book is clearly the single best source on the history of Cuban music in the United States, and this section draws heavily from it.

2. Some of the more important sources on the history and evolution of music in Cuba include: Emilio Grenet, *Popular Cuban Music* (Havana: Ministry of Education, 1939); Alejo Carpentier, *La Música en Cuba* (Mexico City: Fondo de Cultura Economica, 1972); Francisco López Cruz, *La Música Folklorica en Cuba* (Sharon, Conn.: Troutman Press, 1967); and María Teresa Linares, *La Música Popular* (Havana: Instituto del Libro, 1970).

3. The classic reference on African music in Cuba is: Fernando Ortiz, *La Africanía de la Música Folklorica de Cuba* (Havana: Cárdenas, n.d.). Also see Roberto Nodal, "A Note on Afro-Cuban Music," *Ethnos*, 34:130–140, 1969.

4. Roberto Nodal, "The Afro-Cuban Batá Drums," *LORE* 24:22–29, Spring 1974.

5. Howard I. Blutstein et al, *Area Handbook for Cuba* (Washington, D.C.: U.S. Government Printing Office, 1971), p. 169.

6. Grenet, op. cit., p. 62.

7. Fernando Ortiz, *Los Instrumentos de la Musica Afrocubana* (Havana: Ministerio de Educacion, 1954); Harold Courlander, "Musical Instruments of Cuba," *The Musical Quarterly* 28:229–231, January 1942.

8. John Storm Roberts, "Salsa: The Latin Dimension in Popular Music," *BMI*, The Many Worlds of Music Series, Issue 3, October 15, 1976, p. 5.

9. Roberta Singer and Robert Friedman, "Puerto Rican and Cuban Musical Expression in New York," accompanying notes to *Caliente-Hot*, Recorded Anthology of American Music, 1977, New World Records, NW 244 Stereo, p. 2.

10. Roberts, *The Latin Tinge*, op. cit., p. 9.

11. Singer and Friedman, op. cit., p. 2.

12. For an in-depth discussion of the *rumba, mambo, cha-cha-chá,* and *salsa* periods, see Roberts, *The Latin Tinge*, op. cit., p. 76–211.
13. Larry Birnbaum, "Machito: Original Macho Man," *Down Beat* 47:25–27, December 1980; Arnold Jay Smith, "Tito Puente and Machito: Sounds from the Salsa Source," *Down Beat* 43:16, April 22, 1976.
14. Singer and Friedman, op. cit., p. 1.
15. Arnold Jay Smith, "Ray Barretto's Crossover Crisis," *Down Beat* 43:18, April 22, 1976.
16. Birnbaum, op. cit., p. 27.
17. James R. Curtis and Richard F. Rose, "The Miami Sound: A Contemporary Latin Form of Place-Specific Music," *Journal of Cultural Geography* 4:110–118, Fall-Winter, 1983.
18. Enrique Fernández, " 'Tropical Night' Promos Put Focus on Latin Beat," *Billboard*, April 10, 1982, p. 44.
19. Two general references are: Martha de Castro, *El Arte en Cuba* (Miami: Ediciones Universal, 1970); and *Pintores Cubanos* (La Habana: Ediciones Revolución, 1962).
20. Quoted in Griffin Smith, "At Last—Miami has a Cuban Art Exhibit," *The Miami Herald*, April 30, 1972, p. 1H.
21. Gary Russell Libby, Cuban Foundation, Daytona Beach, Florida, Permanent Exhibit Catalogue of "Two Centuries of Cuban Art: 1759–1959," 1980, n.p.
22. Blutstein, op. cit., pp. 174–175.
23. Ricardo Pau-Llosa, "Art in Exile," *Américas* 32:8, August 1980.
24. Ibid., p. 4.
25. José Gómez-Sicre, *Pintura Cubana de Hoy* (La Habana, 1944); and Gilbert Chase, *Contemporary Art in Latin America* (New York: The Free Press, 1970), pp. 60–67.
26. Mirta Blanco, "Pintores Latinoamericanos en Miami," *Vanidades Continental* 18:34, May 30, 1978.
27. Ricardo Pau-Llosa, "The Artist in Exile: Four Cuban Painters Continue Creating in New Environment," *The Miami Herald*, August 31, 1975, p. 5K.
28. Ibid.
29. Blanco, op. cit., p. 35.
30. Ibid., p. 34.
31. Lillian Dobbs, "Cuban Art Exhibition at Lowe Becomes a Reality," *The Miami Herald*, September 20, 1978, p. 1C.
32. Blanco, op. cit., p. 34.
33. Helen L. Kohen, "Bright Days for Art in South Florida," *Art News* 79:99, December 1980.
34. Lillian Dobbs, "Common Bonds of Four Aren't Evident in Their Works," *The Miami Herald*, December 5, 1979, p. 36.
35. Ibid.
36. Center for Inter-American Relations, New York City, Exhibit Catalogue of "Six Cuban Painters Working in New York," held January 15–February 23, 1975, n.p.
37. Frances Wolfson Art Gallery, Miami-Dade Community College, Miami, Florida, Exhibit Catalogue of "Latin American Art: A Woman's View," held October 5–November 13, 1981, n.p.
38. The Lowe Art Museum, University of Miami, Miami, Florida, Exhibit Catalogue of "Contemporary Latin American Art," held September 14-October 8, 1978, p. 80.
39. Miami-Dade Public Library and the Cuban Museum of Art and Culture, Miami, Florida, Exhibit Catalogue of "Hispanic Graphics Today," held October 6–20, 1978; and Bacardi Art Gallery and the Cuban Museum of Art And Culture, Miami, Florida, Exhibit Catalogue of "Selections of Cuban Art from the Olartecoechea Collection," held April 30–May 19, 1982.
40. Ileana Fuentes-Pérez, personal communication, April, 1983.
41. Maria F. González, "Six Out of Cuba," *Marquee* 3:42–27, February–March 1983; and Barbara Gutiérrez, "Mariel Artists Want to Say 'Thanks' with Festival," *The Miami Herald*, February 7, 1982, p. 1B.
42. Intar Latin American Gallery, New York City, Exhibit Catalogue of "10 Out of Cuba," held May 24–July 31, 1982, preface.

43. Guilio V. Blanc, "New Cuban Paintes," *Unveiling Cuba* 1:11, April 1983; and Guilio V. Blanc, "*Pintores Prohibidos*," *Unveiling Cuba* 1:9, January 1982.

44. Quoted in Bacardi Art Gallery, Miami, Florida, Exhibit Catalogue of "GALA, Fourth Annual Exhibition," held April 30–May 18, 1973, n.p.

45. Jose R. de Armas and Charles W. Steele, *Cuban Consciousness in Literature: 1923–1974* (Miami: Ediciones Universal, 1978), p. 134.

46. Blutstein, op. cit., p. 160.

47. Ibid., p. 165.

48. Andrés Rivero Collado, *Enterrado vivo* (México: Dinamismo, 1960).

49. Matías Montes Huidobro and Yara Gonzalez, *Bibliografía crítica de la poesía cubana (exilio 1959–1971)* (Madrid: Plaza Mayor, 1973).

50. Rosa M. Abella, "Five Years of the Cuban Novel," *The Carrell* 7:21, June 1966.

51. Seymour Menton, *Prose Fiction of the Cuban Revolution* (Austin: University of Texas Press, 1975), p. 275.

52. Ibid., pp. 216–234.

53. Ibid.; de Armas and Steele, op. cit., p. 227.

54. Menton, op. cit., p. 229.

55. de Armas and Steele, op. cit., p. 134.

56. Roberto G. Fernandez, "El Cuento Cubano Del Exilio: Un Enfoque" (Ph.D. dissertation, Florida State University, 1977), pp. 57–86.

57. Menton, op. cit., p. 246.

58. See, for example, José Sánchez-Boudy, *Historia de la literatura cubana (en el exilio)* (Miami: Ediciones Universal, 1975).

59. Guillermo Martinez, "Cuban Arts, Literature in Exile," *The Miami Herald*, February 24, 1983, p. 19A.

9
Cuisine and Foodways

Food habits are among the most tenacious of all cultural practices. Immigrant groups in the United States, particularly first- and second-generation émigrés, have been extremely reluctant to abandon their native cuisine. Eating, of course, involves more than just the biological act of ingesting nutrients for basic nourishment. It also is part of a foodways complex that is an essential component of all cultural systems. Foodways include not only a preference for a specific diet, but also methods of preparation and cooking, as well as a host of dining customs and rituals. In this sense, foodways are imbued with powerful social meanings and surrounded by norms which define accepted patterns of behavior. They are often intertwined with a folklore that may relate the consumption of food to collective feelings about concerns as central as health and happiness. Because of the frequency of eating, foodways become habitualized. And, like most daily habits and rituals, they tend to subconsciously offer a measure of personal stability and comfort.

For most immigrants the prospects of suddenly breaking these long-standing and generally pleasurable habits may provoke considerable anxiety. It is perhaps not surprising, then, that grocery stores and restaurants specializing in native foods are usually among the first ethnic businesses to open in areas where immigrants have settled. Beyond the food and service they offer, these establishments often become important social institutions in their own right. They are places that bring people together and enrich community life and strengthen ethnic ties. Moreover, since many ethnic restaurants are visually prominent landscape features and often draw on a clientele from the greater community, they may become important landmarks that help shape the image of the area in the eyes of the local population. In this context, it is not unrealistic to suggest that for some individuals from the host society a desire to dine at a particular restaurant may be their only voluntary experience with that ethnic culture or neighborhood.

Although food preferences and dining habits among immigrant groups in the United States generally broaden and become more "Americanized" through time, as long as an internal sense of ethnicity remains, many of the older foodways will endure, especially during holidays and other special occasions. The number and sheer variety of ethnic restaurants now found in virtually all American cities of even moderate size attest to the survival of ethnic cuisines and illustrate how thoroughly they have become an essential aspect of American eating and dining patterns.

Historical Roots of Cuban Cuisine

Many traditional Cuban foods and eating customs persist among Cubans living in the United States. Like the cuisine of other countries, Cuban foodways reflect a combination of environmental and historical influences. The island's moderate tropical climate, diverse terrain, and large expanses of fertile soils were favorable for the development of productive agriculture. Although sugar cane and tobacco have long been the two principal cash crops and account for much of the arable land, a relatively wide variety of crop plants are also grown, including grains (mostly corn and rice), vegetables (particularly tubers), as well as fruits and nuts. Pastureland is abundant and livestock, especially cattle and sheep, have been raised since the beginning of the Spanish colonial period. Hogs and chickens are also raised and allowed to forage. In addition to terrestrial food resources, many species of edible fish are found in local waters, including a variety of shellfish. In short, Cuba's environmental conditions supported a wide range of food sources that permitted the development of a comparatively diverse diet.

Among the host of cultural-historical forces that helped shape Cuban foodways, clearly the most significant impact was made by the Spanish during their long period of colonial rule. Not only did such traditional Spanish dishes as *arroz con pollo* and *paella* enter the Cubans diet, but from appetizers to deserts, and from cookery to eating customs, the Spanish influence was pervasive. The custom in Spain, for example, of eating a hearty, leisurely noon meal (*almuerzo*), and a light late-evening supper (*comida*) became an established Cuban dining habit. The Spanish preference for spicy, rich food cooked in either oil or wine likewise became a characteristic feature of Cuban cuisine. Environmental conditions, of course, prohibited the introduction of some staple crops grown in Spain, including wheat. Yet, many of the crop plants and animals that the Spaniards brought with them from Iberia survived in their New World setting, such as rice, citrus fruits, cattle, sheep, chickens and pigs. Pigs, in particular, adapted extraordinarily well in the absence of predators and endemic disease and quickly became the major source of meat. The Spanish supplemented these foodstuffs with native biota, including tropical fruits and fish, based in part on knowledge gained from the Arawak Indians. The Arawaks also cultivated a number of root crops, of which the most important was yuca, and it soon became a staple.[1] Through the process of diffusion, corn, beans, squash, and other New World crops were introduced into Cuba and greatly contributed to the diet.

Another cultural influence emerged as a consequence of the African slave trade. The homeland of the slaves was west Africa where root crops, especially yams, plantains, and grains were staple foods. The tubers and grains (except rice) were usually ground into a flour and then meshed or stewed into a thick porridge which was dipped into a vegetable and/or meat sauce.[2] Their knowledge of cultivation practices and cooking methods involving tubers, grains, plantains, and vegetables such as okra had a tremendous impact on the emerging Cuban cuisine. The Afro-Cuban influence is further evident in the use of certain spices and sauces, as well as in a variety of dishes, particularly stews.

The various Spanish, Indian, and African contributions all merged together into a foodways complex that was unique to Cuba. Of course, this basic foundation was supplemented through time by many influences on the cuisine from other areas, especially Europe, China, and the United States.

The Cuban-American Diet

The Cuban-American diet is still dominated by traditional Cuban foods. This is particularly true for first- and second-generation Cubans living in Miami and the general vicinity of New York City where Latin-Caribbean food products are readily available. Individual food preferences, of course, display considerable variation; the diet of some Cuban-Americans, for example, is essentially the same as it was in Cuba, whereas others have adopted a cuisine that is not much different than the American population in general. Younger Cuban-Americans who were born or raised in the United States typically have the most diverse diet, including the usual attraction for popular American fast foods. (The busy McDonald's restaurant on Flagler Street in the heart of Miami's Little Havana is clear testimony.) Even those who prefer traditional Cuban dishes use many American food products, although this is done more often for convenience than out of necessity. Quick rice, for example, has largely replaced the use of the regular, uncooked variety. Of course, advertising has exposed, if not created a desire for, a host of new products. It seems inevitable that these changes will continue and the diet will broaden, becoming more characteristically American as the process of acculturation speeds ahead. Dining habits, for example, have already been significantly altered. Work and school schedules often prohibit a family from having a large noon meal at home. The evening meal is now generally more substantial and served earlier than it was in Cuba. In spite of these and other changes in older foodways, at the present time the traditional Cuban diet remains an important component of Cuban-American culture.

Cuban food is characterized by dishes that are generally hearty, somewhat starchy, and usually spicy (though rarely hot).[3] The liberal use of spices and seasonings is an essential feature of Cuban cooking. Food preparation often begins with a sautéed blend of butter or olive oil, garlic, onions, and lime juice, called a "sofrito." Green peppers, tomato sauce, and vinegar are also common ingredients. The pungent aroma of garlic clearly dominates this blend, which is used in preparing many of the basic dishes, including soups and stews, vegetables, rice, and meats. The spicy quality of Cuban food is further enhanced by marinating meat before cooking, usually in lime, lemon, sour orange, or grapefruit juice. Most cooking is done in vegetable or olive oil, and this too adds a distinctive flavor to the food.

The main course of most Cuban meals includes an entrée of meat, chicken, or fish. Although beef is eaten more frequently now than it was in Cuba, pork remains overwhelmingly the most important meat in the diet. Among the various methods of preparation, roasting pork is probably the most preferred. Two of the favorite pork entrées are *lechón asado* (pork roast) and *masas de puerco* (fried pork chunks). A roast suckling pig is the traditional dish served for the New Year's and Christmas Eve celebrations. Pork is also the meat used most often in sandwiches. A plain roasted pork sandwich (*pan con lechón*), for example, is extremely popular for a quick lunch. The so-called Cuban sandwich is larger and more substantial, made with pork, ham, and swiss cheese served on a grilled french-style bread. Another popular sandwich, often eaten as a nighttime snack, is the "*media noche*" (midnight), which has the same ingredients as the Cuban sandwich but is lighter and served on an elongated soft roll prepared in an egg batter. At parties and other social gatherings, meat croquettes made with ham, pork or chicken are commonly offered as appetizers or snacks.

Beef is the second most important meat in the diet. Steaks are particularly popular, especially thin-sliced sirloin (*palomilla*) and flank (*falda*) steaks. Shredded beef (*ropa vieja*) and dry shredded beef (*tasajo*) dishes, as well as pot roast (*boliche*), are also popular. One of the most common dishes is *picadillo*, a spicy beef hash. There is also a Cuban version of the hamburger, called a *frita*, which is a grilled patty mixture of beef and pork and spices served with pencil-thin french fries and onions inside the bun.

Chicken and seafood entrées are served much less frequently than either pork or beef. Chicken was relatively expensive in Cuba, and hence did not become well established in the cuisine. Roasted chicken (*pollo asado*) is the preferred manner of cooking. *Arroz con pollo* and *paella*, however, are also favorite dishes. Chicken is also used in a variety of casseroles, soups, and stews. During holidays, turkey and black beans and rice is a common meal. Seafood dishes emphasize shellfish, especially shrimp, lobsters and crabs. They are often mixed together with pieces of fish and prepared "Spanish style" in a spicy tomato sauce, called *enchilado*. When fish is the main course, it is typically served whole or in halves and in a well-seasoned sauce or breaded. It may be baked (*al horno*) or fried.

Vegetables and fruits are essential foods in Cuban cuisine. Undoubtedly, the most important staple in the diet is a combination of black beans and rice, prepared in a variety of ways. The beans are generally prepared in a thick sauce made with fat, pork, lard, and other ingredients. Most commonly the beans and rice are served separately, then the beans are usually ladled over the rice. They may also be prepared together and cooked with various meats and seasonings. Two popular mixed beans and rice dishes are called *congrí*, which uses kidney beans, and *moros y cristianos*, which uses black beans. A variety of other beans, especially kidney and white beans, are important in the diet, and often substitute for the traditional black beans.

A number of tropical root crops are also mainstays in the cuisine, including most importantly yuca, malanga, ñama, and boniato. They are usually boiled and prepared with various seasonings. Corn and potatoes are also important vegetables in the diet. Potatoes are most often cooked as french fries (*papas fritas*) or boiled and served in soups and stews. Baked potatoes are rarely prepared. Corn is a common ingredient in a variety of soups and stews, and is also used in making Cuban tamales, which are prepared with a mixture of corn meal, spices, and bits of meat. Though a fruit, fried ripe plantains (*plátanos maduros fritos*) or green plantains (*plátanos verdes*) are sliced and served like a vegetable. They are a standard food in the cuisine. Green plantains are also crispy-fried to make chips, known as *mariquitas*, or *tostones* for a thicker chip. The smaller, sweet banana is also eaten as a fruit (*platanos manzanos*). Many other tropical fruits are popular, including papaya (*fruta bomba*), coconut (*coco*), mango, mamey, and guava. Grapes are also eaten. In keeping with an old Spanish custom, at midnight on New Year's Eve, for example, it is customary to eat twelve grapes, symbolic of the months of the year. For lunch and dinner, a tossed green salad with a dressing of wine vinegar and oil is usually served in restaurants, but not as often in the home. The salad is generally eaten with the meal.

Desserts are integral to Cuban cuisine. Puddings, pastries, and especially custards (*flan*) are the main dessert foods. There is a wide assortment of puddings made from a variety of ingredients. The most commonly served include egg pudding (*natilla*), rice pudding (*arroz con leche*), coconut pudding (*pudín de coco*), bread pudding (*pudín de pan*), sweet potato pudding (*boniatillo*), and a "diplomatic" pudding (*pudín diplomático*) that is usually flavored with a sweet liquor, and served with a layer of cake and chopped dried fruit. The pastries are often filled or topped with preserved fruits, jelly, or fruit pastes; guava and mango pastes are particularly popular. *Casco de guayabe* (guava shells) served with cream cheese, for example, is a typical Cuban dessert. Small meat-filled pies (*empanadas de carne*), sweet breads, cakes, and Cuban crackers (*galletas*) are also standard pastries. Custards are probably the most popular of all the desserts, especially an egg custard prepared with a thin, caramelized sugar sauce. Two other popular custards are *tocino del cielo*, which is a sweet custard, and coconut custard (*tocino de coco*). During holidays, most notably at Christmas, candies such as *cocitas* (a sweet pralinelike candy) and Spanish *turrones* (candy nougats made from almonds) are special festivity foods.

Beverage preferences are relatively diverse. Traditional non-alcoholic drinks include sugarcane juice (*guarapo*), iced coconut milk (*coco frío*), and various fruit juices, particularly mamey, papaya and orange. Fruits are also blended with ice cream to make milkshakes called *batidos*. Along with American soft drinks, there are a number of Cuban sodas such as *Materva, Jupiña* (pineapple), Iron Beer (a root beerlike soda) as well as sweet, malted, soda beverages called *malta* which are very popular. Beer and *sangría* are standard alcoholic drinks. Wine preferences tend toward red Spanish wines. Liquor preferences, however, vary considerably, especially among the middle- and upper-classes. Still, rum remains a favorite, particularly for mixed drinks. Rum and coke served with a slice of lime (called a *Cuba libre*) is a traditional mixed drink, but daiquiris, piña coladas and rum with fruit juices are also popular.

Undoubtedly, the most important beverage is coffee. In fact, consumption of the syrupy, dark, bittersweet espresso known as *café cubano* is an institutionalized aspect of the cuisine. It is not uncommon for adults, and often children too, to drink several demitasse cups of it daily. Served steaming hot, *café cubano* is consumed not only with meals at home or in restaurants, but also at stand-up sidewalk counters, in grocery stores, bakeries, beauty salons, and funeral parlors. (In fact drinking *café cubano* is such an established aspect of the funeral ceremony—which lasts all night—that one Cuban-owned funeral parlor in Miami has installed its own coffee counter.)[4] In the minds of many Cubans *café cubano* is considered to be, ironically, both a stimulant and a depressant. Although the coffee beans are the same as those used in American coffee, they are roasted longer and at a higher temperature, which produces a darker bean. Brewed in small espresso coffee machines, *café cubano* is much stronger than American coffee. In fact some Cubans refer to American coffee as "*agua sucia*" (dirty water). If served black (*café solo*), it is often accompanied by a small glass of cold water. *Café con leche* (coffee with milk) is also an extremely popular coffee beverage. It is made by mixing *café cubano* in a cup with hot, sweetened milk. It is served most frequently for breakfast. A typical light breakfast (*desayuno*), for example, consists of white bread or crackers with butter and *café con leche*; the bread is sometimes dipped into the coffee. (Eggs and the standard breakfast meats are served for more substantial morning meals.) Some Cuban mothers feel that children should drink *café con leche* every morning in order to avoid sickness. In the United States it has become popular among many Cubans to drink their *café cubano* "cortadito," in which a dash of milk is added to "cut" the darkness and strength of the coffee.

Among the four or five leading commercial brands of Cuban coffee, the largest is Bustelo, a division of the Tetley Tea Corporation. It reportedly sells in Florida alone over 500 million pounds of Cuban coffee annually.[5]

Grocery Stores and Restaurants

The persistence of traditional Cuban food in the Cuban-American diet is related in large part to the fact that most are still first- and second-generation immigrants. In areas of concentrated settlement, especially in Miami and Union City-West New York, another critical factor has been the establishment of a vast network of Cuban-owned or -operated grocery stores and restaurants that cater to their culinary needs. In Miami, for example, there are currently an estimated 700 Cuban grocery stores (called *bodegas*), and over 400 Latin restaurants. The demand for Latin food products generated by these retail establishments has, in turn, led to the growth of a large number of manufacturing and wholesale distribution businesses, often Cuban-owned as well, that specialize in these products.

Although virtually all of the larger American supermarkets in Miami now carry a line of Latin foods, and most Cubans do a majority of their grocery shopping in these supermarkets, the *bodegas* serve a substantial percentage of the Cuban population. Research has shown that a majority of Cubans shop in both American chain supermarkets and Cuban grocery stores. In 1980, for example, a survey revealed that 85.7 percent of the Latins in Miami shopped in American supermarkets, whereas 65.6 percent shopped in Cuban markets. When the survey was conducted again in early 1983, the percentages had changed. The number of Latins shopping in American supermarkets had now declined to 67.4 percent; the number shopping in Cuban markets however, had increased to 80.3 percent. The study concluded that the change was primarily a consequence of the influx of more than 100,000 Mariel refugees since April 1980.[6]

The *bodegas* are able to compete for a variety of reasons, some of which are totally unrelated to the products they sell and service they offer. Generally, the *bodegas* are small, family-run, and conveniently located. They are often within walking distance of many of their customers. Beyond the usual convenience foods, the typically cluttered shelves of the *bodegas* offer a wide selection of traditional Cuban foods and items, often in brands unavailable in local supermarkets.[7] In addition to stocking a larger choice of the most popular products, they also carry many items imported from Latin America and Spain. Another attraction for customers is that most *bodegas* include a *carnicería* (butcher shop), where they can special order Latin cuts of meat for specific Cuban dishes. It also is not uncommon for *bodegas* to have a sidewalk counter where fresh pastries, sandwiches, beverages (always *café cubano*), and cigars and candies are sold; inside are Spanish-language newspapers and magazines.

More than just specialized grocery stores, these places serve an important social function. Posters on the windows tell of community and cultural events and political campaigns that affect their lives. They are informal gathering spots where friends and neighbors, owners and patrons, reminisce, share news and gossip. They offer stability, and a feeling of continuity that reaffirms ethnic ties and contributes to a sense of community, while lessening the strains of acculturation. They are, in this sense, important threads in the social fabric.

Cuban restaurants, like *bodegas*, play an important role in community life and social organization. For most middle-class Cuban-Americans, dining out in Cuban restaurants is a frequent and enjoyable activity. It also is an essential feature of their social system, a cultural practice that reinforces their common heritage and bonds of kinship. Beyond this cohesive social function as meeting place, Cuban restaurants help perpetuate a variety of traditional foodways. They may, for example, serve dishes that are not normally prepared at home. For younger Cuban-Americans in particular, this exposure maintains or increases their familiarity with the cuisine, which of course is critical in its survival. More than just the cuisine, the dining experience itself may help sustain many of the traditional and more formal eating and dining customs, customs that may not be observed in the home environment.

Most of the estimated 400 Latin restaurants in Miami are Cuban. They offer the range of Cuban cuisine and dining experiences, from elegant supper clubs with tuxedoed waiters and valet parking, to *mama y papa* cafes with three stools, a sidewalk counter, and one very-used grill.[8] A number of larger and well-known restaurants combine Cuban with Spanish or Basque cuisines. Although some specialize in particular food items, such as steaks, most of the bigger restaurants offer an astounding variety of dishes. Menus listing thirty or forty entrées are not uncommon. There are no Cuban chain restaurants, although a few of the more popular establishments have opened a second or third restaurant.

Unlike Mexican restaurants, for example, there is no dominant theme to the exterior facades or decorative motifs. Occasionally, however, restaurants that feature Spanish-Cuban cuisine may have characteristic Spanish elements such as stucco facades, wrought-iron grillwork and red barrel-tile roofs. Interior decor also varies widely, from opulent to unpretentious. A number of the restaurants have photographs, paintings or murals of street scenes from Havana, rural Cuban landscapes or Spanish themes. But in general the decor reflects the individual owner's tastes, rather than distinctive elements of the Cuban culture. A number of the better known restaurants are named and patterned as much as possible after restaurants that existed in pre-Castro Cuba; in some cases they are owned and staffed by the same people.

The majority of restaurants are located along the main thoroughfares in the predominantly Cuban sections of the metropolitan area, especially in the incorporated areas of Miami, Hialeah and Westchester. The greatest concentration occurs within the Little Havana district of Miami, especially along *Calle Ocho*. There are now over forty Cuban restaurants on *Calle Ocho*.[9] They help define the character of Little Havana, and are perhaps its major attraction for Anglos, as well as many Cuban-Americans.

Notes

1. Carl O. Sauer, *The Early Spanish Main* (Berkeley: University of California Press, 1969), p. 183.

2. Paul Bohannan, *Africa and Africans* (Garden City, N.Y.: Natural History Press, 1964), pp. 136–138.

3. There are very few Cuban cookbooks available in the United States. One in English is by Raquel Rabade, *The Cuban Flavor: A Cookbook* (Miami: Downtown Book Center, 1979). Also see Margaret Stanley Boon, "Cubans in City Context: The Washington Case" (Ph.D. dissertation, the Ohio State University, 1977), pp. 140–144.

4. Liz Balmaseda, "Cuban Way of Death Keeps Traditions Alive," *The Miami Herald*, July 31, 1982, p. 1C.

5. Lesley Valdes, "It Costs More, You Drink Less, But Ummm!" *The Miami Herald*, January 11, 1979, p. 1D.

6. Andres Oppenheimer, "Mariel Made Area's Latins More Latin, Survey Finds," *The Miami Herald*, April 29, 1083, p. 1C; Strategy Research Corporation, "Latin Market Survey," Miami, Florida, April 1982.

7. Fabiola Santiago, "La Bodega," *The Miami Herald*, March 10, 1983, p. 1E.

8. Harvey Steiman, *Guide to Restaurants of Greater Miami* (Chatsworth, Cal.: Brooke House, 1977).

9. Lourdes Meluza, "Set Your Own Pace in Little Havana," *The Miami Herald*, March 5, 1983. p. 1C.; and Christine Brown Arnold, "An Anglo's Guide to Little Havana," *The Miami Herald*, December 2, 1977, p. 1D.

10
Politics and Ideology

The political attitudes and activities of Cuban-Americans would probably be of little consequence to most Americans had they not immigrated to the United States from a communist country and not concentrated their settlement in the two metropolitan areas of Miami and Union City–West New York. If, instead, they were dispersed throughout all fifty states, their numbers in any particular location would have been so small that they would have been inconsequential in affecting either local or national politics. In fact, it has only been recently that Cubans have played a major role in the politics of Miami and Union City–West New York because it was not until the 1970s that a significant percentage began to acquire American citizenships status with its concomitant voting rights. In addition, the second-generation Cuban-Americans, who were the first to be born in the United States, were only just beginning to reach voting age in 1980.

While surveying the politics of Cuban-Americans it is relevant to distinguish between their exile and immigrant political roles. As noted in Chapter 3, many of the Cuban refugees who arrived during the early 1960s believed that their stay in this country would be of short duration. They were convinced that the Castro government would soon lose control and they would be able to return home to a free Cuba. For instance, in 1966 the University of Miami's Center for Advanced International Studies conducted a poll in which they asked a sample of Cubans living in metropolitan Miami if they thought that there would be a successful counterrevolution in Cuba against the Castro government. Less than 22 percent said no, while 51 percent answered affirmatively, and 27 percent said they did not know.[1] As time wore on, however, it became apparent that their stay in the United States would be longer than originally anticipated. They began to adjust to American lifestyles and their desire and hopes for returning to their island of origin decreased. Until this time their political thoughts were directed primarily toward the politics of Cuba, but by the late 1960s it became apparent that they were beginning to become more interested in American politics. This fundamental shift in focus, from an exile perspective to that of permanent immigrants, became clear for the majority by the 1970s.

Exile Politics

Given the fact that many of the Cuban migrants who arrived in the United States in 1959 and during the early 1960s expected to be returning soon to their homeland, it is logical that they would involve themselves in political activities oriented toward Cuba.[2] In 1960 a number of Miami-based groups were formed that became active in exile politics. One that received a great deal of attention from the news media was the Anti-Castro Liberation Alliance. It maintained close ties with the Cuban underground and frequently reported news regarding the achievements of anti-Castro guerrilla forces in Cuba. Among its leaders were two well-known former Castro military officers, Pedro Diaz Lanz and Nino Diaz.

In 1961 political activities increased among the exile organizations and on January 23, 1961, a meeting was held in Miami in an attempt to organize approximately 60 exile groups into an effective force for the overthrow of the Castro government. The meeting was not a success because it quickly became apparent that the only common bond they had was the desire to unseat the Havana regime. They could not agree on who should coordinate their efforts or what type of government would replace Castro's if they were successful. However, in the following March two of the strongest exile groups merged, The Revolutionary Movement of the People and The Democratic Revolutionary Front. The new organization was named the National Revolutionary Council and was headed by the former premiere of Castro's government, José Miro Cardona. It had as its focus four primary goals: (1) the overthrow of Castro, (2) the holding of free elections for a new government, (3) the return of property confiscated by the Castro government to its former owners, and (4) the continuation of economic and social reform in Cuba within a democratic framework.

On April 7, 1961, it was reported in the press that Cuban exile forces had been training in the United States and Central America for almost nine months for an invasion of Cuba. It was estimated by *The New York Times* that between 5,000 and 6,000 men were involved in these exercises. The Revolutionary Council was supposedly directing the operations, but it is clear that the United States Central Intelligence Agency also provided advice and funding. A period of frenzied political activity developed within the Little Havana community of Miami. The preparations for an attack on Cuba were an open secret. Plans were discussed on the streets, in Cuban cafes, in restaurants, and almost everywhere else Cubans exiles congregated. Local newspapers frequently reported on incidents in the military camps located in south Florida. Many exile doctors joined the cause and made large purchases of medical supplies and blood plasma. Special boats equipped with high-powered engines and powerful radio transmitters made frequent runs from the Florida Keys to Cuba to make contact with the anti-Castro underground forces on the island. When the Bay of Pigs invasion was announced on April 17, political interest was at its high point. Cuban males flocked to the various exile organizations to volunteer their services. A number of Americans also offered to join the rebel forces, as did a large number of former Hungarian freedom fighters.

The Bay of Pigs invasion was a dismal failure, with most of the rebels being either captured or killed. Although many exiles became disillusioned with this turn of events, some of the groups continued to plan for another invasion. However, a second full-scale invasion never materialized. Still, during the rest of 1961 and throughout 1962 arms were transported clandestinely to Cuba and many small-scale raids took place. The results of the Cuban Missile Crisis in 1962 marked the turning point in Cuban exile activities, since the United States government agreed not to intervene militarily in Cuba as a condition for the Soviet Union's withdrawal of its offensive missiles from the island. A survey of Miami Cubans conducted in 1963 determined that almost 43 percent had changed their opinion of the United States government as a result of the Missile Crisis. About two-thirds of these people indicated that their opinions were less favorable than before.[3] Many refugees realized that without United States backing, the odds against their cause being successful were overwhelming. In 1963 the Cuban Revolutionary Council went out of existence.

It is easy to gain the mistaken impression that most of the Cuban exiles who arrived during the early 1960s were wealthy extremists with Fascist leanings who only wanted to recoup the property and social position they had lost as a result of Castro's revolution. It is true that the early exiles came from all walks of life in Cuba, although the wealthy were more than proportionately selected from the island's population. They were not all supporters of Batista or against Castro's movement in 1959. A survey conducted in 1963 of Cuban exiles living in Miami found that 70 percent of the people interviewed were in favor of the downfall of Fulgencio Batista's government. A second similar survey undertaken in 1967 found that 55 percent of its respondents agreed with the demise of Batista's regime.[4] Another survey in Miami conducted in 1963, found that 23 percent of the immigrant Cuban adults interviewed had participated in some manner in anti-Batista activities prior to Castro's victory.[5] Furthermore, most surveys that were undertaken during the early 1960s have indicated that between one-third to one-half of the Cuban exiles at one time supported Fidel Castro's revolution.[6] When asked if a revolution was necessary in Cuba in

1959, 46 percent of the respondents to a survey conducted in 1967 said that they felt it was.[7] Another study carried out in the early 1970s found that only 14 percent of its respondents felt that revolutionary reform was necessary, but another 48 percent agreed that some type of extensive reform should have taken place. Approximately 32 percent said that a little reform was called for and only 6 percent were in favor of no reform.[8]

Since 1963 the membership and activity levels of Cuban exile organizations have continually declined. The majority now realize that it is not possible for them to be a factor in most political events taking place in Cuba. Most of the former exile military leaders have faded into American life and now concentrate their efforts on promoting the well-being of their families and other Cubans living permanently in the U.S. There are still, however, a few hardliners who cannot accept the realities of the existing situation. Some have joined one of several secretive militant organizations, such as Alpha 66 and Omega 7, which occasionally promote acts of violence as a means of trying to suppress an increasingly more liberal view of Cuban politics. They especially oppose efforts to restore diplomatic and trading relations between the United States and Cuba. For instance, in January 1983 two businesses in Miami were bombed by members of Omega 7. One of the businesses affected was a Cuban-American cigar factory that has been bombed seven times during the last three years. The other was a Cuban-owned travel agency that has been active in promoting tours to Cuba. A third bomb was discovered unexploded outside of the offices of a local Spanish-language periodical, *Replica* which has supported a resumption of trade relations between Cuba and the United States.[9] These acts of terrorism are limited to an extremely small number of militants and are not condoned by the vast majority of Cuban-Americans.

There is an apparent negative relationship between participation in exile political organizations and adaptivity to life in the United States. Many of those who continue to participate in exile political groups have not been very successful in adjusting to living in this country. As a consequence, they continue to dream of the overthrow of Castro and their triumphant return to Cuba. The types of persons who are most likely to fall into this category are middle aged or elderly males who were either lawyers or businessmen in Cuba before moving to the United States.

It is generally conceded that older people have more difficulty adapting to new living conditions. It has also been found that a person is most receptive to change during the pre-adolescent ages. Another significant finding is that immigrant Cuban women have more readily adjusted to living in the United States than their male counterparts. Four reasons have been offered as an explanation for this. First, Cuban women have been more readily hired than men in many lines of work. Also, it has been suggested that females find it easier to accept employment in positions that are below their qualifications and regard this condition as less of a threat to their egos than Cuban males. Second, American society affords more independence for women than did the traditional male-dominated Latin society that characterized Cuba until 1959. Third, it has been reported that the adversity that many Cuban families have faced in their adjustment to life in the United States has sometimes strengthened husband-wife relationships. It is now more difficult for a husband to maintain a mistress in the United States than it was in Cuba, especially if he is not as well-off financially here. Fourth, some psychologists suggest that women are innately more flexible than men and for this reason also they adjust more easily to new circumstances.[10]

When it comes to occupational classes, it is clear that among Cuban professionals, former lawyers and businessmen have had the greatest difficulty in adjusting to American life. A survey conducted in the early 1970s found that only 16 percent of those who were lawyers in Cuba were able to continue this profession in the United States. The comparable figure for businessmen was 59 percent. On the other hand, 97 percent of those who were engineers and scientists in Cuba were practicing the same profession in America. The figure for medical doctors was only slightly lower at 91 percent. For teachers the figure was 69 percent. Certainly, the ability of a refugee to continue his or her profession in this country helps in the adaptation process. Conversely, an inability to adjust in this manner will become a source of frustration. Many of the exiles who have this problem, like those who show poor adjustment patterns in other areas of their lives, will tend to cling to the past. This makes them more likely to become involved in an exile political organization. Through such involvement they are able to sublimate their frustrations by associating with other people who may be in a similar situation and by plotting for a triumphant return to Cuba.[11]

The anti-Castro lobby at the national level received a major boost in 1981 with formation of the Washington-based Cuban-American National Foundation. Composed of an influential group of Cuban-American businessmen, the foundation coalesced around the campaign to establish Radio Martí, a proposed station backed by the federal government to broadcast "the truth" about the United States and about Castro to Cuba.[12] Through the Coalition for a Free Cuba, the Foundation's political action committee, sizable contributions have been given to the election campaigns of various candidates from Texas to Florida who support the Radio Martí proposal and whose records are anti-Castro. On May 20, 1983, the Foundation sponsored a trip to Miami by President Reagan to visit Little Havana and to address the Cuban-American community. These efforts illustrate not only a continuing interest in exile politics, but also reflect the growing involvement of Cuban-Americans in the domestic political process.

United States Politics

An obvious prerequisite for voting participation in the American political system is United States citizenship. But before an individual applies of citizenship a decision must be made to remain permanently in the United States, or at least to designate it as his or her home country. The vast majority of the earliest arrivals from Cuba after the Castro revolution had intended to return as soon as Castro was overthrown. A survey conducted in Miami in 1966 found that 83 percent of the Cuban respondents said they would return to Cuba if the island were to become free.[13] A similar survey in West New York found that 71.2 would either certainly or probably return.[14] However, as time wore on these percentages were reversed. A study conducted in Dade County in 1977 determined that 93 percent intended to remain permanently.[15] A follow-up study in West New York undertaken in 1979 found that less than 25 percent wanted to return to live in Cuba.[16] A longitudinal investigation carried out in Miami in 1973, 1976, and 1979 questioned a sample of newly arrived Cuban immigrants about their desire to return to Cuba if the Castro government were to be overthrown. In 1973, 60.0 percent said they would return. In 1976 the figure had declined to 50.5 percent and by 1979 it had fallen to only 22.6 percent.[17] Clearly there is a negative relationship between length of residence in the United States and the desire to return to Cuba. The United States has become an area of permanent residence for most Cuban-Americans and a place where economic, social, and political roots are deepening as time progresses.

The increasing preference for remaining in the United States is paralleled by a growing desire for American citizenship. Again, length of residence is directly related to both the achievement of citizenship and the desire to attain citizenship status. One obvious reason for the link between length of residence and becoming an American citizen is that the United States government requires that once an individual receives legal permanent residency status, a five year wait is necessary before that person can apply for citizenship.[18] The decision to become an American citizen is another important indicator of assimilation because it requires that the person becoming naturalized renounce the citizenship that was held before. To a Cuban, this usually formalizes the realization that returning to Cuba to live is no longer practical or desirable. In 1970 approximately 25 percent of all Latins living in metropolitan Miami were United States citizens. By 1978 the figure had risen to 43 percent. Furthermore, of those who were not yet citizens, 77 percent planned to apply.[19] In West New York, none of the Cubans questioned in a 1968 survey was an American citizen. At that time 44 percent wanted to become citizens; 33.9 percent did not want citizenship status; and 22 percent could not make up their minds. In 1979 there was a dramatic change in these figures. By that time 40.3 percent had attained citizenship status; another 43.7 percent wanted to become citizens; 6 percent did not want citizenship; and 10 percent had no preference.

Once citizenship has been attained, the political behavior of Cuban-Americans can be described as being participatory, personal, anti-communist, and conservative. It is participatory in the sense that an exceptionally large percentage of Cuban-American citizens both register to vote and exercise their voting rights at the polls. In 1978, 84.3 percent of the Cubans living in West New York who were eligible to vote registered to vote. In this same year, only 62.6 percent of the total eligible-to-vote population for the United States registered. In addition, the Cuban's voting participation rate was about 10 percentage points higher than for the entire American population.[21] In November 1981, the city of Miami held a mayoral election. Of those eligible to vote, the voter turnout rates were 58 percent for Latins, 38 percent for Anglos, and somewhat more than 50 percent for blacks.[22] These figures suggest that Cubans will exert even more of an influence in future elections in both Miami and the Union City–West New York as more of them become eligible to vote.[23]

Cuban-American politics are personal, in the sense that most Latin American politics are personal. This tendency represents a refusal to deal with the government as a bureaucratic and impersonal institution. It is a face-to-face approach, in which there is a belief that to obtain a favor a person needs to know (or have access to) a contact, someone who personally knows someone else in a position of power. In English the system is known as "power brokering," while in Spanish it is called *personalismo*. Most Cuban-American politicians are well aware of the political expectations that friends and relatives have once they achieve an elected position. How they react to such pressures varies, but it is true that it helps to have friends and relatives in influential positions, at least as much as in conventional American politics.[24]

Persons of Cuban descent tend to be both strongly anti-communist and conservative in their political leanings as a result of their experiences with the Castro government in Cuba. Both tendencies favor membership in the Republican Party. A study of voting patterns in neighborhoods in Dade County, both before and after they became dominated by Cuban residents, showed a marked shift in voting preferences. First the majority supported the Democratic Party candidates and later voted in favor of the Republican

Party. In addition, a survey of over 500 Cuban emigrants living in greater Miami found that 73 percent supported the Republican Party and most favored conservative issues.[25] It has further been estimated that during the 1980 presidential election more than 90 percent of Dade County's Cuban-born voters cast their ballots for Ronald Reagan.[26] The general preference for the Republican Party has significantly changed the reputation of Miami, which used to be known as a staunchly liberal enclave that traditionally could be counted on to vote in favor of the Democrats. The Cuban-American support for Republicans can be linked to strong feelings against communism, the Bay of Pigs fiasco and the results of the Cuban Missile Crisis during which the United States agreed not to invade Cuba. Many Cubans clearly remember that the latter two events occurred during the administration of a Democratic President, John F. Kennedy. In addition, many Cubans feel that Jimmy Carter, the last Democratic President, ineffectively handled the issue of Soviet weapons and troops being stationed in Cuba during 1980. There is, however, some hope for support for Democrats by Cuban-Americans. One study has shown that the Cuban preference for Republican candidates weakens as their length of residence in the United States increases.[27]

Cuban Municipalities in Exile

Many immigrant groups in America have formed sociopolitical organizations. In most cases they function principally as voluntary mutual support societies. In this capacity, they serve as adaptive institutions that attempt through various organizational activities to lessen the strains of adjustment and acculturation.[28] For arriving émigrés, for example, they may hold orientation sessions, offer educational and language classes, and provide information about housing, job placement, and government assistance programs; direct financial and material relief are also common. Concurrently, they endeavor to strengthen the consciousness of a group's culture by encouraging the maintenance of traditional practices and institutions. This role is particularly important in helping preserve a sense of ethnic identity for second- and third-generation immigrants. Politically, they tend to be more involved during the early period of development in the politics of the homeland, especially if their immigration was motivated by political reasons. Through time, however, the emphasis usually shifts to domestic political concerns; although the politics of the mother country may continue to hold greater interest for older first-generation émigrés. These general characteristics apply to the largest network of voluntary sociopolitical associations in the Cuban-American community in Miami, known as *municipios en el exilio* (municipalities in exile).

In pre-Castro Cuba, there were 126 *municipios*, or townships, that existed in the six provinces of Pinar del Río, La Habana, Matanzas, Las Villas, Camagüey and Oriente. Administratively, they were comparable to counties in the United States. They ranged in size, according to the 1953 Cuban National Census (the last federal census taken before the revolution), from Havana with a population of 787,765 to La Salud (also in the Province of La Habana) with a population of 5,863. In respect to the percentage of population classified as urban, they extended from Regla (a suburb of Habana) with 100 percent to Consolacion del Norte in Pinar del Río with only 12.1 percent of its population residing in urban places.

Beginning in the mid-1960s, at the time of the Freedom Flights, the former residents of various *municipios* living in Miami joined together to lend assistance to new arrivals who came from their home township. Through time their activities were expanded to include social and political functions, and formal organizations were established. Currently, there are 114 officially recognized associations of municipalities in exile in Miami.[29] Membership and participation in the sponsored programs and organizational activities vary widely. Some of the larger *municipios*, such as Havana and Santiago de Cuba, have in excess of 1,000 members. Most of the associations gather only periodically, once or twice a year (often on the birthday of their patron saint), typically in rented halls or at restaurants. Over 20 of the *municipios*, however, have permanent buildings.[30] They are located primarily in Little Havana or in Hialeah. Inside, the buildings are usually decorated with portraits of famous Cuban patriots (especially José Martí), old photographs, flags, and assorted memorabilia from Cuba.

The *municipios* differ from a majority of other immigrant associations in at least three ways: (1) membership is open to a broad spectrum of social, occupational, and age groups (though older members clearly predominate); (2) they are united by a single federation (*Municipios de Cuba en el Exilio*), but function independently; and (3) political ideology and activism are central organizational goals.

The stated aims of the parent federation, which represents 110 of the *municipios*, apply generally to those of all the associations. These goals are: (1) to promote the values of their cultural heritage: (2) to promote democracy and to combat communism; and (3) to extend aid to newly arriving refugees.[31] In respect to their political role, each of the *municipios* is represented on the *Junta Patriotica Cubana*, which is an umbrella organization that coordinates the anti-Castro efforts of nearly 200 Cuban exile groups. Fund-raising is one of the important ways in which the *municipios* aid the anti-Castro campaign. In general, the *municipios* have attempted to avoid local political issues that might disrupt the unity that binds the organizations. Some, however, provide information about citizenship and

Figure 10.1 The headquarters of the Municipio de Santiago de Cuba en el Exilio *are housed in this building located in Little Havana. (Photo by Jeff Murphree.)*

have been involved in voter registration drives. On an informal, if not formal, basis interest in local politics appears to be increasing.

The *municipios* also offer a variety of activities and programs to help perpetuate Cuban traditions and to maintain contact among members. In addition to the gatherings and civic and charity efforts, there are also celebrations in honor of religious and patriotic holidays that hold special significance for Cubans. Some local *municipio* customs have likewise been preserved. In the *Municipio de Santiago de Cuba en el Exilio*, for example, at midnight on New Year's Eve the flag is raised in front of the *municipio's* building in the heart of Little Havana. Tradition holds that if the flag waves it will be a good year; if it does not, it is considered a bad omen.[32] Most of the *municipios* also publish monthly newsletters. They typically contain information about births, deaths, marriages, and social news of interest to their members. Many as well have articles and photographs dealing with the history of the *municipio* in Cuba. In an effort to reach out to the greater community, in April 1983 over 90 of the *municipios* participated in the First Annual Municipalities in Exile Fair, held in the Orange

Bowl.[33] Beyond the food and entertainment that was provided, each of the *municipios* set up booths that displayed exhibits and information about their history and their role in exile.

Notes

1. Laureano F. Batista, "Political Sociology of the Cuban Exile, 1959–1968" (M.A. thesis, University of Miami, 1969), p. 147.
2. Much of this section draws freely from Patrick Lee Gallagher, *The Cuban Exile: A Socio-Political Analysis* (New York: Arno Press, 1980), pp. 121–145.
3. Batista, op. cit., p. 148.
4. Ibid., p. 138.
5. Richard R. Fagen, Richard A. Brody, and Thomas J. O'Leary, *Cubans in Exile: Disaffection and Revolution* (Stanford, Calif.: Stanford University Press, 1968), p. 51.
6. Thomas J. O'Leary, "Cubans in Exile: Political Attitudes and Political Participation" (Ph.D. dissertation, Stanford University, 1967), p. 33; and Batista, op. cit., p. 139.
7. Batista, op. cit., p. 143
8. Gallagher, op. cit., p. 191.
9. Richard Wallace, "Bombs Rock Little Havana Firms," *The Miami Herald*, January 12, 1983, p. 1D.
10. Gallagher, op. cit., pp. 135–139.
11. Ibid., pp. 139–143.
12. Helga Silva, "Group Is a Cuban-Born Who's-Who," *The Miami Herald*, May 21, 1983, p. 9A.
13. Batista, op. cit., p. 146.
14. Eleanor Meyer Rogg, *The Assimilation of Cuban Exiles: The Role of Community and Class* (New York: Aberdeen Press, 1974), pp. 93–95.
15. Aida Thomas Levitan, "Hispanics in Dade County: Their Characteristics and Needs" (Miami: Latin Affairs, Office of County Manager, Metropolitan Dade County, printed report, Spring 1980), p. 20.
16. Eleanor Meyer Rogg and Rosemary Santana Cooney, *Adaption and Adjustment of Cubans: West New York, New Jersey* (New York: Monograph No. 5, Hispanic Research Center, Fordham University, 1980), p. 18.
17. Alejandro Portes, Juan M. Clark, And Manuel Lopez, "Six Years Later, The Process of Incorporation of Cuban Exiles in the United States: 1973–1979," *Cuban Studies* 11:1–24, July 1981.
18. William Francis Mackey and Von Nieda Beebe, *Bilingual Schools for a Bilingual Community* (Rowley, Mass.: Newbury House Publishers.1977), p. 39.
19. Levitan, op. cit., p. 23.
20. Rogg and Cooney, op. cit., p. 29.
21. Ibid., p. 29.
22. James Kelly, "Trouble in Paradise: South Florida Hit by a Hurricane of Crime, Drugs and Refugees," *Time* 118:22–32, November 23, 1981.
23. Nicholas Acocella, "Politics: Little Havana in Little Italy," *Attenzione* 21:93–96, January 1980.
24. William R. Amlong, "Politics Cuban-Style Rule Miami,"*The Miami Herald*, May 5, 1981, p. 1B.
25. Paul S. Salter and Robert C. Mings. "The Projected Impact of Cuban Settlement on Voting Patterns in Metropolitan Miami, Florida," *The Professional Geographer* 24:123–131, May 1972.

26. Guillermo Martinez, "Cuban-Americans Love Reagan's Latin Stand," *The Miami Herald*, May 2, 1983, p. 23A.
27. Francisco Raimundo Wong, "The Political Behavior of Cuban Migrants" (Ph.D. dissertation, University of Michigan, 1974), pp. 61–65.
28. Saskia Sassen-Koob, "Formal and Informal Associations: Dominicans and Colombians in New York," *International Migration Review* 13:314–332, Summer 1979.
29. Sandra Dibble, "Memories Live On in *Municipios*," *The Miami Herald*, July 18, 1982, Neighbors Section, pp. 32–34.
30. Ileana Oroza, "The Traditionalist," *The Miami Herald*, July 4, 1978, p. 16A.
31. Paul Wasserman and Jean Morgan, eds., *Ethnic Information Sources of the United States* (Detroit: Gale Research Company, 1976), p. 102.
32. Dibble, op. cit., p. 34.
33. Barbara Gutierrez, "Exile Municipal Groups Go to Town with First Festival," *The Miami Herald*, April 8, 1983, p. 9C.

11

The Cuban-American Family and Youth: Acculturation and Assimilation

Change is a central and unavoidable aspect of the immigrant experience in America. Initially, the acceptance of American ways may be resisted, especially among the first generation immigrants clinging to familiar and comfortable cultural patterns of their homeland. For them, the new culture is unknown and often suspect. Yet in spite of the most diligent and self-conscious efforts of immigrant groups to preserve their heritage, changes inevitably occur. The dynamics of acculturation and assimilation, however, proceed differentially; some elements (such as language and adornment) tend to vanish quickly, whereas others (such as religion and cuisine) may persist for generations, perhaps even indefinitely. Typically the pace of change accelerates along generational lines as rates of out-marriage, movement from traditional ethnic enclaves and, of course, acceptance of the ways of the host culture increase.

Although these changes are institutional and exist at a group level, they are also personal. Perhaps most immediately and intimately, they are felt in the home and among the youth. In this context, it is often the family that suffers the brunt of conflict between the new and the old cultures. The accepted structure of the family and the role of its members may be questioned and ultimately re-aligned. This, clearly, is the case among Cuban-Americans.

In this final chapter, therefore, the initial focus is on the Cuban-American family and youth. In order to place these topics into a broader perspective, the concern shifts lastly to the perplexing and often controversial question of assimilation as it relates specifically to the Cuban-American experience.

The Cuban-American Family

Generally speaking, the family has played a somewhat different role in traditional Cuban society than it has in the United States. Prior to 1959, a

Cuban's self-confidence, sense of security, and identity were established primarily through family relationships. In contrast to the individulalism of the United States, which values an individual in terms of his or her abilities to compete independently for socioeconomic status, the culture of Cuba viewed life as a network of personal relationships. The Cuban relies and trusts persons; he or she knows that in times of trouble a close friend or relative can be counted upon for needed assistance. A Cuban relies less on impersonal secondary relationships and generally does not trust or place much faith in large organizations. At least this was the case in Cuba prior to Castro's revolution. Such an attitude is not unique to Cuba but rather is typical of most Latin American societies.

One way in which the greater emphasis that is placed on the Cuban family can be illustrated is through its use of surnames. English custom in United States society dictates that family names be derived partilinealy. In Latin American societies it is more common for a person to have two surnames, representing both the father's and mother's sides of the family. For instance, a man with the name of Ricardo Gomez Gonzales had his name derived in the following way. His given name is Ricardo and his two surnames are Gomez and Gonzales. Gomez was his father's family name and Gonzales was his mother's family name. Suppose that a woman by the name of Maria Garcia Rivera married Mr. Gomez. Her new name would become Maria Garcia de Gomez. She would retain her father's surname, drop her mother's name, and add her husband's father's name after the "de." In fact, for formal occasions, even more complicated combinations of names frequently are used. To avoid confusion, many Cuban-Americans have adopted the American custom of using only the surname of the father.

Another characteristic of traditional Cuban society that illustrated a reliance on personal relationships is the institution known as *compadrazgo*. It is somewhat similar to the tradition of godparents in the United States, except that it is usually taken more seriously by Cubans and often involves a higher level of personal obligation. Under the *compadrazgo* system a set of *compadres* are selected for each child. These are best thought of as being "companion parents" with the child's natural parents. Sometimes they are selected when the parents are married, but they might be decided upon at the time of the child's baptism or perhaps confirmation. The *compadres* are sometimes relatives, but often they are not. But if they are not blood relatives, they become de facto members of the family upon becoming *compadres*. The purpose of a *compadre* is to offer both economic and moral assistance to the family whenever it is needed. He or she may feel freer to give advice in regard to family problems than a brother or sister of the father or mother would. It is essential that *compadres* live close to the family they are associated with, so that frequent contact can be made and the necessary obligations honored.

In the traditional Cuban family there was a sharp distinction between the role of men and women, with a double standard being applied in work, play, and sex. The wife was expected to stay at home and attend to the running of the household and care for the children. A pattern of male-dominance prevailed, where most of the major family decisions were made by the husband. The tradition of *machismo* dictated that males demonstrate virility through physical strength, courage, and business success. It was common, and considered proper, for males to have extra-marital affairs. Whether or not a husband had a regular mistress was frequently more affected by economics than conscience. Daughters and wives were to be protected against temptation. A strict tradition of chaperoning was in effect for respectable, unmarried women who dated.[1]

Sociologists have developed a concept known as *resource theory* for explaining the position of decision-making power that the members of any particular family have relative to each other. An individual gains in power if the resources that he or she contributes to the family increases. These resources may be economic, intellectual, or emotional.[2] One of the important circumstances that affected the adjustment of Cuban immigrants was the economic difficulties that many faced upon their arrival in the United States. Often, the husband would be unable to find work, or would find work at a lower status level than he had experienced in Cuba. As a result, it became necessary for many wives to enter the labor force to help contribute to the support of the family. In 1980 slightly over half of all women over 16 years of age of Cuban descent in the United States were in the labor force. A survey of women in West New York found that less than one-fourth worked in Cuba before coming to the United States.[3] And as the wife's resource contribution to the family became greater through her employment, usually her power to make decisions also increased, while that of her husband declined. A recent study of Cuban women in Washington, D.C., concludes that their entrance into the labor force is the single most important change in their lives as immigrants.[4] As a result, the traditional patriarchal family structure for Cuban-Americans began to change toward greater equality in decision-making abilities for husbands and wives. Length of residence in the United States and degree of association with Americans were also positively associated with level of equality or independence within the family.[5] As a result, Cuban-American families are less male dominated and the roles of husbands and wives are less segregated than the traditional Latin American family norm that typified Cuba before 1959.

Despite the fact that Cuban family structure has changed in the United States, it is still different enough from the American norm to cause some conflict between first- and second-generation Cuban-Americans. Studies of acculturation stresses among Cubans living in the United States have found that the second generation, which was the first born in America, generally adopts Anglo attitudes and behavior patterns more quickly than their parents. Sometimes a crisis in authority emerges, as the parents find themselves being led and instructed in new ways by their children. Many of the traditional norms of the Cuban family became labeled old-fashioned. Chaperoning for dating, for example, has become a focal point of tension in many families. Many second-generation Cuban-Americans feel they are caught between two cultures, being neither completely Cuban nor American. They want to maintain selected aspects of both cultures, and as a result feel that they do not belong to (or are not completely accepted by) either.

Another aspect of the Cuban-American family that distinguishes it from the contemporary American family is the tendency for Cuban households to include relatives in the nuclear family. The U.S. Census Bureau indicates that about 9 percent of all persons of Cuban descent live in households where they are "other relatives" (other than wife or child) of the head of the household. The corresponding figure for all persons of Spanish origin is about 6 percent, while for the non-Spanish it is approximately 4 percent.[6] Often this additional relative is a widowed and dependent grandparent, who came to the United States after the nuclear family arrived. Because so many Cuban-American women work, the elderly became important as housekeepers and babysitters and for passing on the culture and language to the new-generation children.[7]

One important factor that is having an impact on the survival of the traditional Cuban family in the United States is the high out-marriage rate of Cuban-Americans. For 1970, 17 percent of all women of Cuban descent had married non-Cubans.[8] However, many of the marriages to Cubans took place in Cuba before arrival in the United States. When only second-generation, American-born women are considered, it was found that 46 percent of those married had married non-Spanish husbands. The comparable figures for women of Puerto Rican and Mexican descent were 33 and 16 percent, respectively.[9] Second-generation Cubans have exhibited an extraordinarily high rate of out-marriage, which would appear to indicate a very rapid tendency toward assimilation. A recent comparative study of out-marriage patterns of Hispanic groups living in New York City determined that Cubans had the highest out-group marriage rates. It also found that the degree of out-marriage is much higher among second-generation,

American-born children than for their foreign-born Hispanic parents. In addition, persons with higher socioeconomic status, those who were older at the time they married, and those who had been married more than once, all showed higher out-marriage rates. The relative degree of spatial concentration proved to be the strongest determinant of exogamous marriage rates. Groups that were more dispersed residentially throughout New York City exhibited higher out-marriage rates.[10] The rate of intergroup marriage was also considerably higher for Cubans living in New York than for those living in New Jersey and Florida, possibly because more Cubans live in New Jersey and Florida.[11]

It is clear that most of the Cubans who immigrated to the United States have carried with them the tradition of the Cuban family. This tradition emphasizes personal relationships, the use of both maternal and paternal family names, the institution of *compadrazgo*, and a double standard for male and female behavior. However, the longer the period of residence in the United States the more this tradition erodes. For instance, most second-generation Cuban-Americans seldom use their maternal surnames, the significance of *compadres* has become diluted, the sexual double standard is weakening, and out-marriage is becoming very common. Nevertheless, despite these changes, the typical Cuban-American family is still significantly different from the typical United States family norm.

Cuban-American Youth

It has been a quarter of a century since the Castro Revolution. The 1980 census (which was taken before the massive Mariel exodus) revealed that 40.6 percent of the total Cuban-American population was below the age of 25.[12] In Dade County alone it is estimated that there are over 225,000 Cubans in this age group. Although a majority were born in Cuba, most left the island at an early age; Cuba is often just a vague memory for them. Many others, of course, were born in this country. For these Cuban youths, most or all of their lives have been spent in the United States and they have been duly influenced by American values and institutions. Yet at the same time their Cuban heritage is typically instilled by strong familial ties and a social system that places great value in the preservation of Cuban culture in the United States. Consequently, they are the products of two cultures. In this sense, they form a new subcultural group unique in its mixture of elements drawn from the two traditions.

There are, of course, potential advantages as well as liabilities that young Cuban-Americans face in this position between two cultures. Ideally, it affords them the opportunity of capitalizing on the best features of each group and of establishing an extended social network that bridges the gap between the two. Some Cuban youths, in fact, have shaped a pattern of existence in which they feel equally comfortable in either setting and enjoy the differences. In order to accomplish this transition they must have command of both languages. Their bilingual skills and familiarity with the two cultures also greatly enhance their employment opportunities, especially in Miami.

At the opposite extreme, for a number of young Cuban-Americans this situation has led to an identity crisis; they do not feel completely Cuban or American. This has led a few to Anglicize their names, either informally or officially, in order to feel more American.[13] Some lack sufficient development in either Spanish or English to function effectively and without fear of embarrassment in more formal setting in either culture. For these young people, their economic opportunities and lifestyle alternatives may be severely restricted. It is not unusual for them to limit their voluntary social interactions to fellow young Cubans who share similar circumstances. Because of its large concentration of Cuban-American youths, Miami may be the only place where some young Cubans raised in south Florida feel a sense of belonging and a measure of security in numbers.[14]

Individual rates of adjustment for young Cuban-Americans vary widely between the two extremes suggested above. It is probably true that all face a certain amount of conflict resolution between the often opposing values and traditions of their Cuban heritage and the American society in which they live. In most cases, concessions are made to both cultures. Double-role-playing is also common. At home, for example, they may "act" more Cuban than at school or with friends in which they "act" more American. The degree to which either Cuban or American elements are stressed tends to vary as well by age or life stage. During the early and middle teenage years, for instance, American ways are often emphasized. This is largely a consequence of peer group pressure and an emerging sense of independence. At marriage and especially at the stage of early parenthood, however, there is frequently a reaffirmation of their Cuban heritage as they begin to consider the values they wish to pass on to their children.[15]

Some of the established Cuban traditions that have generated considerable conflict in the past between Cuban-American parents and children are gradually changing. The custom of a chaperon (usually a parent or older relative) accompanying unmarried couples on dates is one example. Although chaperons are still part of the social scene for a vast majority of younger teenagers, many parents now allow older teenagers and young adults to go on dates alone; group functions and double dating, however, are strongly encouraged. Other customs have not changed as quickly, especially regarding girls and young women, who tend to be extremely protected by their families. Unmarried females are still expected to live at home until they marry, even if they work and could afford to move into their own house or apartment. It has been suggested that this is one reason why a higher percentage of Cuban-American female college students attend schools in or near their hometowns than do their male counterparts.[16]

Cuban-American youth have fashioned a distinctive lifestyle that freely incorporates elements of both cultures. In some cases these elements are mixed together to create a synthesis that is unique and somewhat particular to the place in which the fusion occurs. It is a dynamic lifestyle that is continually in flux and evolving in response to new influences and shifts in popular culture. It also serves an important social function for many young people in the Cuban-American community by fostering a sense of subcultural identity.

Language is the most obvious area where this process has occurred. Spanish and English words and phrases are mixed and jumbled together to form a new linguistic synthesis that has been popularly labeled "Spanglish."[17] For perhaps a majority of Cuban-American youths it is the language they feel most comfortable speaking, at least among themselves. Yet while Spanish may be spoken at home and Spanglish when with Cuban friends, English-language movies and television programs are preferred over those in Spanish.

Music is another cultural element that has tremendous crossover appeal. Most Cuban-American young people have been thoroughly exposed to and appreciate both Latin and American music. They may listen to radio stations that play American rock or jazz or country and western, and then turn the dial to a Spanish language station and catch the latest *salsa* sounds. Some of the Spanish radio stations in Miami aimed at a younger audience, such as WQTU-FM ("Super Q"), incorporate popular American rock tunes into their program. The two musical traditions are also commonly fused, giving rise to new musical expressions.[18] A number of popular young Cuban-American groups in Miami, such as the Miami Sound Machine, Alma, and Clouds, have enjoyed commercial success in recent years by blending contemporary Latin and American musical styles.

A host of other cultural elements from both traditions are likewise mixed. On the dance floor, for example, they may perform the latest disco dance on one occasion, and then on another dance the *rumba* or *chachachá*. Traditional Cuban food is generally served and enjoyed at home, but when dining out they prefer to go to an American fast-food restaurant and have the standard order of hamburgers, french fries, and a Coke. And while many Cuban-American girls and young women may prefer to wear the latest fashion in jeans, their mothers may insist that the jeans be tailored and pressed to avoid a casual appearance, which many Cuban parents consider to be inappropriate.

In certain instances, the results of these mixtures have been criticized by some Cuban-Americans, including young people, as representing the worst of both cultures. One phenomenon that has drawn criticism by many is the *Fiesta de Quince Anos*. On a Cuban girl's fifteenth birthday, it is customary to commemorate the occasion by giving a party. It is similar to a "coming out" or debutante celebration, and traditionally marked the age when girls were considered marriageable, or more recently, allowed to increase their social activities, including dating. In Cuba, the wealthy typically held *quince* parties at social clubs; *quinces* for the working class were more family-oriented and generally took place at home. In the United States, especially in Miami, they have become a major social event for many middle-class Cubans.[19] The parties have grown conspicuously in size and expense. It is not unusual for some families to spend thousands of dollars on the party, which may necessitate a "quince loan." In some cases, the parties have evolved into such big affairs that they would be more appropriately classified as extravaganzas, even spectacles, that attempt to exceed each other in grandeur and consumption.[20] One father, for example, rented the Orange Bowl for his daughter's *quince*! Girls have arrived at their parties in horse-drawn carriages, in helicopters, and in simulated rockets, while other have popped out of cakes and emerged from birdcages. A humor columnist for *El Herald*, George Childs, wrote about his vision of the ultimate *quince*: a girl is fired out of a cannon two blocks away, lands in a specially created fountain, while the Goodyear blimp drops 15 boys dressed as Robin Hood and 15 girls float down in Cleopatra costumes.[21] *Quince* celebrations have been used by some Cuban-Americans as a symbol of the success they have attained in the United States, one way of showing their financial well being. But they have been criticized as examples of American commercialization and materialism misapplied to an important Cuban tradition that could seriously damage its original meaning.

The Question of Assimilation

The idea that the United States is a melting pot for different ethnic groups is as old as the country itself. It was long held that the immigrants who arrived from the various European nations would melt into a new citizen, known as "the American." In 1908 Israel Zangwill's play *The Melting Pot* was first performed on Broadway in New York City. It was a story about a Russian Jew who had escaped the harsh realities of Russian anti-semitism by immigrating to the United States. The play was an instant success and at the same time popularized the phrase "melting pot." This notion of an amalgamation of nationalities became the theme of most assimilation studies, which indicated that the immigrants had become an integral part of

American society by the time of the third generation.[22] In 1963 Glazer and Moynihan finished what would become known as a classic study of the major ethnic groups in New York City, *Beyond the Melting Pot.* After careful analysis, they reached the conclusion that there was a basic flaw with the melting pot thesis—it never melted. After several decades of residence in the city, the blacks, Puerto Ricans, Jews, Italians, and Irish were still visibly different from each other. As time wore on and the process of assimilation began to take place, identity based on national origin tended to weaken. It was no longer possible to identify these people by their language, culture, or customs. Instead, identification began to rest more on common interests which became related to ethnic background, rather than constituting an ethnic background themselves. In other words, the ethnic groups became interest groups that maintained social cohesion through identification with issues and special events. For instance, Nazi persecution and the establishment of Israel became the focus of identification for the Jews; the reemergence of the Catholic school controversy in New York City did the same for the Irish and Italians; racial attitudes and discrimination was the central issue for the city's blacks; and the unique migration experiences of Puerto Ricans became their focus.[23]

CURRENT ASSIMILATION THEORY

As a result of the work of Glazer and Moynihan, and others who reached similar conclusions, the melting pot hypothesis has been discarded by most researchers studying ethnic topics and replaced by the concept of cultural pluralism. The notion of a pluralistic society does not imply that an immigrant culture will continue forever without change within American society. It recognizes that eventually every ethnic group's lifestyle will evolve into a form that is predominantly American. However, it also suggests that this process is best achieved when the culture of the immigrant group is given an opportunity to continue without restrictions.[24]

Most immigrant groups that have migrated to the United States in large numbers have established ethnic neighborhoods in their first origins, much as the Cubans have done in Miami and Union City-West New York. Invariably, this process has been criticized by many native residents because it was felt that these immigrant communities would prevent their members from assimilating into American society. However, it has become obvious to most researchers that these fears were unfounded. It has been a consistent finding in ethnic studies that as the immigrant population progressed through its second and third generations, the inevitable process worked itself out. As a result, the third generation was predominantly American, and no longer a product of foreign culture.

The significance of the philosophy of cultural pluralism is that it recognizes the benefits that are derived from not discouraging cultural maintenance. Virtually all ethnic studies over the past 30 years have found that culture is a stabilizing factor that helps a newly arrived immigrant adjust to a new social order. An ethnic enclave provides an island of security from which a gradual and less painful transition and acceptance of the American lifestyle can take place. On the other hand, a disintegration of culture is often attended by instability, insecurity, unrest, and possibly even hostility.[25]

In a study of Spanish-Americans, Jaffe, Cullen, and Boswell suggest that there is a natural life cycle that all ethnic groups evolve though as they gradually become more American and identify less with their countries of origin. Although the evolution toward becoming more American seems to be a process with very few exceptions, it proceeds at different speeds with different groups. For some it may take less than a century, but for others it may take much longer.[26]

Whatever the length of time, the assimilation process normally follows two phases. The first is cultural assimilation, whereby the ethnic group establishes working relationships with the new society through secondary group associations. During this phase most of the members begin to learn enough English so that they can transact business relationships. They also develop the ability to seek work and perform it satisfactorily. They are able to find a suitable place to live and learn to observe the law. In addition, they begin to participate in political life and take advantage of the educational system. The second phase is social assimilation, and essentially involves primary group relationships. During this stage the members of the ethnic groups gain entrance into elite cliques, clubs, and institutions of the Anglo majority. Large-scale intermarriage takes place and personal identification is more with American society. Feelings of prejudice and discrimination are lost and value conflicts become a thing of the past.[27]

WHERE DO CUBAN-AMERICANS FIT?

The Cuban-Americans have made remarkable progress in their adjustment to life in the United States. In the third chapter it was noted that the first immigrants to arrive from Cuba after the Castro takeover in 1959, were above average in terms of their educational background and entrepreneurial skills. As happened with most other ethnic groups, these first arrivals were able to establish an economic and cultural base that would ease the difficulties of adjustment for later waves of Cuban refugees, who were not so wealthy or skilled. The Cubans who chose not to locate in the ethnic enclaves of Miami and Union City—West New York settled mainly in other large cities where they received considerable government assistance under the Cuban Refugee Program.

By almost any measure it is clear that Cubans are becoming rapidly assimilated into American society, although they still are readily visible as an ethnic minority. Most of the first-generation immigrants from Cuba and their second-generation American-born children are well on the way toward social or structural assimilation. We think that this rapid assimilation can be seen most clearly in terms of five key indicators: (1) the residential patterns of Cuban-Americans, (2) their changing occupational structure, (3) family characteristics and fertility, (4) changing language patterns, and (5) their desire to remain in the United States and become citizens.

The degree to which an ethnic groups is residentially segregated from a host population is one primary indicator of cultural assimilation. As noted in chapter 5, during the early 1960s the Cuban-Americans living in metropolitan Miami were concentrated in the Little Havana area. By 1980 they had dispersed widely throughout Dade County.[28] Although there is still a tendency for Cubans to live in Cuban-dominated neighborhoods, there are many exceptions, especially in the outer fringe of the Cuban enclave. For instance, a poll conducted by *The Miami Herald* in 1978 of 500 non-Latins living in Dade County determined that 71 percent of the whites and 58 percent of the blacks surveyed live in neighborhoods where they had Cuban neighbors.[29] Clearly the Cubans are less segregated than either the black or Mexican-American populations living in the United States.

In addition to their residential patterns, it was noted in Chapter 6 that Cuban-Americans also are becoming more similar to Anglo Americans in terms of their occupational patterns. After a usual decline in occupational status upon their initial arrival in the United States, most experience considerable upward mobility as their length of residence increases. The younger and more highly educated Cuban immigrants have been especially successful in approaching the American occupational norms. Cubans now exhibit occupational characteristics that are more similar to those of the non-Spanish white population than to those of all Spanish-Americans. This is a significant finding, since the type of job a person has affects many other assimilation characteristics, such as income, place of residence, size of family, and general aspiration levels.

The fertility patterns and family structure of Cuban-Americans provide further evidence of their convergence toward non-Latin, Anglo culture. As noted in Chapter 6, the birthrates of Cuban females are now somewhat below those of white American women. The labor force participation rates for women of Cuban descent indicate that there are many working Cuban mothers, as is the case for many Anglo mothers. In this last chapter it has been shown that the patriarchical character of the traditional Cuban family is becoming weakened in the United States, as it evolves toward the American norm and away from the Latin American model. In addition, the American-born children of the Cuban immigrants are intermarrying at exceptionally high rates with non-Hispanic whites. This is perhaps the strongest piece of evidence of their American assimilation.

Most Cuban-Americans have given up the hope and desire of returning to Cuba, even if Castro were to be overthrown by a democratic regime. As a result, most either have (or would like to have) United States citizenship status. Those who possess citizenship exhibit high levels of participation in the American electoral process. Politically, they have become very well integrated into the American system. The increasing desire for United States citizenship is an indication that these individuals are identifying themselves more as Americans and less as Cubans. This tendency provides further evidence of social assimilation.

As noted in Chapter 7, in terms of language, Cuban assimilation appears to be occurring primarily along generational lines. That is, the second- and third-generation Cuban-Americans have developed the greatest facility with English. A recent study conducted by a University of Florida linguistic anthropolgist determined that Cubans are learning English as fast or faster than any other group of immigrants in United States history.[30] Typically, the second generation is bilingual, while the third usually is fluent only in English. Although the first generation is more comfortable when speaking Spanish, an increasing percentage is learning English. Still, their difficulty with understanding English is usually considered to be one of the most severe problems they have had to face while living in the United States. Nevertheless, there is an unmistakable drift toward the use of English and away from the use of Spanish as the generations increase.

THE FUTURE ASSIMILATION OF CUBAN-AMERICANS

It is our view that Cuban-Americans will continue to rapidly assimilate into American society. In fact, we feel that the evidence presented here indicates that the Cubans are assimilating as rapidly as any other non-English speaking immigrant group in the history of the United States. However, there are several factors that could retard the assimilation process for Cubans. One of these is their continued concentration in both Miami and Union City–West New York. The tradeoff benefit is that although this may somewhat slow their rate of acculturation, it does ease the adjustment processes for the more recently arrived migrants and many of the elderly who may never assimilate. A second retarding factor is related to Fidel Castro's ability to continue to play a prominent role in the news. Each time he makes a pronouncement it is played up by the news media, reminding the Cuban-Americans about their homeland and their hatred for the Castro government. The political actions of the United States government regarding the current Cuban regime also reawakens these memories. A third factor that could slow the assimilation of Cubans into American society would be another large wave of immigration from Cuba, like the Mariel wave that occurred in 1980.[31] This would provide an infusion of new migrants who would need to begin the assimilation process all over again.

Some studies of immigrant groups living in the United States have noted a tendency for the third generation to try to recapture some of the elements of the culture of their immigrant grandparents. The second generation would often rapidly abandon the cultural traits of their parents because they were viewed as a handicap toward their upward social mobility in American society. This tendency is embodied in the sociological concept known as the *three generations concept*.[32] Although the third generation of Cuban-Americans is only beginning to appear, there is no evidence to suggest that the three-generations hypothesis will apply in the case of Americans of Cuban descent. All available evidence seems to indicate the opposite. The assimilation momentum built up by the first generation and increased by the second should continue to be sustained during the third and subsequent generations. Eventually, the Cuban element in the United States will become indistinguishable from the rest of the American population. Precisely when this will occur will depend to a large extent on future events such as conditions in Cuba, any further immigration from the island, and the rate of dispersal of the second- and third-generation Cuban-Americans out of the Miami and Union City—West New York enclaves. Even when assimilation runs its course, the Cuban heritage of Miami will not be completely lost to history. The impact that the Cuban-Americans have on the city's landscape and in reorienting much of its economy toward Latin America is likely to be felt well into the future.

Notes

1. Marie LaLiberte Richmond, *Immigrant Adaptation and Family Structure Among Cubans in Miami, Florida* (New York: Arno Press, 1980), pp. 33–39.

2. R. O. Blood and R. L. Hamblin, "The Effect of the Wife's Employment of the Family Power Structure," *Social Forces* 36:347–352. 1957; and S. J. Bahr, "Comment on the Study of Family Power Structure: A Review 1960–1969," *Journal of Marriage and the Family* 34:239–243, 1972.

3. Eleanor Meyer Rogg and Rosemary Santana Cooney, *Adaptation and Adjustment of Cubans: West New York, New Jersey* (New York: Monograph No. 5 Hispanic Research Center, Fordham University, 1980), p. 4.
4. Margaret Stanley Boone, "Cubans in City Context: The Washington Case" (Ph.D. dissertation, Ohio State University, 1977), p. 18.
5. Eleanor Meyer Rogg, *The Assimilation of Cuban Exiles: The Role of Community and Class* (New York: Aberdeen Press, 1974), p. 134; and Rogg and Cooney, op. cit., p. 4.
6. U.S. Bureau of the Census, Current Population Reports, Series p-20, No. 354, "Persons of Spanish Origin in the United States," March 1979 (Washington, D.C.: U.S. Government Printing Office, 1980), p. 42.
7. Lisandro Perez, "Cubans," in *The Harvard Encyclopedia of American Ethnic Groups*, ed. Stephen Thernstrom (Cambridge, Mass.: The Becknap Press of Harvard University Press, 1980), p. 259.
8. Joseph P. Fitzpatrick and Douglas T. Gurak, *Hispanic Intermarriage in New York City: 1975* (New York: Monograph No. 2, Hispanic Research Center, Fordham University, 1979), pp. 23–25.
9. A. J. Jaffe, Ruth M. Cullen, and Thomas D. Boswell, *The Changing Demography of Spanish American* (New York: Academic Press, 1980), pp. 63–68.
10. Fitzpatrick and Gurak, op. cit., pp. 83–86.
11. Ibid., pp. 24–25.
12. U.S. Bureau of the Census, *Current Population Reports*, series p-20, No. 361: "Persons of Spanish Origin in the United States," March 1980 (Washington, D.C.: U.S. Government Printing Office, 1981), p. 5.
13. Louise Montgomery, "Hispanics Take New Names to Make It in New Country," *The Miami Herald*, July 18,1977, p. 1B.
14. John Dorschner, "Growing Up Spanglish in Miami," *The Miami Herald*, September 11, 1977, Tropic Section, p. 7.
15. Ileana Oroza, "Young Exiles: A Generation in Abyss," *The Miami Herald*, July 4, 1978, p. 1A.
16. Dorschner, op. cit., p. 8.
17. William D. Montalbano, "Spanglish Spoken Here," *The Miami Herald*, April 1, 1979, Tropic Section, pp. 30–33.
18. James R. Curtis and Richard F. Rose, "The Miami Sound: A Contemporary Latin Form of Place-Specific Music," *Journal of Cultural Geography*, forthcoming.
19. Montalbano, op. cit., pp. 52–54.
20. Ena Naunton, "Miami-Born Tradition," *The Miami Herald*, April 8, 1979, p. 6G.
21. Dorschner, op. cit., p. 17.
22. Nathan Glazer and Daniel Patrick Moynihan, *Beyond the Melting Pot* (Cambridge, Mass.: The M.I.T. Press, 1970), pp. 288–289.
23. Ibid., pp lxxviii-lxxxiii, 1–23, 288–292.
24. Joseph P. Fitzpatrick, *Puerto Rican Americans* (Englewood Cliffs, N.J.: Prentice-Hall, 1970), pp. 29–31.
25. Fitzpatrick, op. cit., pp. 31–34.
26. Jaffe, Cullen, and Boswell, op. cit., pp. 9–20.
27. Fitzpatrick, op. cit., pp. 34–43; and Milton M. Gordon, *Assimilation in America* (New York: Oxford University Press, 1964), p. 71.
28. Fredrick Tasker and Helga Silva, "Latin Centers Spread, Transforming Country," *The Miami Herald*, February 14, 1982, p. 1B.
29. Morris S. Thompson, "Cubans Fare Better, Black Family Says," *The Miami Herald*, July 5, 1978, pp. 1A, 20A.
30. "Prof: Cuban Learn English Quickly," *The Miami Herald*, May 13, 1983, p. 4B.
31. Andres Oppenheimer, "Mariel Made Area's Latins More Latin, Survey Finds," *The Miami Herald*, April 29, 1983, p. 1C.
32. Bernard Lazerwitz and Louis Rowitz, "The Three Generations Hypothesis," *The American Journal of Sociology* 69:529–538, March 1964.

Index

Acculturation: diet and, 160–61; geographic dispersion and, 113; indications of, 77–78; language and, 116; rate of, 191; religion and, 126, 132; of second generation, 183
Actors, 155
Adjustment: exile politics and, 171–72; of youth, 184–85
"Aerial Bridge," 48–50
Afro-Cuban influence: on cuisine, 160; on literature, 152, 154; on music, 137–38; on visual arts, 142
Age composition, 100–102, 109, 110
Agrarian Reform Law, 20
Agriculture in Cuba, 12–14, 20, 43
Aid, F., 124
Airlift, Freedom Flights, 48–50
American society, Cubans in contemporary, 1–10; as ethnic minority, 1–3; national view of, 3–10
Anglicisms in Spanish, 123
Anti-Castro Liberation Alliance, 169
Anti-Castro lobby, 172–73
Antonio Maceo Minipark, 91–92
Arawak Indians, 160
Architecture of Little Havana's commercial district, 92–93
Arnaz, D., 9
Art festivals, 150
Artistic expression, 136–57; community support, 148–50; creative literature, 151–54; music, 136–41; theater and dance, 154–55; visual arts, 141–50
Artists, 143–48; established, 143–45; migrating during Mariel boatlift, 150; younger, 145–48
Assimilation, 187–92; American citizenship and, 173–74; Castro's effect on, 192; cultural, 189; current theory, 188–89; ethnic segregation and, 67–68; future, 191–92; geographic dispersion and, 113; identity and, 188; linguistic, 124, 191; out-marriage rate and, 183; residential patterns and, 190; social, 189, 190; viewpoint, 85–86
Associations, immigrant, 175–78
Athletics, recognition in, 9
Ayapá: Cuentos de Jicotea (Cabrera), 154

Baseball, recognition in, 9
Batista, F., 17–18, 41, 73, 170
Bay of Pigs invasion, 7, 21, 43, 48, 170, 175; memorial to, 92, 93
Beef entrees, 161
Beverage preferences, 163
Beyond The Melting Pot (Glazer & Moynihan), 188
Bilingualism, 120–21, 126–27, 185
Black Cuban-Americans, 103–4
Black market, 34
"Blue-jeans revolution," 52
Boatlift: Camarioca, 48, 51; Mariel, 4–6, 10, 51–57, 150
Bodegas, 94, 164, 165
Bolero, Cuban, 137
"Book of the Block," 25
Boswell, T.D., 189
Botánicas, 132, 133
"Brain drain," 2, 47, 57
Brito-Avellana, M., 147
Brody, R.A., 41
Bugalú music, 140–41
Business: entrepreneurial accomplishments in, 8–9; grocery store and restaurants, 96, 158, 164–66; in Miami, 8–9, 85–89, 92–96

Cabrera, L., 154
Café cubano, 163–64
Cafeterías, 95–96
California, Cuban-Americans in, 62, 108–11
Calle Ocho, 89–91, 166
Camacho cigar factory, 88
Camarioca boatlift, 48, 51
Cardona, J.M., 169
Carnival Miami, 89–91
Carter, J., 175
Castro, F.: allowance of Cuban-American visitors to Cuba, 52; effect on assimilation, 192; emergence of, 18; Freedom Flights

period and, 48, 50; "golden exiles" period and, 41–45; major social changes in Cuba since, 24–35; Mariel boatlift and, 4, 6; out-migration, ambivalence toward, 47; revolution, 1, 19–23, 35, 103, 104, 170–71
Catholicism, Roman, 125–29, 132–33
CDRs, 25–26, 43
Central Planning Board, 21–22
Cespedes, C.M. de, 15
Chachachá rhythm, 140
Chaperon custom, 185
Charanga, 139, 140
Chicken entrees, 161–62
Children. *See also* Youth: education in Cuba of, 26–28; family role in Cuba and, 31–32
Childs, G., 187
Cigar factories, 87, 88
Cintas, O.B., 150
Cintas Foundation, 150
Cities, concentration of settlement in, 64–66
Citizenship, 173–74, 191
Clark, J.M., 118, 120
Clave rhythmic pattern, 138
Clergy, Spanish-speaking, 126–27
CNPC, 116, 118, 119
Coffee: consumption, 163–64; production in Cuba, 12
Collado, A., 152
Colonialist view, internal, 86
Committees for the Defense of the Revolution (CDRs), 25–26, 43
Communist Party of Cuba, 25
Community support of visual arts, 148–50
Compadrazgo system, 181–82
Concentrated pattern of settlement, 2, 56, 61–66
Conjunto, 139, 141
Contagious diffusion process, 85
Cooney, R.S., 118–19
Creative literature, 151–54
Criminals in Mariel boatlift, 53–54
Criollo paintings, 142
Cruz, C., 89
Cuba, 11–37; advantages of emigration from, 53, 57; agriculture in, 12–14, 20, 43; desire to return to, 169–70, 173; diet in, 159–60; economy of, 15, 18–19, 21–23, 34, 35, 52, 53; education in, 26–28; exile politics and plan to attack, 169–70; family structure in, 31–33; historical perspective of, 11–23; housing in, 29–30; impact of Seven Years War on, 12; investment priorities in, 30–31; labor productivity in, 22–23; literature in, 151–52; major social changes since Castro, 24–35; mass organizations in, 24–26; Protestantism in, 129; provinces prior to 1976, 13; public health in, 28–29; rationing in, 33–34; revolution, 1, 19–23, 35, 103, 104, 170–71; sexual prejudices in, 32–33; slavery in, 14–15; Spanish domination of, 12–16; U.S. interest in annexing, 14–15; -U.S. relations, 16–21, 22, 43, 171; urban and rural growth in, 30–31
Cuban-American National Foundation, 172
Cuban-Americans: black, 103–4; distribution in U.S. of, 63; as ethnic minority, 1–3; national view of, 3–10; population, 40; visiting Cuba, 52
Cuban Consciousness in Literature (de Armas and Steele), 151
Cuban Family code, 32
Cuban Memorial Plaza, 92, 93
Cuban National Planning Council (CNPC), 116, 118, 119
Cuban Refugee Center, 74
Cuban Refugee Program, 64, 67, 75, 86, 113, 190
Cuban Refugee Resettlement Center, 56
Cuban Women's Federation, 32
Cuentos negros de Cuba (Cabrera), 154
Cuisine and foodways, 158–67; diet, 160–64; grocery stores and restaurants, 96, 158, 164–66; historical roots of, 159–60
Cullen, R.M., 189
Cultural assimilation, 189
Cultural pluralism, 188–89
Culture. *See also* Artistic expression; Cuisine and foodways; Language; Religion: of Miami, Little Havana's impact on, 89–97; preservation of, 3; "queue," 33–34; Spanish influence on, 16
Customs. *See also* Family: chaperon, 185; dining, 165

Dade County: bilingualism of, 121; cities, selected population characteristics, 82; Cuban-American population in, 71, 73, 74–75, 76, 80; ethnic segregation in, 68; impact of Mariel boatlift on, 53–54, 55; Latin population in 1970s in, 78–85; returnees to, 67; suburbanization trend in, 81–83, 85
Dance, 154–55; music, 139–41
de Armas, J.R., 151, 153
Decision-making power in family, 182
Democratic party, support of, 174–75
Demographic profile, 100–114; age and sex composition, 100–102, 109, 110; compared to Spanish and non-Spanish Americans, 100–108; educational attainment levels, 106–7, 109–110; employment,

occupation and income, 104–6, 109–11, 112; fertility levels, 107–10, 190–91; racial characteristics, 102–4; by residence, 108–11
"Demonstration effect" of migration, 47, 52
Desserts, 162–63
Dictatorships in Cuba, 17–18, 35
Diet, 159–64
Diffusion process, contagious, 85
Dining customs, 165. *See also* Cuisine and foodways
Dispersion, geographic, 113
Domino Park, 91–92

Economic enclave in Miami, 85–89, 117–18
Economy of Cuba, 15, 18–19, 21–23, 34, 35, 52, 53
Education: attainment levels in, 106–7, 109–10; in Cuba, 26–28; of "golden exiles," 45; opportunities, 127; use of Spanish language and, 116–17
El Guarjiro cigar factory, 87
"El Manicero" (Grenet), 139–40
Emigration. *See* Migration, history of Cuban
Employment demographics, 104–6, 109–11, 112
English, proficiency in, 117, 118
Enterrado vivo (Collado), 152
Entertainment field, 9
"Entrants-Status Pending," 57
Entrees for meals, 161–62
Ethclass concept, 68
Ethnic area, Jordan and Rowntree model of, 83–85
Ethnic identity, 115, 137, 175
Ethnic minority, 1–3
Ethnic segregation, 67–68
Exile, municipalities in, 175–78
Exile politics, 168–73
Exports, economic enclave in Miami and, 86–87

Fagen, R.R., 41
Falero, E., 147, 148
Family, 180–84; assimilation and structure of, 190–91; changes in Cuba, 31–33; settlement and role of, 75; traditional Cuban, 180–82; in U.S., 182–84
"Family Reunification Flights," 48–50
Fernández, R., 153
Fertility levels, 107–10, 190–91
Festivals, 89–91, 150
Fiesta de Quince Anos, 187
First Agrarian Reform Law, 20
First-generation, language problems of, 120
Fishman, J.A., 124
Fitzpatrick, J., 125
Florida. *See also* Miami: demographics of Cuban-Americans in, 108–11, 112; early migration to, 39, 41; settlement in, 62, 64, 65–66
Food. *See* Cuisine and foodways
Freedom Flights period, 48–50
Freedom Tower, 44
Fruits in diet, 162
Fuentes-Pérez, I., 150
Fundamental Law of 1959, 32

Geographic dispersion, 113
Ghetto, Jordan and Rowntree model of, 84
Glazer, N., 188
Goizueta, R., 8
"Golden exiles" period, 41–47
Gómez, J.M., 17
Gomez, M., 15
Gómez-Sicre, J., 142, 150
González, J., 147, 149
Gort, W., 74
Granma (yacht), 18
Great Depression, 18
Grenet, E., 138, 139–40
Grillo, F., 140
Grocery stores, 158, 164–66
Guantanamo Bay, U.S. Naval Base at, 17
Gutierrez, O., 145

Havana, growth rate of, 30–31
Health, public, in Cuba, 28–29
Hebrew Immigrant Aid society (HIAS), 130
Hialeah, settlement in, 78, 79, 81, 85
Hierarchical process of settlement, 85
Hofman, J.E., 124
Home, use of Spanish language at, 116–17
Housing, 29–30, 96

Identity: assimilation and, 188; crisis of youth, 185; ethnic, 115, 137, 175; subcultural, 122
Illinois, Cuban-Americans in, 62, 108–11
Illiteracy in Cuba, 26
I Love Lucy (TV), 9
Immigrant associations, 175–78
Immigrant politics, 168–69
Immigration policies, 58, 103
Improvisation in music, 138
Income: demographics, 104–6, 109–11, 112; language use and, 117
Institution Nacional de Reforma Agraria (INRA), 20
Integrated parishes, 126
Internal colonialist view, 86
International trade, Miami's economic enclave and, 89
Investment priorities in Cuba, 30–31

Jaffe, A.J., 189
Jews, Cuban, 130–31
Jordan, T.H., 83–85
Jorge, A., 41
José Martí Park, 92
Journals, literary, 154
Junta Central de Planificacion (JUCEPLAN), 21–22
Junta Patriotica Cubana, 176

Kennedy, J.F., 7, 8, 175
Kennedy Administration, 7

Labor force, 104–5, 182. *See also* Occupation
Labor productivity in Cuba, 22–23
Language, 115–24; acculturation and, 116; bilingualism, 120–21, 126–27, 185; as cohesive force, 115; linguistic assimilation, 124, 191; problems, 120–21; "Spanglish," 122–24, 186; use and preference, 116–20
Lewis, P.F., 91
Liebman, S.B., 131
Lifestyle of youth, 186
Lilayando (Sánchez-Boudy), 153
Linguistic assimilation, 124, 191
Literacy campaign in Cuba, 26
Literature, creative, 151–54
Little Havana: advantages offered by, 77; authenticity of, 91; black Cuban-Americans in, 103; commercial activities in, 92–96; as core settlement, 84–85; cultural landscape of, 89–97; direction of expansion from, 78, 79; establishment of, 74, 75–78; residential areas of, 96; restaurants and cafeterías, 95–96
Little Havana Development Authority, 74
Lobby, anti-Castro, 172–73
Lopez, M.M., 118, 120
Los Tres Reyes Magos, 129

Maceo, A., 15
Machado, G., 39, 73, 92
Machismo, tradition of, 182
Machito and His Afro-Cubans, 140
Maine (battleship), 15–16
Mambo sound, 140
Manuel, V., 143
Mariel boatlift, 51–57; American response to, 4–6, 10, 54–55; artists migrating during, 150; composition of migrants in, 53–54, 56; motivations behind, 52–53; occupational structure of migrants in, 56–57
Markets: in Cuba, 34; in Little Havana, 94
Marranos, 130
Marriage, 29–30, 183–84
Martí, J., 15, 151
Mass media: coverage in, 6–7; Spanish-language, 119–20
Mass organizations in Cuba, 24–26
Matas, J., 154
McKinley, W., 17
Meals, Cuban, 161–64. *See also* Cuisine and foodways
Melting Pot, The (Zangwill), 187
Melting pot hypothesis, 187–88
"Memorandum of Understanding," 48, 50
Men, role in family of, 182
Menocal, M.G., 17
Menton, S., 152, 153, 154
Merrick, G., 92
Miami, 71–99. *See also* Little Havana: arts community, 148–50; business in, 8–9, 85–89, 92–96; Catholic church in, 125–27; Cuban Jews in, 130; economic enclave in, 85–89, 117–18; ethnic segregation in, 68; growth and expansion of Cuban population in, 72–85; Latin restaurants in, 165–66; literary community in, 154; migration, 39, 40, 43–45, 49–50; occupational structure of Cuban refugees to, 45, 46; origins of migrants to, 51; residential pattern of settlement in, 75–78; return flow to, 66–67; Spanish-language media in, 119–20; supermarkets in, 164–165
Miami Herald, The (newspaper), 54, 67, 120, 190
"Miami Sound," 141
Middle class, fertility levels of, 107–8
Migration, history of Cuban, 38–60; demonstration effect of, 47, 52; early trickle, 39–41; freedom flights period, 48–50; "golden exiles" period, 41–47; historical trends summarized, 57–58; interlude from 1973-1980, 50–51; Mariel boatlift, 4–6, 10, 51–57, 150; missile crisis hiatus, 47–48; motivation for, 38, 43–45, 57–58; process of, 4; purification theme of, 47; selectivity processes and trends, 50–51, 101; significance to U.S., 58; tradition of, 61
Mijares, J.M., 143–44
Militant organization, 171
Minority, ethnic, 1–3
Missile crisis, 47–48, 170, 175
Mobility, socioeconomic, 3, 64–65, 106, 113
Moncarz, R., 41
Montaner, C.A., 154
Moynihan, D.P., 188
Municipalities in exile, 175–78

Municipio de Santiago de Cuba en el Exilio, 177
Murals, wall, 94, 95
Music, 136–41, 186
Musicians, 9

National Commission for Employment Policy (NCEP), 117, 118
National Council of Jewish Women, 130
National Institute of Agrarian Reform, 20
Nationalization activities in Cuba, 21
National parishes, 126
National Revolutionary Council, 169
New Jersey, Cuban-Americans in, 62, 108–11, 112
"New Man" concept, 24
Newspapers, Spanish-language, 119
New York City, Cuban-Americans in, 39–41, 62–63, 130
New York state, Cuban-Americans in, 62–63, 108–11, 112
New York Times, The (newspaper), 169
1980 Refugee Act, 6, 57
Noche Buena, 128–29
Nostalgia in literature, 153
Nuestra Señora de la Caridad, celebration of, 129

Occupation: adjustment according to, 172; assimilation and, 190; of Cuban refugees to Miami, 45, 46; demographics, 104–6, 109–11, 112; of Mariel boatlift migrants, 56–57; of refugees in Freedom Flight period, 49
O'Leary, T.J., 41
Omega 7, 171
Out-marriage rate, 183–84

Padilla, H., 150
Parallel market, 34
Parishes, Catholic, 126–27
Parties, quince, 187
Pau-Llosa, R., 142–45
Peasant markets, 34
Perromundo (Montaner), 154
"Personalismo," 174
Personal relationships, reliance on, 181
Platt Amendment, 17, 34–35
Pluralism, cultural, 188–89
Poetry, 152
Policies, immigration, 58, 103
Political-ideological theme in literature, 152–53
Political prisoners, release of, 50
Politics and ideology, 7–8, 168–79; exile, 168–73; municipalities in exile, 175–78; shift from exile to immigrant, 168–69; U.S., 173–75
Population: Cuban-American, 40, 71, 72–85; redistribution policy in Cuba, 30–31
Pork entrees, 161
Por que (Cabrera), 154
Portes, A., 118, 120
"Power brokering," 174
Prado, P., 140
Prejudices, sexual, 32–33
Prisoners, release of political, 50
Prose Fiction of the Cuban Revolution (Menton), 152
Protestantism, 129–30
Public health in Cuba, 28–29
"Purification" theme of migration, 47

"Queue culture," 33–34
Quince parties, 187

Racial characteristics, 102–4
Radio Martí, 172
Radio stations, Spanish language, 119
Rationing in Cuba, 33–34
Reader's Digest (magazine), 6
Reading material, language patterns based on, 118–19
Reagan, R., 172, 175
Religion, 124–33; acculturation and, 126, 132; Cuban Jews, 130–31; decreasing participation rate in, 128; personalistic character of practicing, 125; Protestantism, 129–30; Roman Catholicism, 125–29, 132–33; Santería, 94–95, 128, 131–33, 137, 153
Republican Party, preference for, 174–75
Resettlement, 64, 67, *See also* Settlement
Residence: assimilation and, 190; demographic profile by, 108–11, 112
Resource theory, 182
Restaurants, 95–96, 158, 164–66
Revolution: "blue-jeans," 52; Castro, 1, 19–23, 35, 103, 104, 170–71; literature and, 151–52
Rhythm: chachacha, 140; clave pattern of, 138
Rights, voting, 174–75
Riveró, E., 145, 146
Rogg, E.M., 118–19
Román, A., 126
Roman Catholicism, 125–29, 132–33
Rosa, E., 124
Rowntree, L., 83–85
Rumba dance music, 139–40
Rural growth in Cuba, 30–31

Saints, worship of, 125, 128
Salsa music, 141
San Alejandro Academy of Arts, 143
Sánchez-Boudy, J., 153
Sandoval, M., 133
Santería, 94–95, 128, 131–33, 137, 153
School. *See* Education
Seafood entrees, 161–62
Second Agrarian Law, 20
Second generation, 113, 118, 121, 173–74, 183
Segregation, ethnic, 67–68
Septeto, 138–39
Settlement. *See also* specific cities and states: Catholic church's role, 127; core, 84–85; ethnic segregation, 67–68; family's role in, 75; hierarchical process of, 85; patterns and process, 2, 56, 61–70; social networks and, 50; suburbanization, 65, 81–83, 85
Seven Years War, 12
Sex composition, 100–102, 109, 110
Sexual prejudices in Cuba, 32–33
Shrines, yard, 96, 97, 128
Slavery in Cuba, 14–15
Socarras, C.P., 73, 92
Social assimilation, 189, 190
Social networks and settlement, 50
Socioeconomic mobility, 3, 64–65, 106, 113
Socioeconomic status, 68, 77–78, 104–6, 111–13
Sofrito, 161
Somoza, A., 92
Soriano, R., 144–45
Soviet Union-Cuban relations, 20–21
"Spanglish," 122-24, 186
Spanish Americans, Cuban-American demographics compared to, 100-108
Spanish-American War, 16, 34
Spanish domination of Cuba, 12–16
Spanish language: anglicisms in, 123; attitudes toward use of, 120–21; clergy speaking, 126–27; mass media, 118, 119–20
"Sparrow and the Maiden, The" (drawing) (Gonzalez), 149
Status, socioeconomic, 68, 77–78, 104–6, 111–13
Steele, C.W., 151, 153
Stolzenberg, R., 117
Stores, grocery, 158, 164–66
Subcultural identity, 122
Suburbanization trend, 65, 81–83, 85
Supermarkets, 164–65
Surnames, use of, 181
Sweetwater, settlement in, 79–81

Television programs, Spanish-language, 118, 119
"Tent City," 55, 92
Ten Years War, 15
Terrorism, 171
Texas, settlememt in, 62, 108–11
Theater, 154–55
Three generations concept, 192
Three Kings Day, 129
Tobacco production in Cuba, 12–14
Trade relation between Cuba and U.S., 171
Trasobares, C., 147
Trends: Cuban migration, 57–58; in labor force history, 104–6; suburbanization, 65, 81–83, 85
26th of July Movement, 18, 25

Union City-West New York, 49–50, 51, 64, 150
Union of Young Communists, 24
United States: -Cuban relations, 16–21, 22, 43, 171; distribution of Cuban-Americans in, 63; family role in, 182–84; interest in annexing Cuba, 14–15; music in, 139–41; Naval Base at Guantanamo Bay, 17; politics, 173–75; significance of Cuban migration to, 58; Spanish-American War, 16, 34
United States Central Intelligence Agency, 169
United States Customs District, 86
United States Department of Immigration and Naturalization Service, 48
Universal theme in literature, 153–54
Urban growth in Cuba, 30–31
Urban Reform Law, 21, 29, 43

Vegetables in diet, 162
Visual arts, 141–50; Afro-Cuban influence in, 142, 152; community support, 148–50; established artists, 143–45; themes in, 142–43; younger artists, 145–48
Voting rights, exercise of, 174–75

Wall murals, 94, 95
Walsh, B.O., 127
Watergate break-in, 7
"White flight," 68
Winsberg, M.D., 74
Women: adjustment compared to men, 171–72; changes in role of Cuban, 32–33; early predominance demographically, 101–2; in labor force, 182; protection of, 185–86
Woodlawn Memorial Park, 92

Yard shrines, 96, 97, 128
Young Pioneers, 24
Youth, 184–87

Zangwill, E., 187